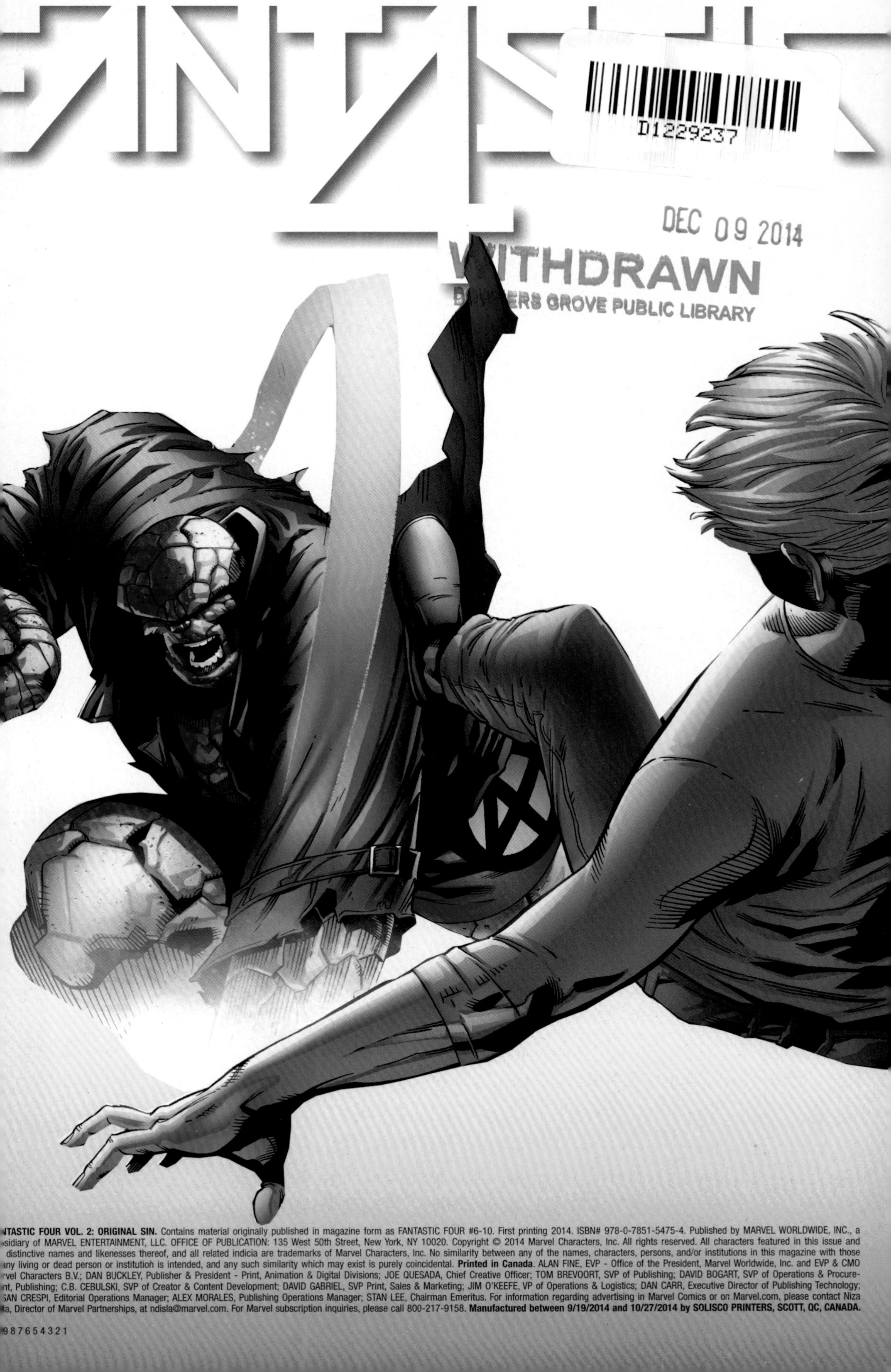

NTASTIC FOUR VOL. 2: ORIGINAL SIN. Contains material originally published in magazine form as FANTASTIC FOUR #6-10. First printing 2014. ISBN# 978-0-7851-5475-4. Published by MARVEL WORLDWIDE, INC., a sidiary of MARVEL ENTERTAINMENT, LLC. OFFICE OF PUBLICATION: 135 West 50th Street, New York, NY 10020. **Printed in Canada**. ALAN FINE, EVP - Office of the President, Marvel Worldwide, Inc. and EVP & CMO rvel Characters B.V.; DAN BUCKLEY, Publisher & President - Print, Animation & Digital Divisions; JOE QUESADA, Chief Creative Officer; TOM BREVOORT, SVP of Publishing; DAVID BOGART, SVP of Operations & Procure-nt, Publishing; C.B. CEBULSKI, SVP of Creator & Content Development; DAVID GABRIEL, SVP Print, Sales & Marketing; JIM O'KEEFE, VP of Operations & Logistics; DAN CARR, Executive Director of Publishing Technology; SAN CRESPI, Editorial Operations Manager; ALEX MORALES, Publishing Operations Manager; STAN LEE, Chairman Emeritus. For information regarding advertising in Marvel Comics or on Marvel.com, please contact Niza la, Director of Marvel Partnerships, at ndisla@marvel.com. For Marvel subscription inquiries, please call 800-217-9158. **Manufactured between 9/19/2014 and 10/27/2014 by SOLISCO PRINTERS, SCOTT, QC, CANADA.**

987654321

FANTASTIC 4   ORIGINAL SIN

Writer: James Robinson
Pencilers: Leonard Kirk [#6-8] & Marc Laming [#9-10]
Inkers: Karl Kesel [#6-7] with Rick Magyar [#7],
Scott Hanna [#8, #9 pgs. 4-6 & #10] &
Marc Laming [#9 & 10 pgs. 1 & 4]
Colorists: Jesus Aburtov with Veronica Gandini [#6]
Original Sin flashback art: Dean Haspiel & Nolan Woodard
Letterer: VC's Clayton Cowles
Cover Art: Leonard Kirk with Jesus Aburtov [#6-7], Nolan
Woodard [#8], Israel Silva [#9] & Jason Keith [#10]
Assistant Editor: Emily Shaw
Editor: Mark Paniccia

Collection Editor: Sarah Brunstad
Associate Managing Editor: Alex Starbuck
Editors, Special Projects: Jennifer Grünwald & Mark D. Beazley
Senior Editor, Special Projects: Jeff Youngquist
Book Designer: Nelson Ribeiro
SVP Print, Sales & Marketing: David Gabriel

Editor in Chief: Axel Alonso
Chief Creative Officer: Joe Quesada
Publisher: Dan Buckley
Executive Producer: Alan Fine

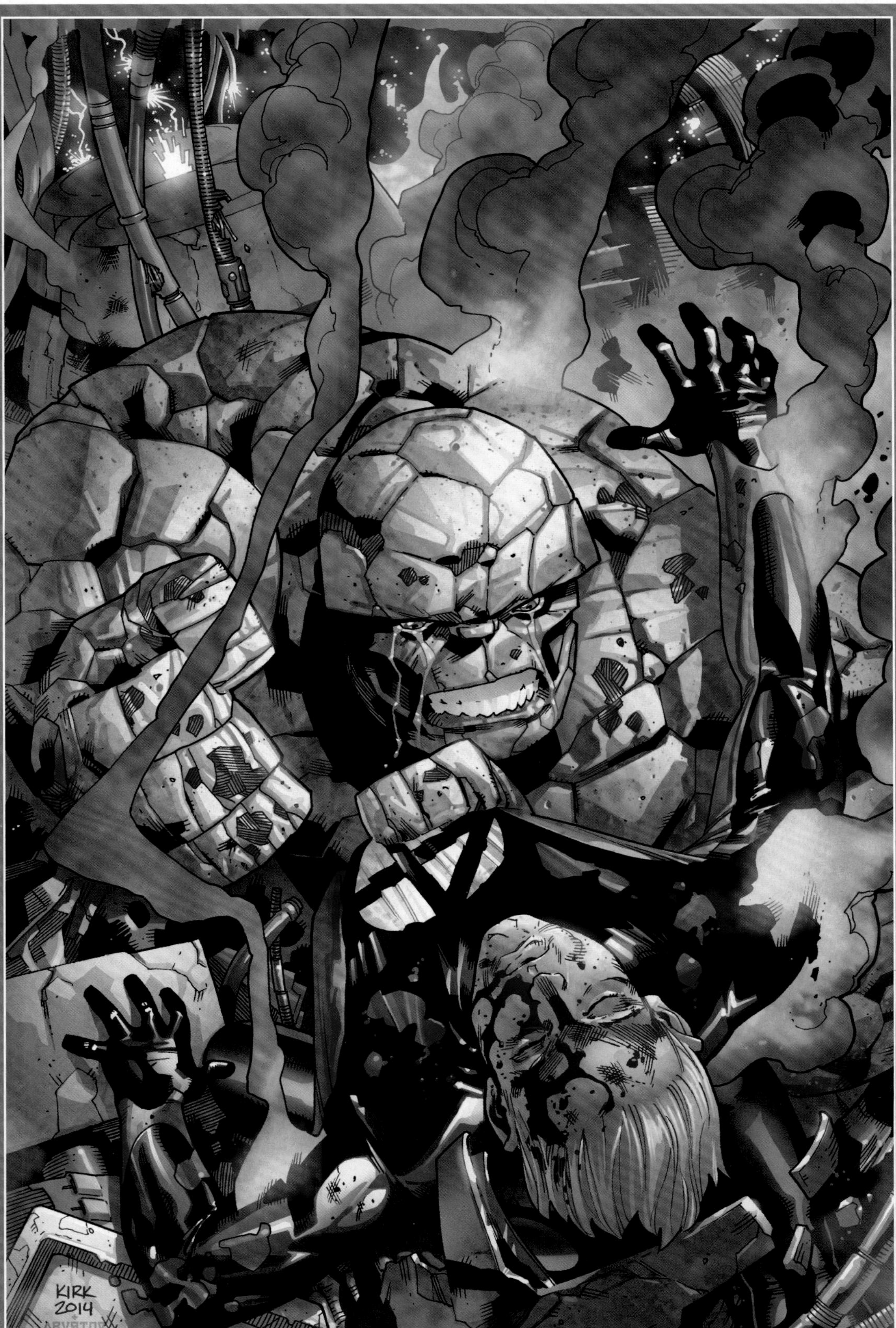
KIRK
2014

SIX

FANTASTIC 4

ORIGINAL SIN

CREATURES FROM FRANKLIN RICHARDS' WORLD BROKE FREE FROM THE BAXTER BUILDING AND RAN AMOK ACROSS MANHATTAN, LEAVING DESTRUCTION WHEREVER THEY WENT.

THE FANTASTIC FOUR WERE SUED FOR THE DESTRUCTION CAUSED BY THE CREATURES. THE TRIAL, HOWEVER, TOOK A BROADER APPROACH, REFERENCING SIMILARLY DESTRUCTIVE EVENTS THAT TOOK PLACE OVER THE ENTIRE HISTORY OF THE TEAM. EVERYTHING FROM GALACTUS AND THE ULTIMATE NULLIFIER TO PROPERTY DAMAGE WAS BROUGHT UP AS EVIDENCE AGAINST THE FANTASTIC FOUR.

THE COURTS RULED IN FAVOR OF THE PROSECUTION. AS PART OF THE RULING, THE CHILDREN OF THE FUTURE FOUNDATION, WITH THE EXCEPTION OF VALERIA WHO IS LIVING IN LATVERIA WITH DOCTOR DOOM -- WERE TAKEN FROM SUE AND REED'S CUSTODY AND BROUGHT TO AN UNDISCLOSED S.H.I.E.L.D. HOLDING FACILITY. THERE THEY MET JIM HAMMOND, THE ORIGINAL HUMAN TORCH AND NEW S.H.I.E.L.D. AGENT, WHO PROMISED TO WATCH OVER THEM.

MEANWHILE, AN ALL-SEEING COSMIC BEING KNOWN AS THE WATCHER WAS MURDERED AND THE SECRETS HE KEPT WERE LEAKED INTO THE MINDS OF MANY MARVEL HEROES. HOW WILL THESE SECRETS IMPACT THE FANTASTIC FOUR?

REED RICHARDS
MR. FANTASTIC

SUSAN RICHARDS
THE INVISIBLE WOMAN

JOHNNY STORM
THE HUMAN TORCH

BEN GRIMM
THE THING

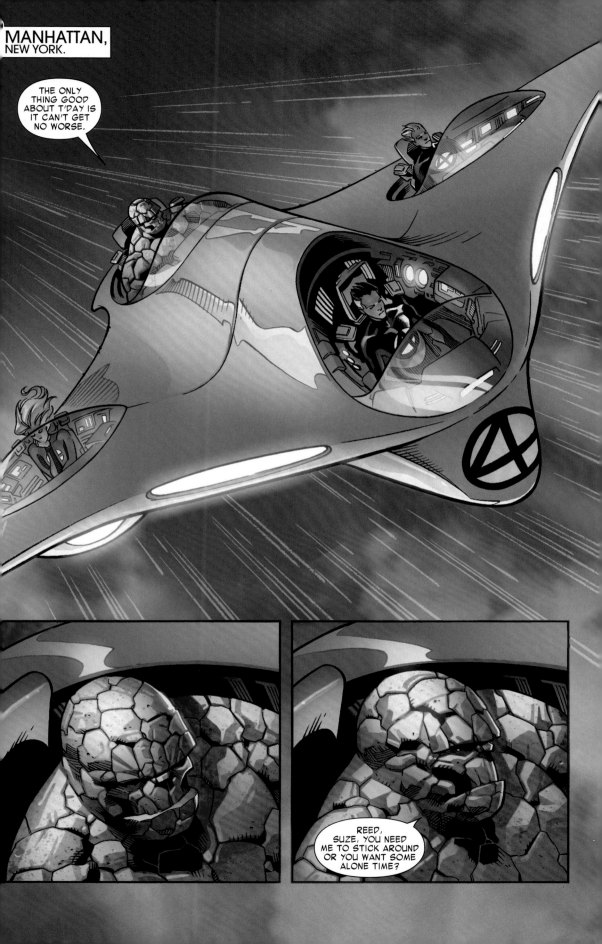

MANHATTAN, NEW YORK.

THE ONLY THING GOOD ABOUT T'DAY IS IT CAN'T GET NO WORSE.

REED, SUZE, YOU NEED ME TO STICK AROUND OR YOU WANT SOME ALONE TIME?

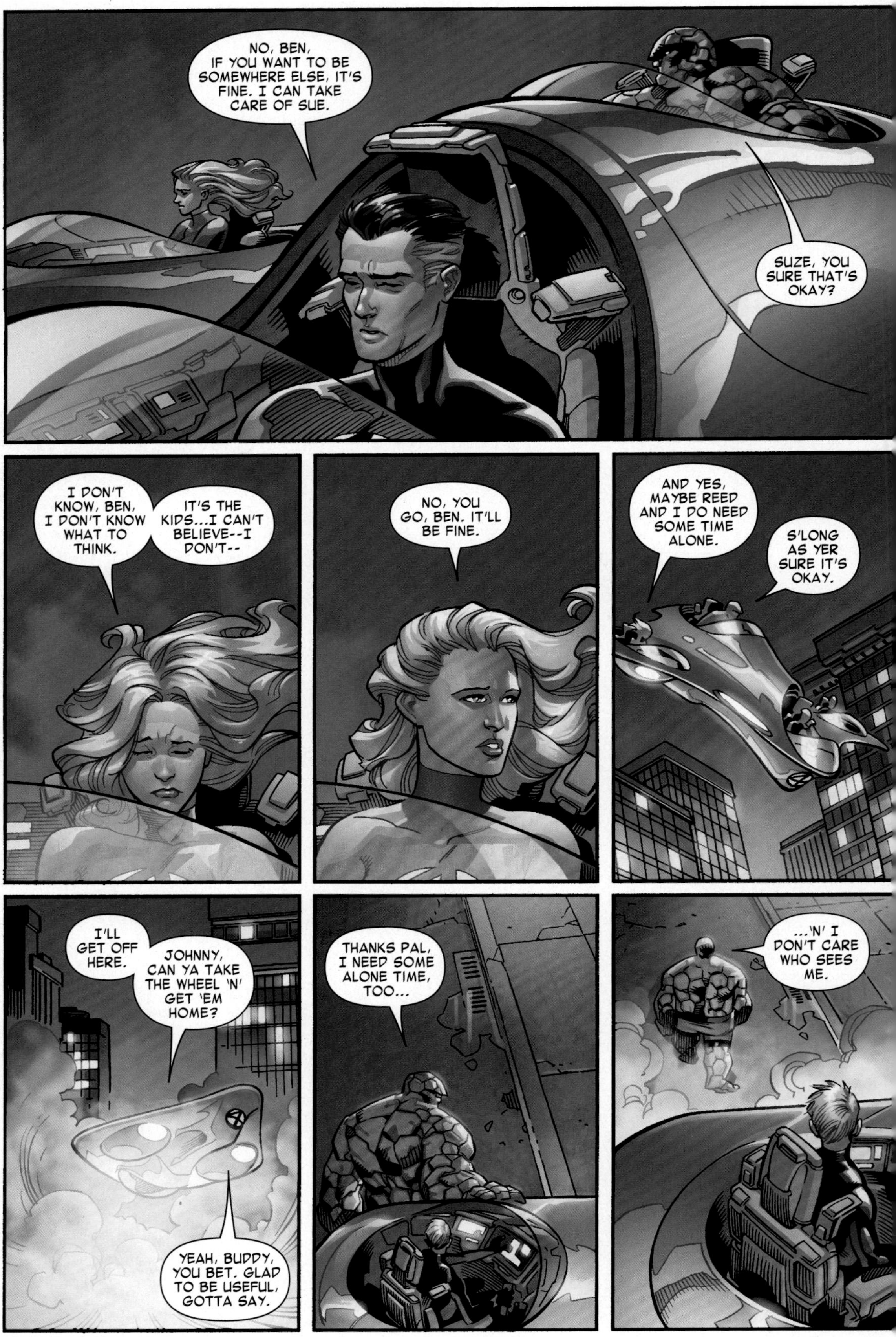
NO, BEN, IF YOU WANT TO BE SOMEWHERE ELSE, IT'S FINE. I CAN TAKE CARE OF SUE.
SUZE, YOU SURE THAT'S OKAY?
I DON'T KNOW, BEN, I DON'T KNOW WHAT TO THINK.
IT'S THE KIDS...I CAN'T BELIEVE--I DON'T--
NO, YOU GO, BEN. IT'LL BE FINE.
AND YES, MAYBE REED AND I DO NEED SOME TIME ALONE.
S'LONG AS YER SURE IT'S OKAY.
I'LL GET OFF HERE.
JOHNNY, CAN YA TAKE THE WHEEL 'N' GET 'EM HOME?
YEAH, BUDDY, YOU BET. GLAD TO BE USEFUL, GOTTA SAY.
THANKS PAL, I NEED SOME ALONE TIME, TOO...
...'N' I DON'T CARE WHO SEES ME.

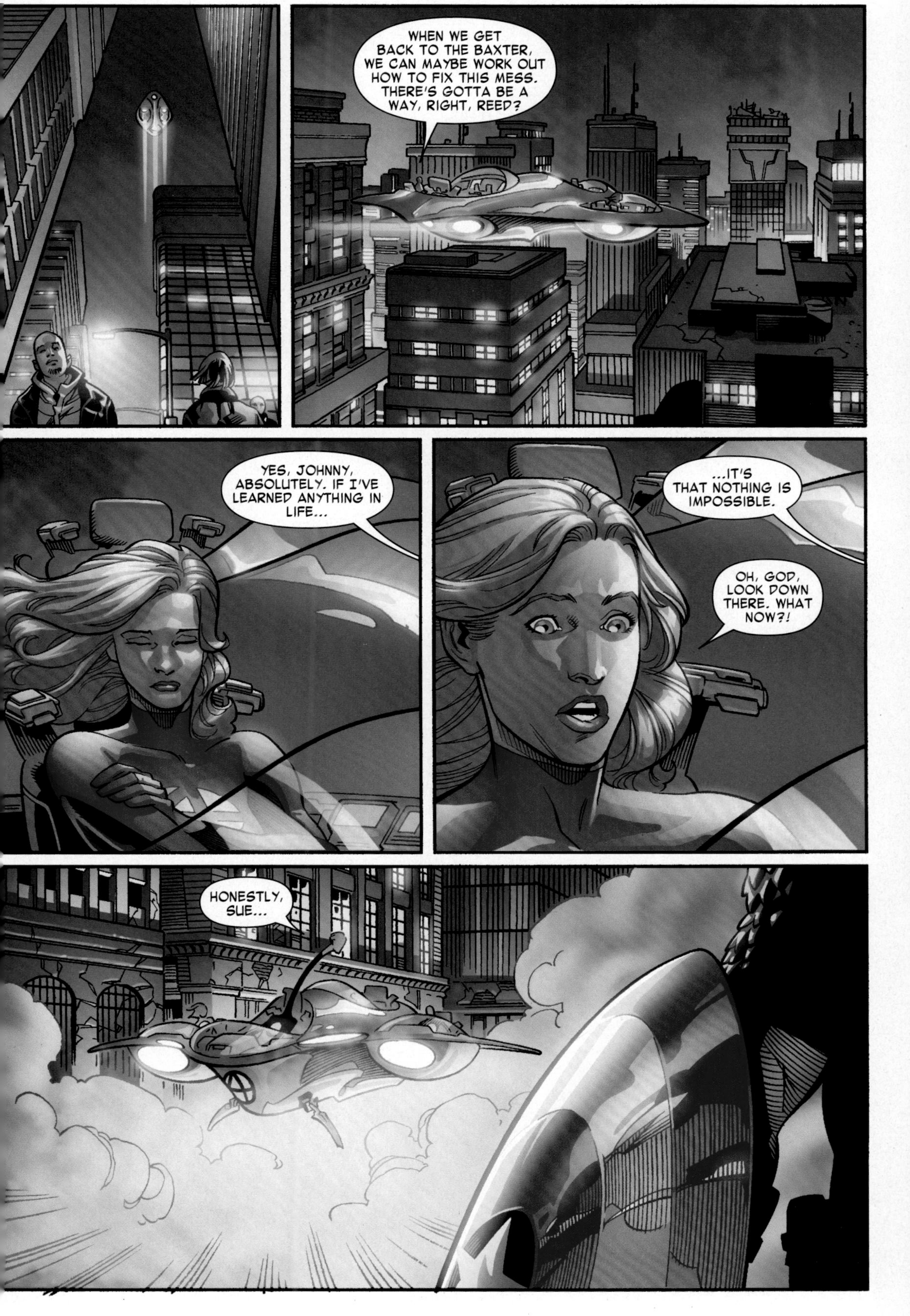
WHEN WE GET BACK TO THE BAXTER, WE CAN MAYBE WORK OUT HOW TO FIX THIS MESS. THERE'S GOTTA BE A WAY, RIGHT, REED?
YES, JOHNNY, ABSOLUTELY. IF I'VE LEARNED ANYTHING IN LIFE...
...IT'S THAT NOTHING IS IMPOSSIBLE.
OH, GOD, LOOK DOWN THERE. WHAT NOW?!
HONESTLY, SUE...

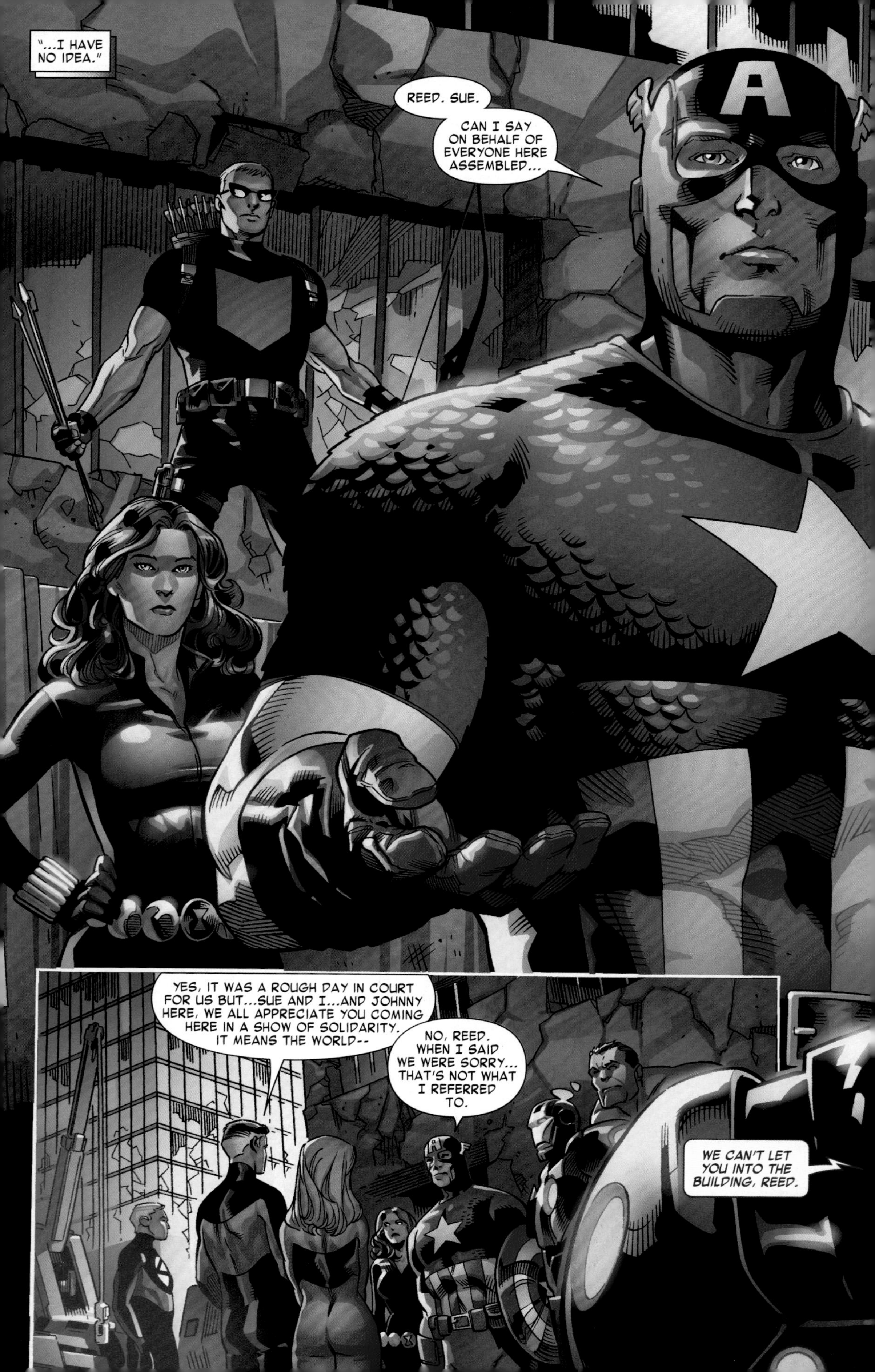
"...I HAVE NO IDEA."
REED. SUE.
CAN I SAY ON BEHALF OF EVERYONE HERE ASSEMBLED...
YES, IT WAS A ROUGH DAY IN COURT FOR US BUT...SUE AND I...AND JOHNNY HERE, WE ALL APPRECIATE YOU COMING HERE IN A SHOW OF SOLIDARITY. IT MEANS THE WORLD--
NO, REED. WHEN I SAID WE WERE SORRY... THAT'S NOT WHAT I REFERRED TO.
WE CAN'T LET YOU INTO THE BUILDING, REED.

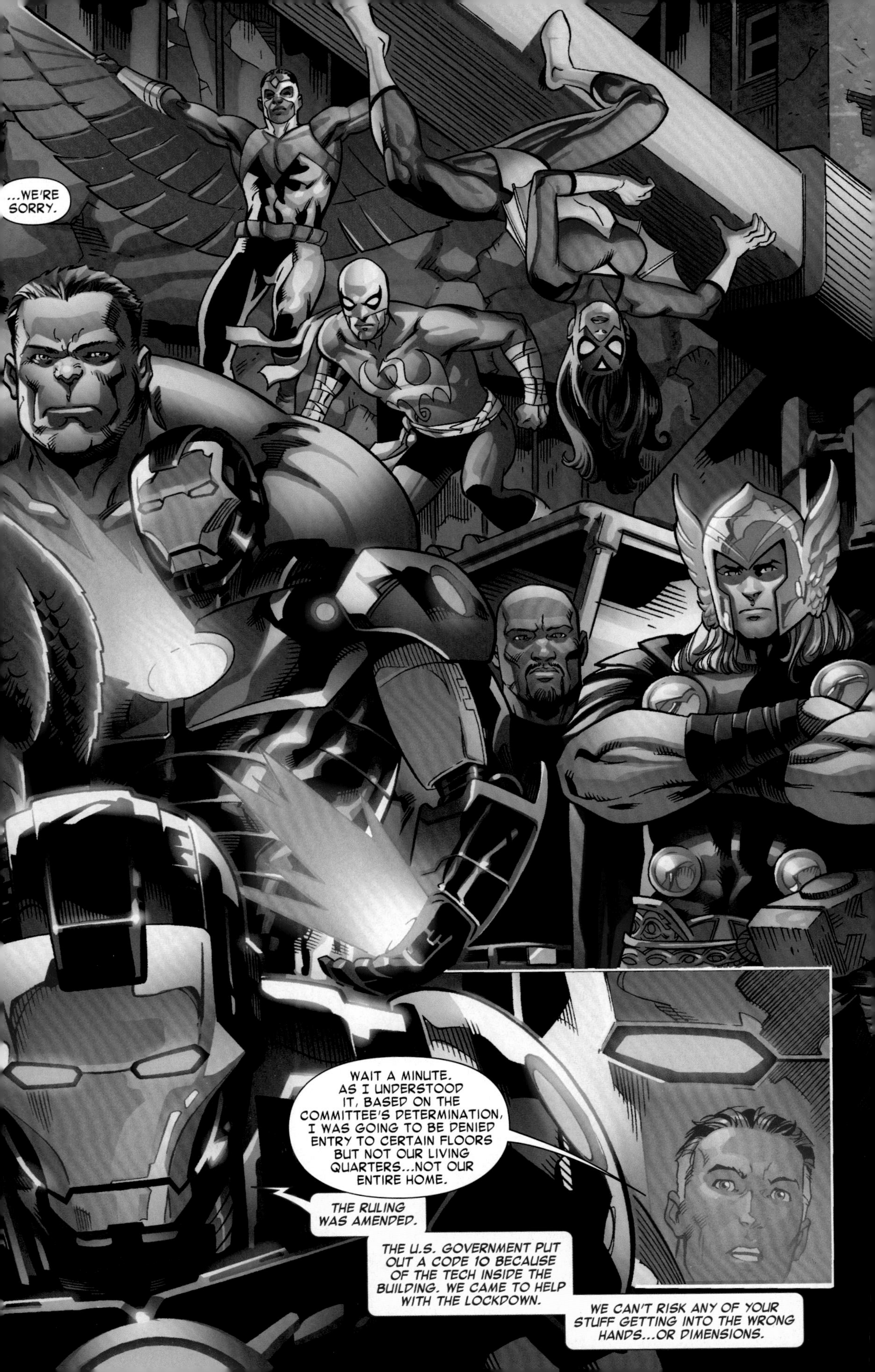
...WE'RE SORRY.
WAIT A MINUTE. AS I UNDERSTOOD IT, BASED ON THE COMMITTEE'S DETERMINATION, I WAS GOING TO BE DENIED ENTRY TO CERTAIN FLOORS BUT NOT OUR LIVING QUARTERS...NOT OUR ENTIRE HOME.
THE RULING WAS AMENDED.
THE U.S. GOVERNMENT PUT OUT A CODE 10 BECAUSE OF THE TECH INSIDE THE BUILDING. WE CAME TO HELP WITH THE LOCKDOWN.
WE CAN'T RISK ANY OF YOUR STUFF GETTING INTO THE WRONG HANDS...OR DIMENSIONS.

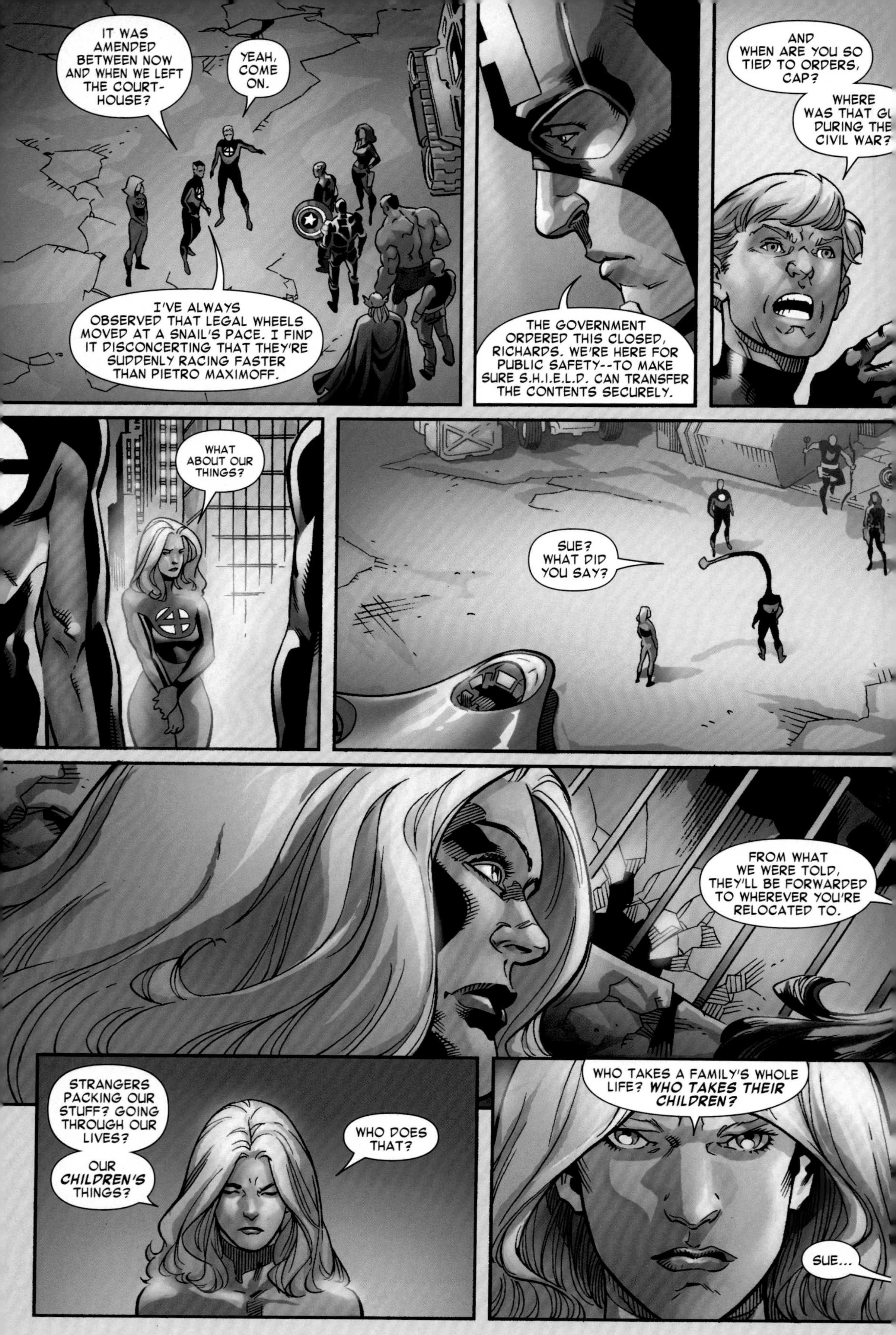
IT WAS AMENDED BETWEEN NOW AND WHEN WE LEFT THE COURT-HOUSE?
YEAH, COME ON.
I'VE ALWAYS OBSERVED THAT LEGAL WHEELS MOVED AT A SNAIL'S PACE. I FIND IT DISCONCERTING THAT THEY'RE SUDDENLY RACING FASTER THAN PIETRO MAXIMOFF.
THE GOVERNMENT ORDERED THIS CLOSED, RICHARDS. WE'RE HERE FOR PUBLIC SAFETY--TO MAKE SURE S.H.I.E.L.D. CAN TRANSFER THE CONTENTS SECURELY.
AND WHEN ARE YOU SO TIED TO ORDERS, CAP?
WHERE WAS THAT G DURING THE CIVIL WAR?
WHAT ABOUT OUR THINGS?
SUE? WHAT DID YOU SAY?
FROM WHAT WE WERE TOLD, THEY'LL BE FORWARDED TO WHEREVER YOU'RE RELOCATED TO.
STRANGERS PACKING OUR STUFF? GOING THROUGH OUR LIVES?
OUR *CHILDREN'S* THINGS?
WHO DOES THAT?
WHO TAKES A FAMILY'S WHOLE LIFE? *WHO TAKES THEIR CHILDREN?*
SUE...

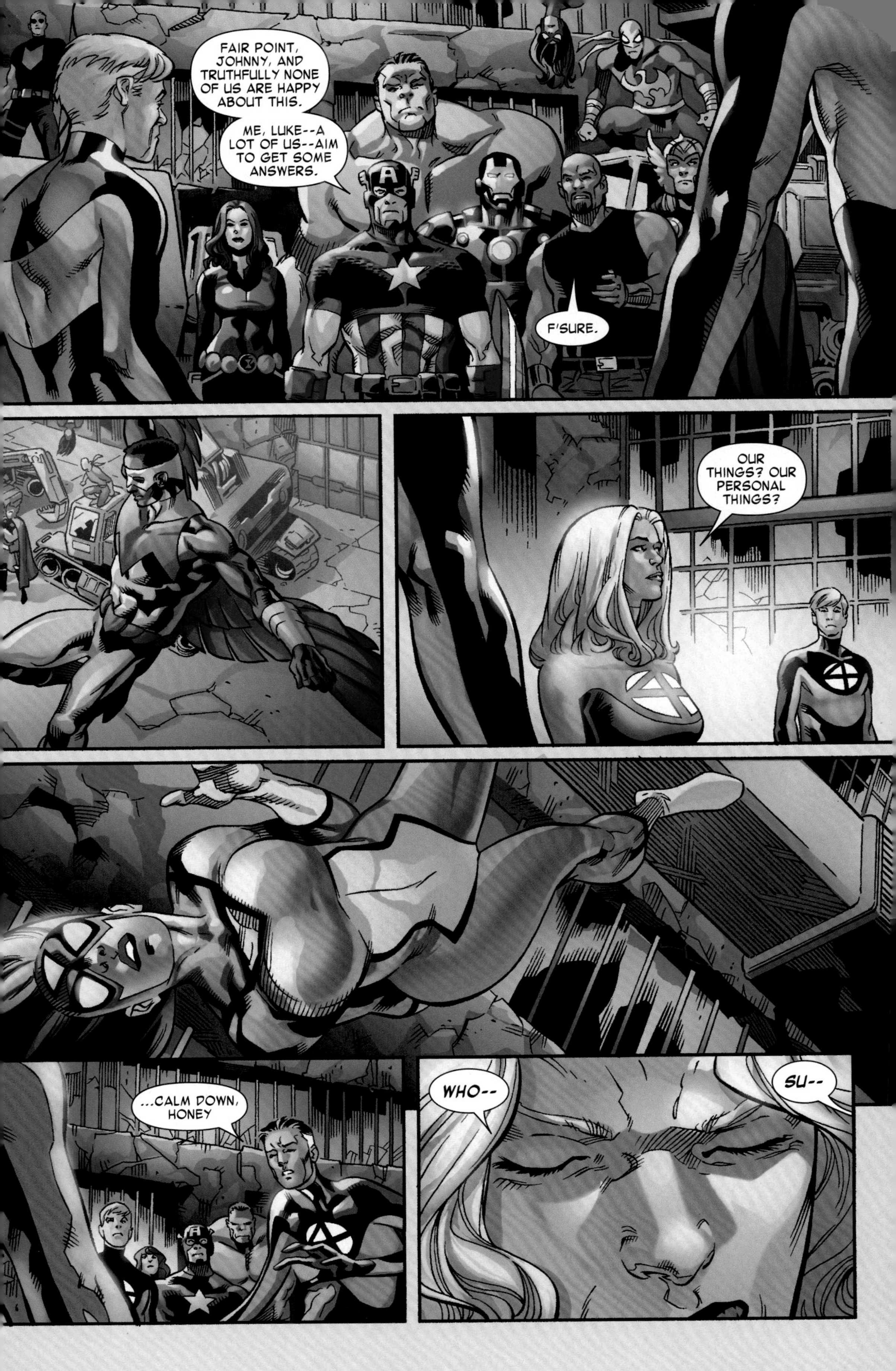
FAIR POINT, JOHNNY, AND TRUTHFULLY NONE OF US ARE HAPPY ABOUT THIS.
ME, LUKE--A LOT OF US--AIM TO GET SOME ANSWERS.
F'SURE.
OUR THINGS? OUR PERSONAL THINGS?
...CALM DOWN, HONEY
WHO--
SU--

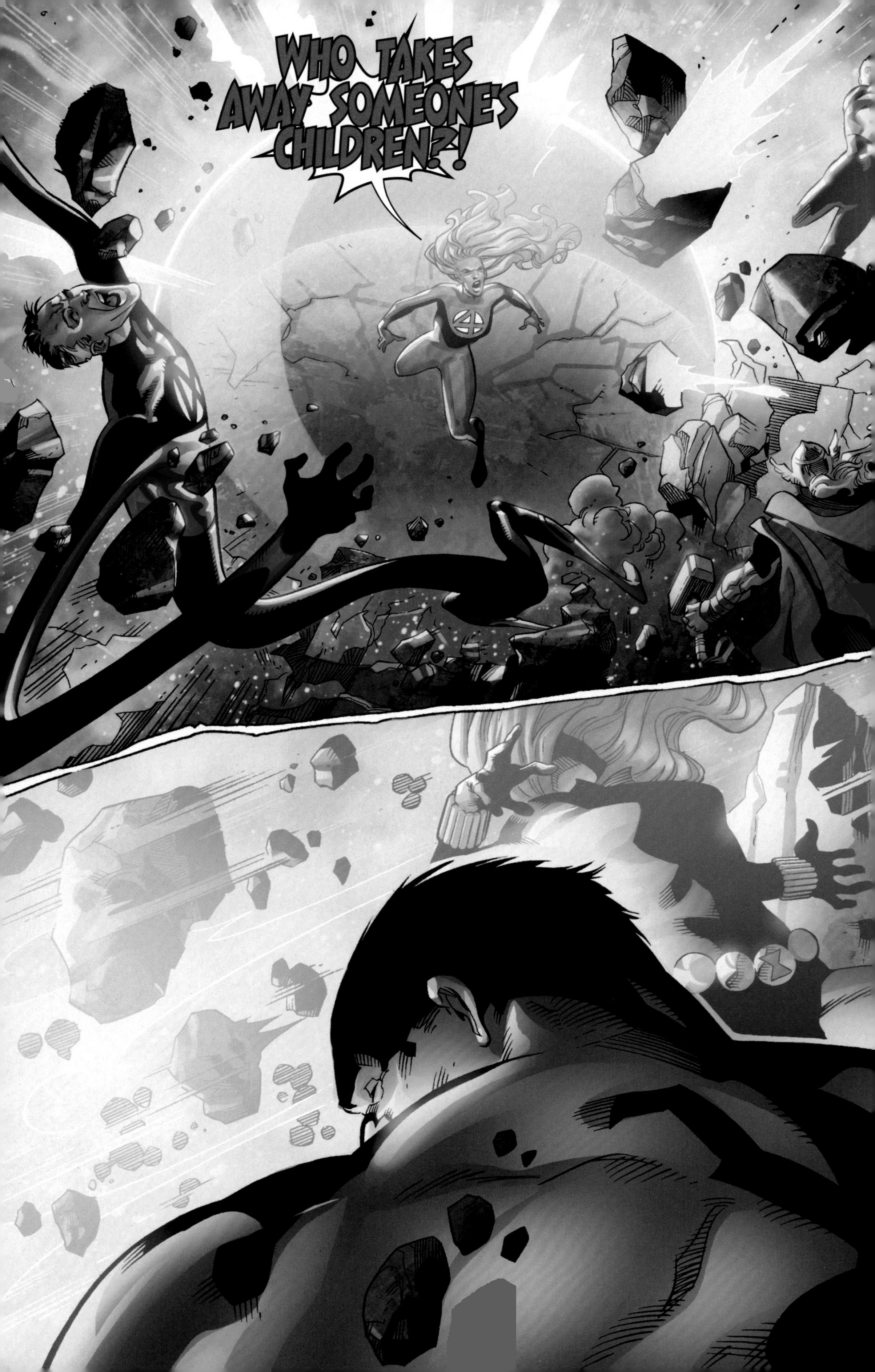
WHO TAKES AWAY SOMEONE'S CHILDREN?!

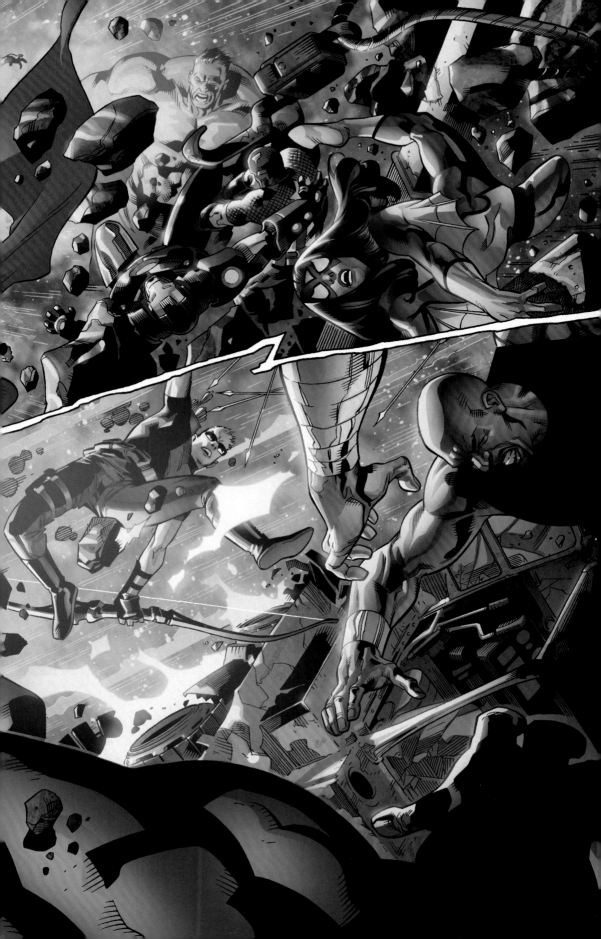

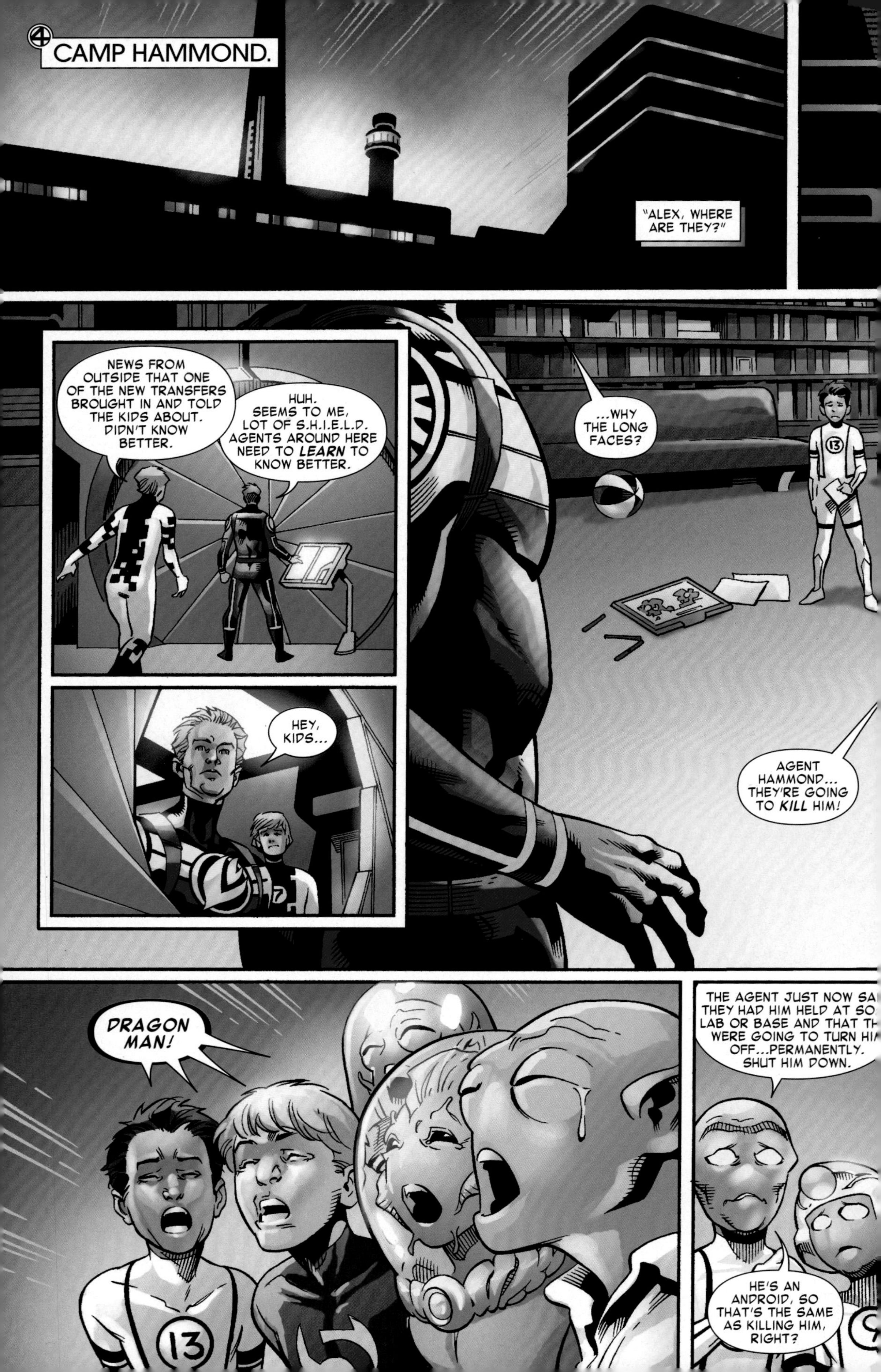

CAMP HAMMOND.
"ALEX, WHERE ARE THEY?"
NEWS FROM OUTSIDE THAT ONE OF THE NEW TRANSFERS BROUGHT IN AND TOLD THE KIDS ABOUT. DIDN'T KNOW BETTER.
HUH. SEEMS TO ME, LOT OF S.H.I.E.L.D. AGENTS AROUND HERE NEED TO LEARN TO KNOW BETTER.
HEY, KIDS...
...WHY THE LONG FACES?
AGENT HAMMOND... THEY'RE GOING TO KILL HIM!
DRAGON MAN!
THE AGENT JUST NOW SA THEY HAD HIM HELD AT SO LAB OR BASE AND THAT TH WERE GOING TO TURN HI OFF...PERMANENTLY. SHUT HIM DOWN.
HE'S AN ANDROID, SO THAT'S THE SAME AS KILLING HIM, RIGHT?

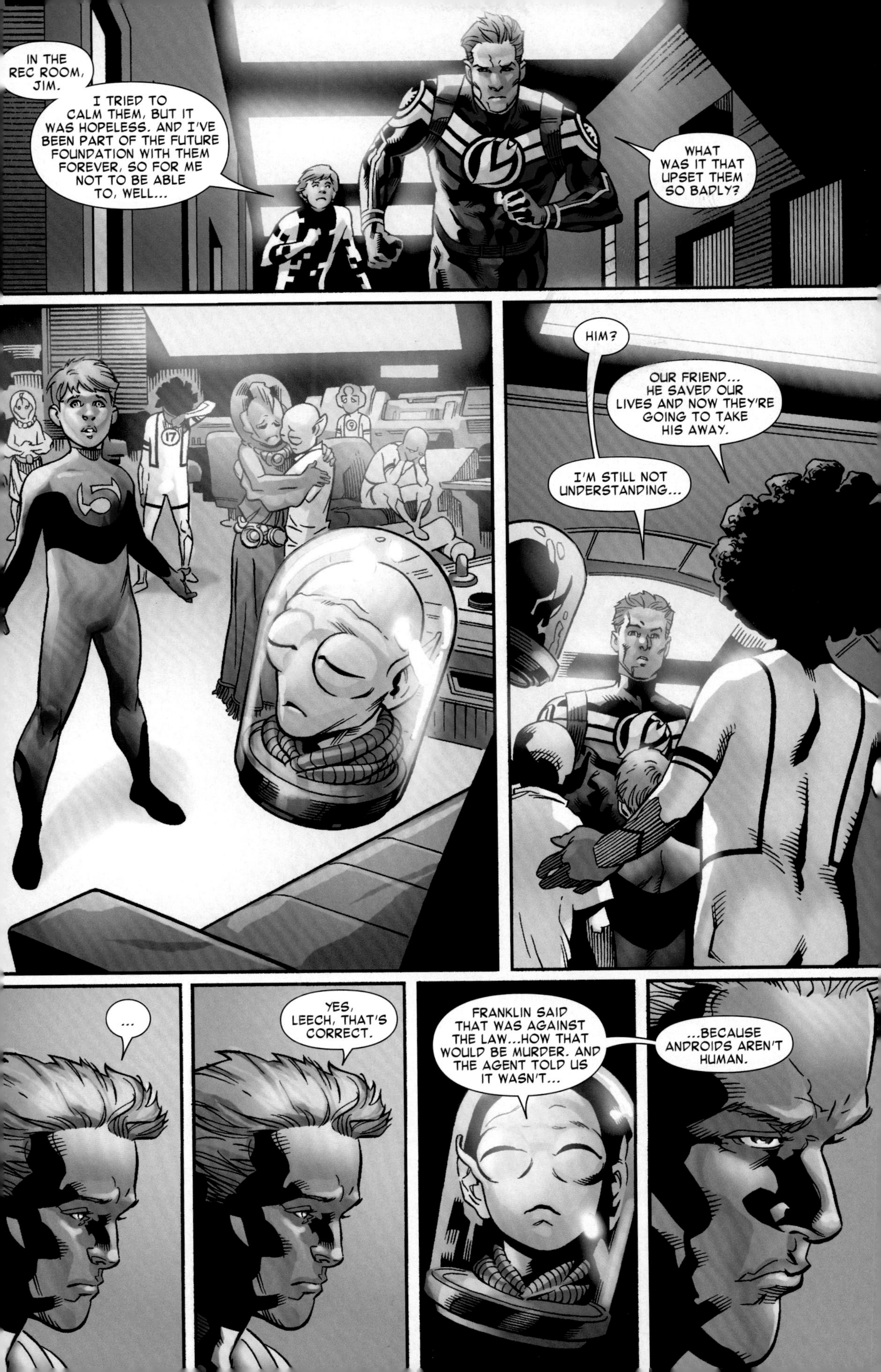
IN THE REC ROOM, JIM.
I TRIED TO CALM THEM, BUT IT WAS HOPELESS. AND I'VE BEEN PART OF THE FUTURE FOUNDATION WITH THEM FOREVER, SO FOR ME NOT TO BE ABLE TO, WELL...
WHAT WAS IT THAT UPSET THEM SO BADLY?
HIM?
OUR FRIEND... HE SAVED OUR LIVES AND NOW THEY'RE GOING TO TAKE HIS AWAY.
I'M STILL NOT UNDERSTANDING...
...
YES, LEECH, THAT'S CORRECT.
FRANKLIN SAID THAT WAS AGAINST THE LAW...HOW THAT WOULD BE MURDER. AND THE AGENT TOLD US IT WASN'T...
...BECAUSE ANDROIDS AREN'T HUMAN.

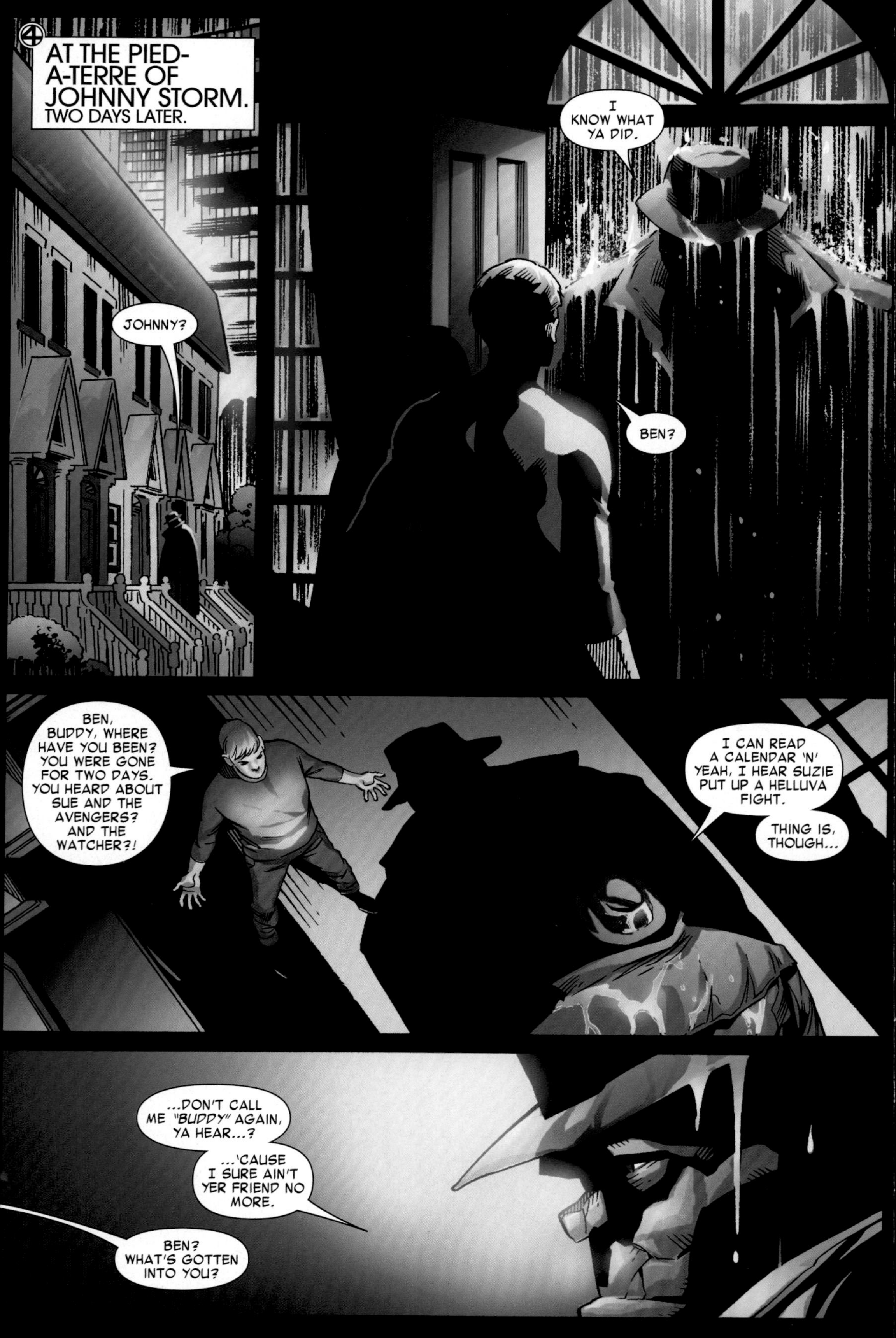
AT THE PIED-A-TERRE OF JOHNNY STORM. TWO DAYS LATER.
JOHNNY?
I KNOW WHAT YA DID.
BEN?
BEN, BUDDY, WHERE HAVE YOU BEEN? YOU WERE GONE FOR TWO DAYS. YOU HEARD ABOUT SUE AND THE AVENGERS? AND THE WATCHER?!
I CAN READ A CALENDAR 'N' YEAH, I HEAR SUZIE PUT UP A HELLUVA FIGHT.
THING IS, THOUGH...
...DON'T CALL ME "BUDDY" AGAIN, YA HEAR...?
...'CAUSE I SURE AIN'T YER FRIEND NO MORE.
BEN? WHAT'S GOTTEN INTO YOU?

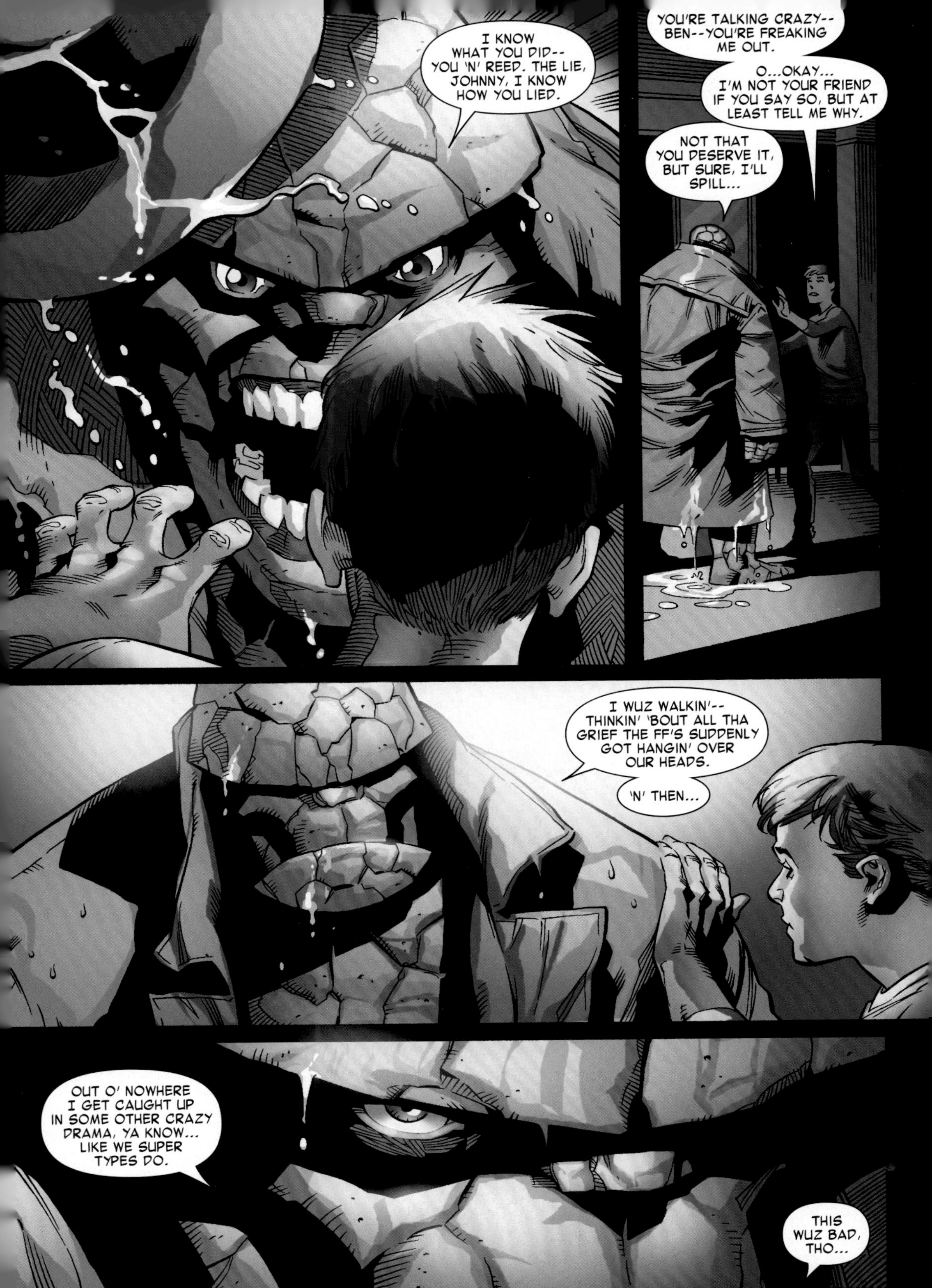
I KNOW WHAT YOU DID--YOU 'N' REED. THE LIE, JOHNNY, I KNOW HOW YOU LIED.
YOU'RE TALKING CRAZY--BEN--YOU'RE FREAKING ME OUT.
O...OKAY... I'M NOT YOUR FRIEND IF YOU SAY SO, BUT AT LEAST TELL ME WHY.
NOT THAT YOU DESERVE IT, BUT SURE, I'LL SPILL...
I WUZ WALKIN'--THINKIN' 'BOUT ALL THA GRIEF THE FF'S SUDDENLY GOT HANGIN' OVER OUR HEADS.
'N' THEN...
OUT O' NOWHERE I GET CAUGHT UP IN SOME OTHER CRAZY DRAMA, YA KNOW... LIKE WE SUPER TYPES DO.
THIS WUZ BAD, THO...

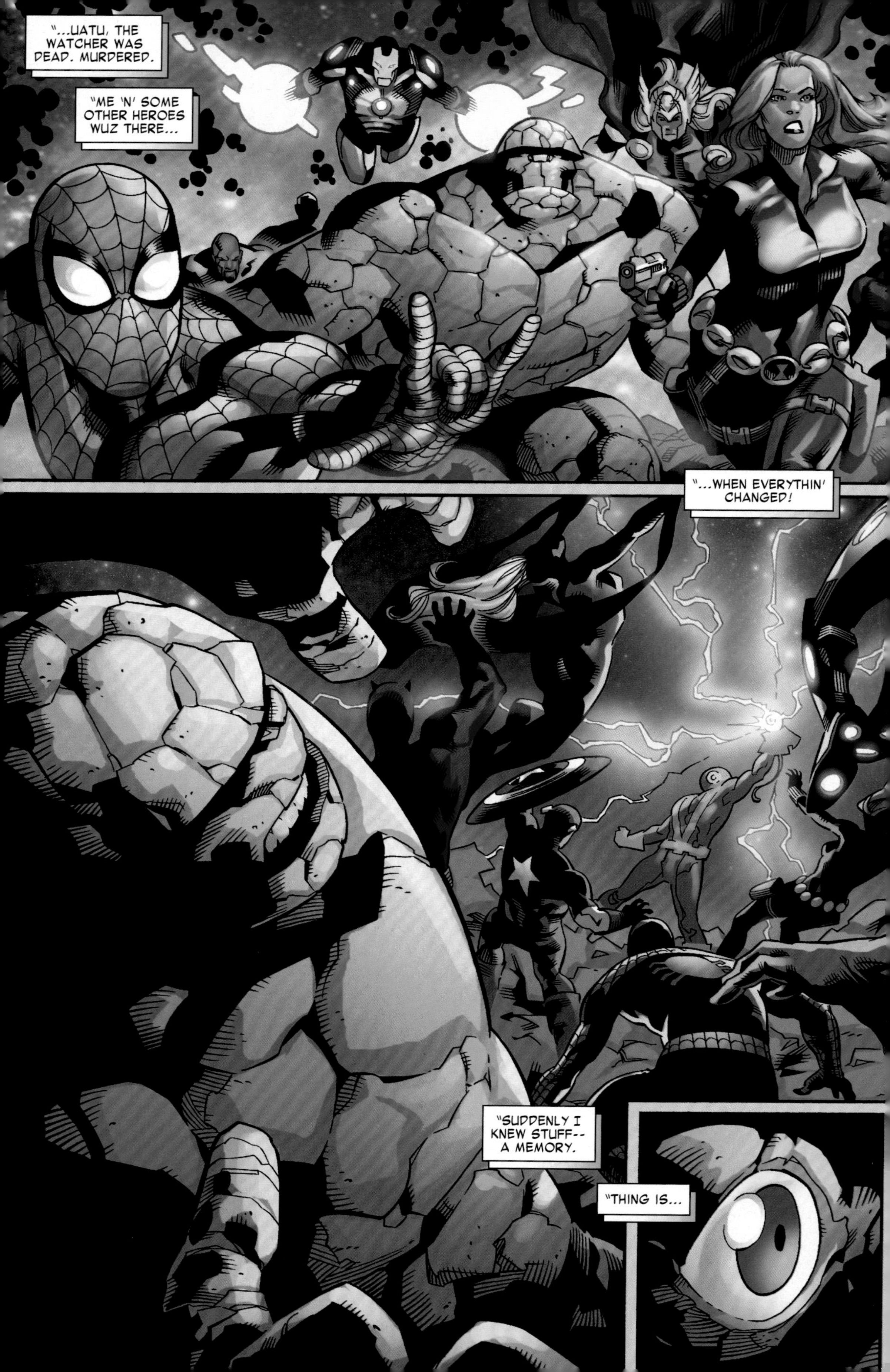
"...UATU, THE WATCHER WAS DEAD. MURDERED.
"ME 'N' SOME OTHER HEROES WUZ THERE...
"...WHEN EVERYTHIN' CHANGED!
"SUDDENLY I KNEW STUFF-- A MEMORY.
"THING IS...

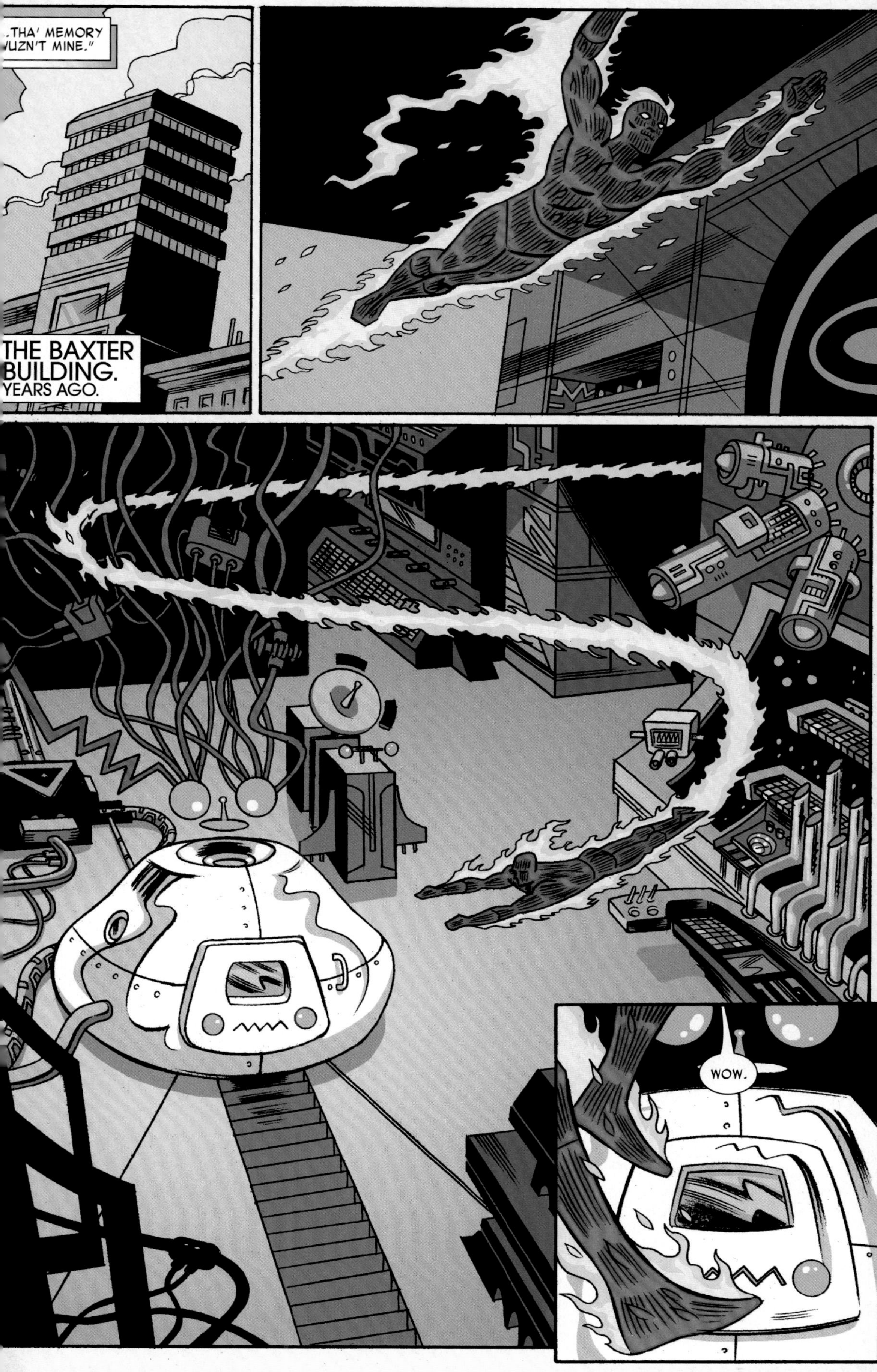
..THA' MEMORY
WUZN'T MINE."
THE BAXTER BUILDING.
YEARS AGO.
WOW.

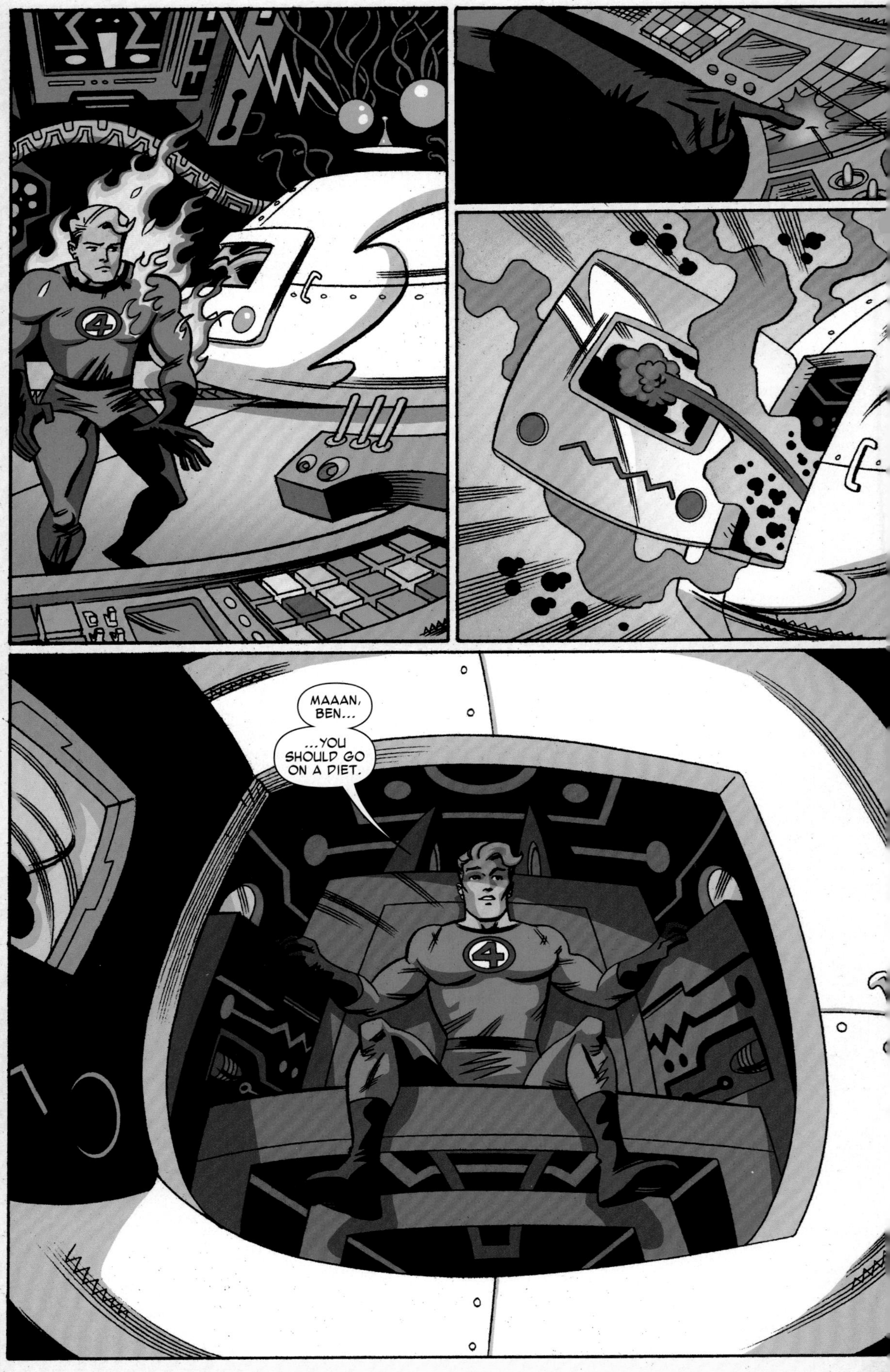
MAAAN, BEN...
...YOU SHOULD GO ON A DIET.

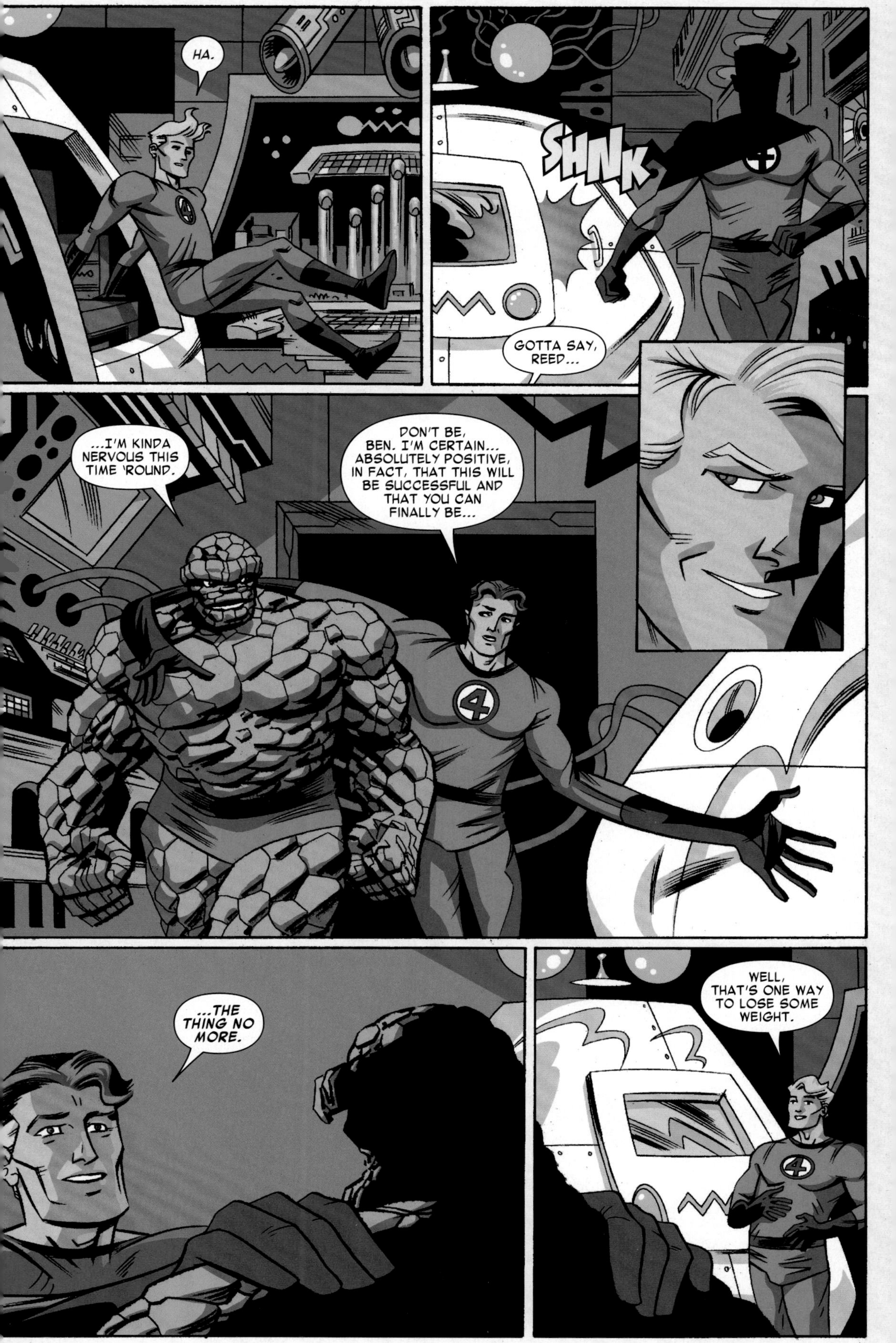
HA.
SHNK
GOTTA SAY, REED...
...I'M KINDA NERVOUS THIS TIME 'ROUND.
DON'T BE, BEN. I'M CERTAIN... ABSOLUTELY POSITIVE, IN FACT, THAT THIS WILL BE SUCCESSFUL AND THAT YOU CAN FINALLY BE...
...THE THING NO MORE.
WELL, THAT'S ONE WAY TO LOSE SOME WEIGHT.

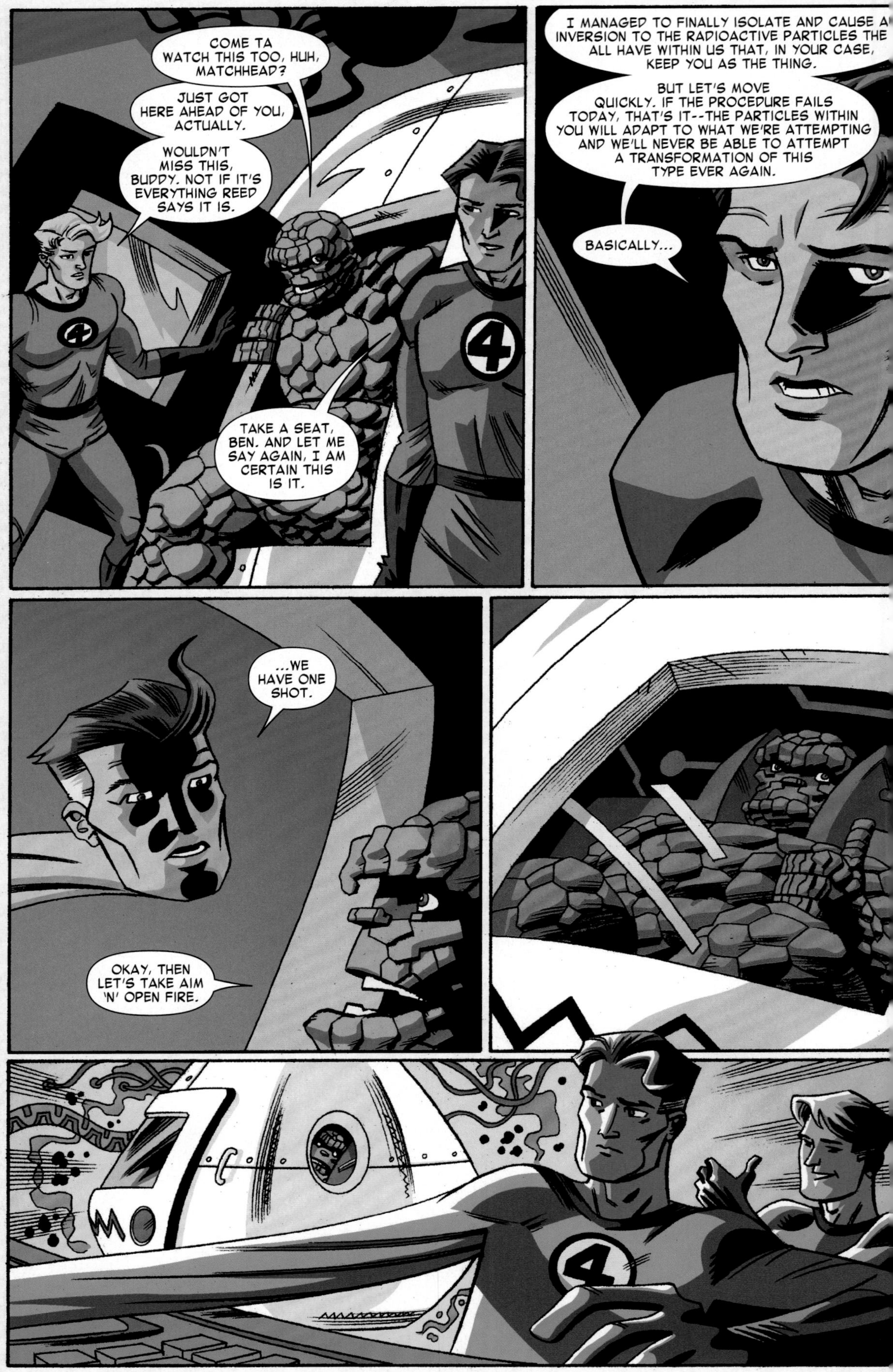
COME TA WATCH THIS TOO, HUH, MATCHHEAD?
JUST GOT HERE AHEAD OF YOU, ACTUALLY.
WOULDN'T MISS THIS, BUDDY. NOT IF IT'S EVERYTHING REED SAYS IT IS.
TAKE A SEAT, BEN. AND LET ME SAY AGAIN, I AM CERTAIN THIS IS IT.
I MANAGED TO FINALLY ISOLATE AND CAUSE A INVERSION TO THE RADIOACTIVE PARTICLES THE ALL HAVE WITHIN US THAT, IN YOUR CASE, KEEP YOU AS THE THING.
BUT LET'S MOVE QUICKLY. IF THE PROCEDURE FAILS TODAY, THAT'S IT--THE PARTICLES WITHIN YOU WILL ADAPT TO WHAT WE'RE ATTEMPTING AND WE'LL NEVER BE ABLE TO ATTEMPT A TRANSFORMATION OF THIS TYPE EVER AGAIN.
BASICALLY...
...WE HAVE ONE SHOT.
OKAY, THEN LET'S TAKE AIM 'N' OPEN FIRE.

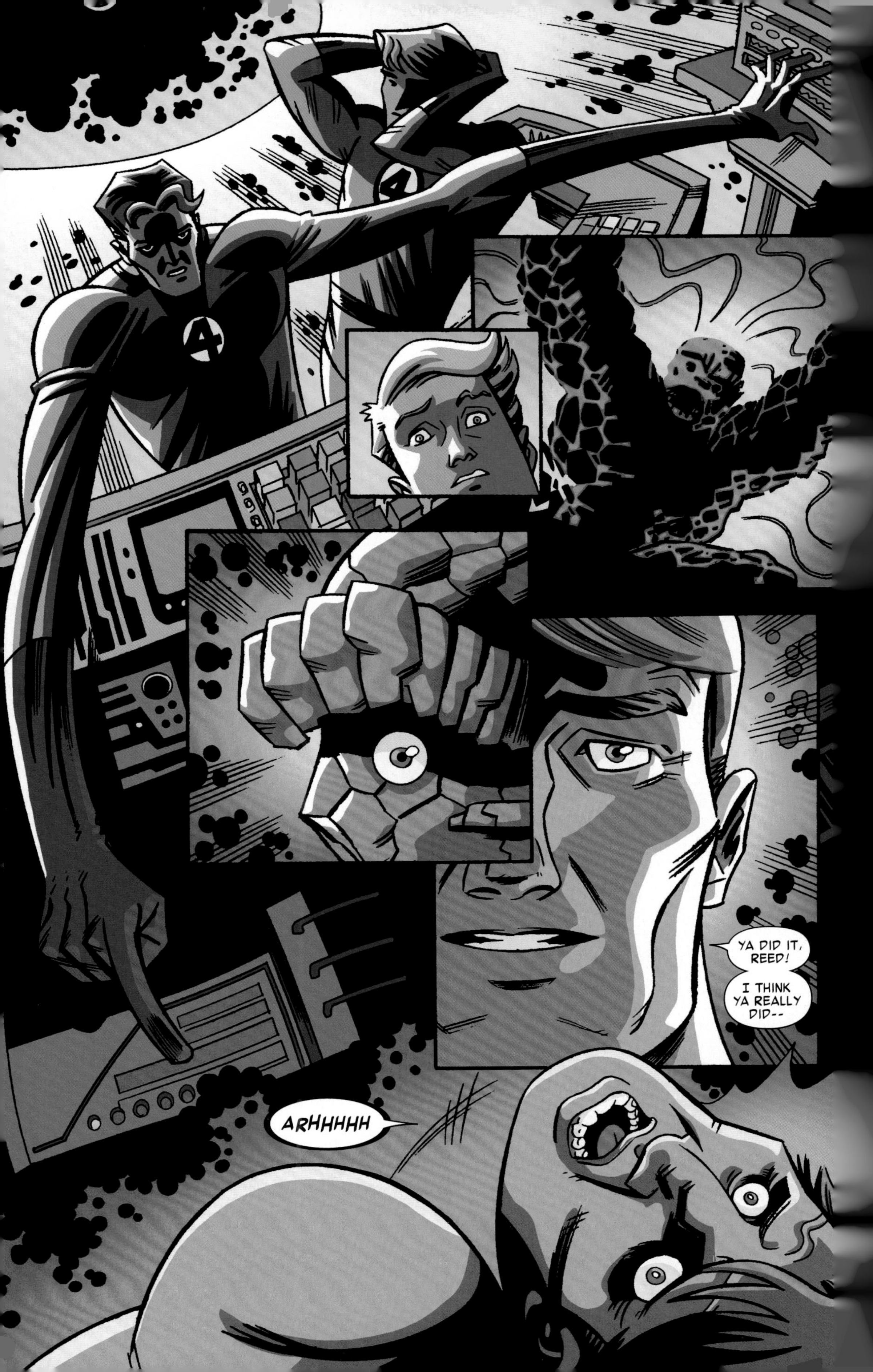
YA DID IT, REED!
I THINK YA REALLY DID--
ARHHHHH

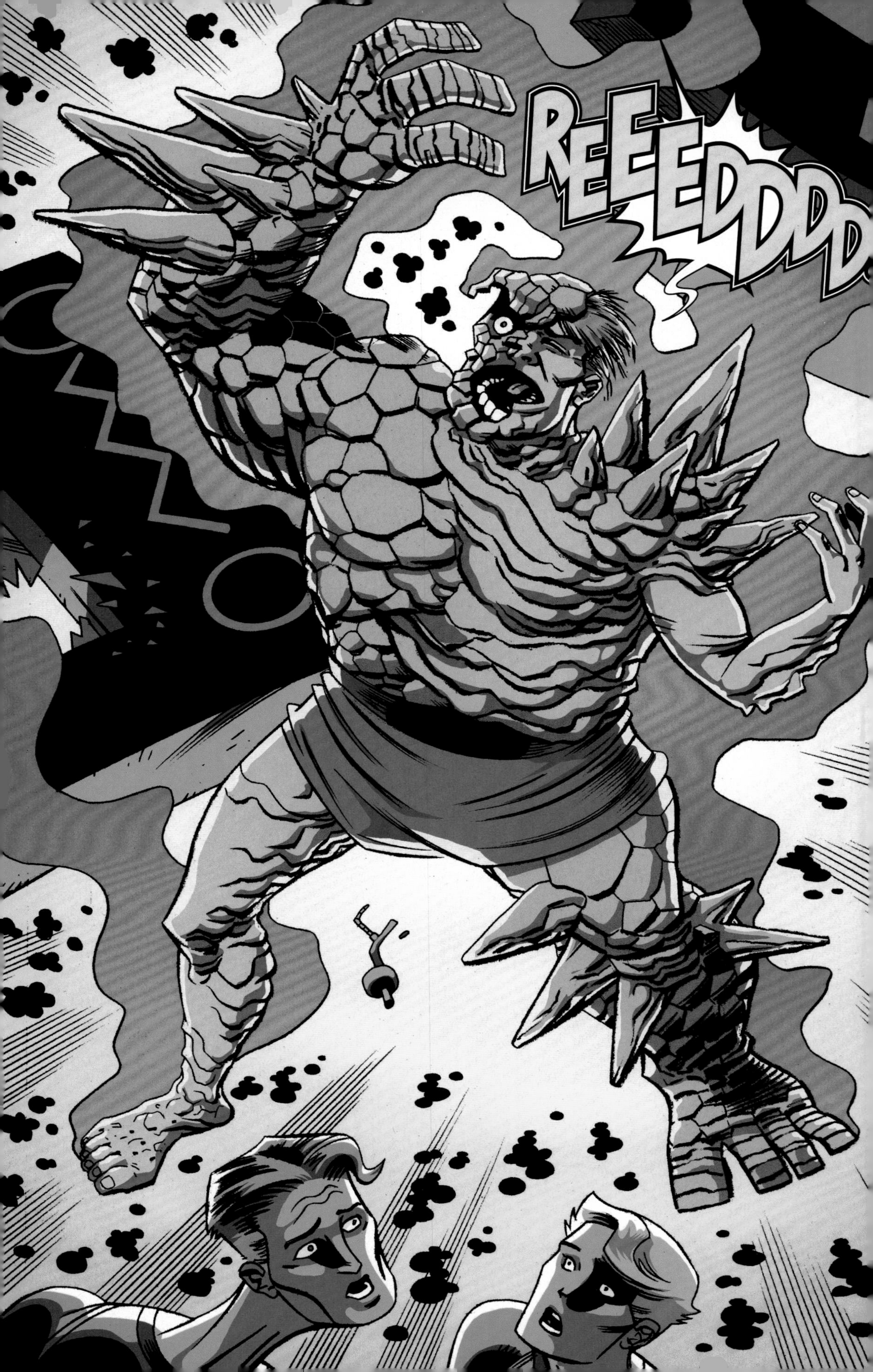
REEEDDDD

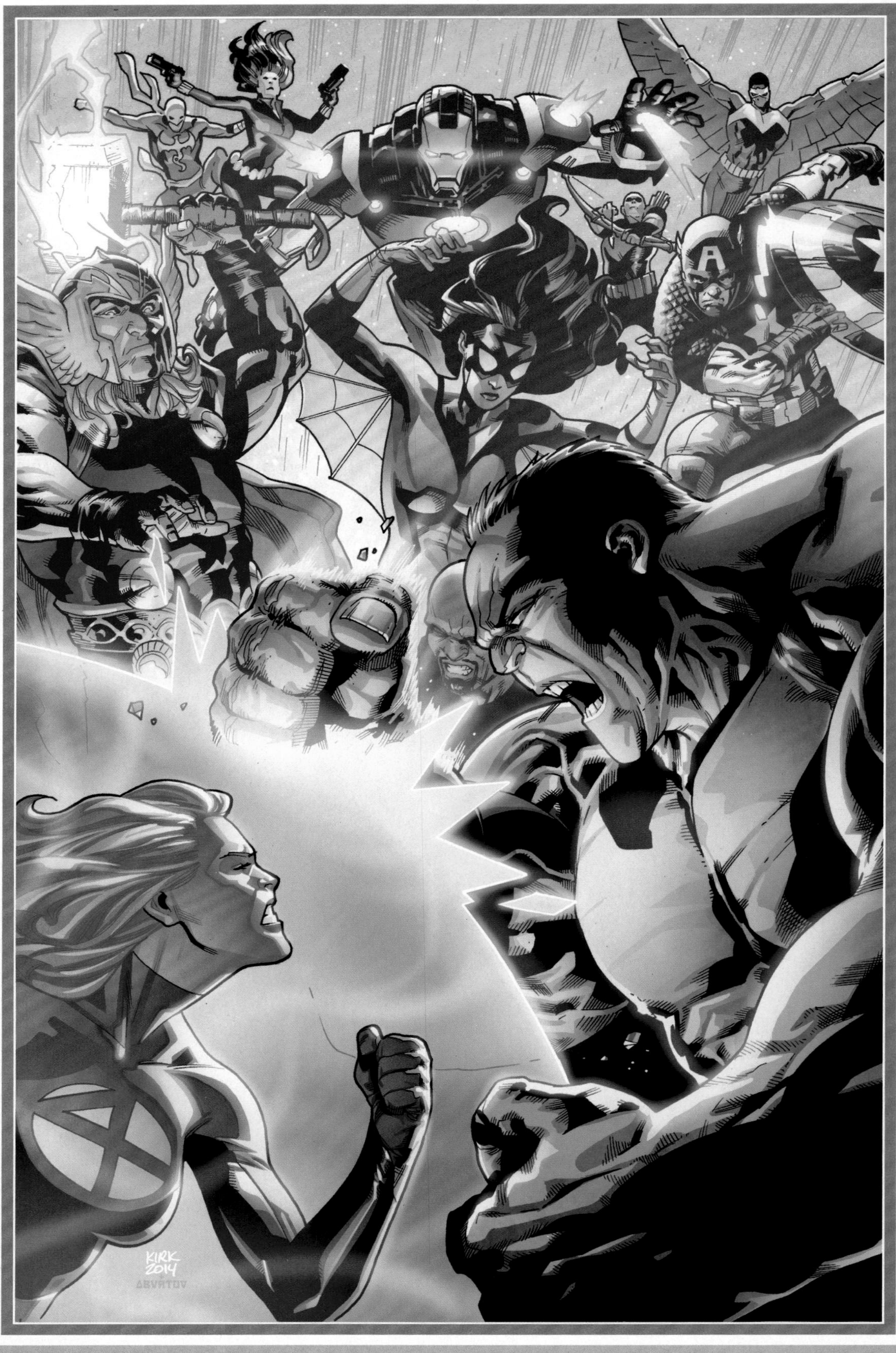
KIRK
2014

SEVEN

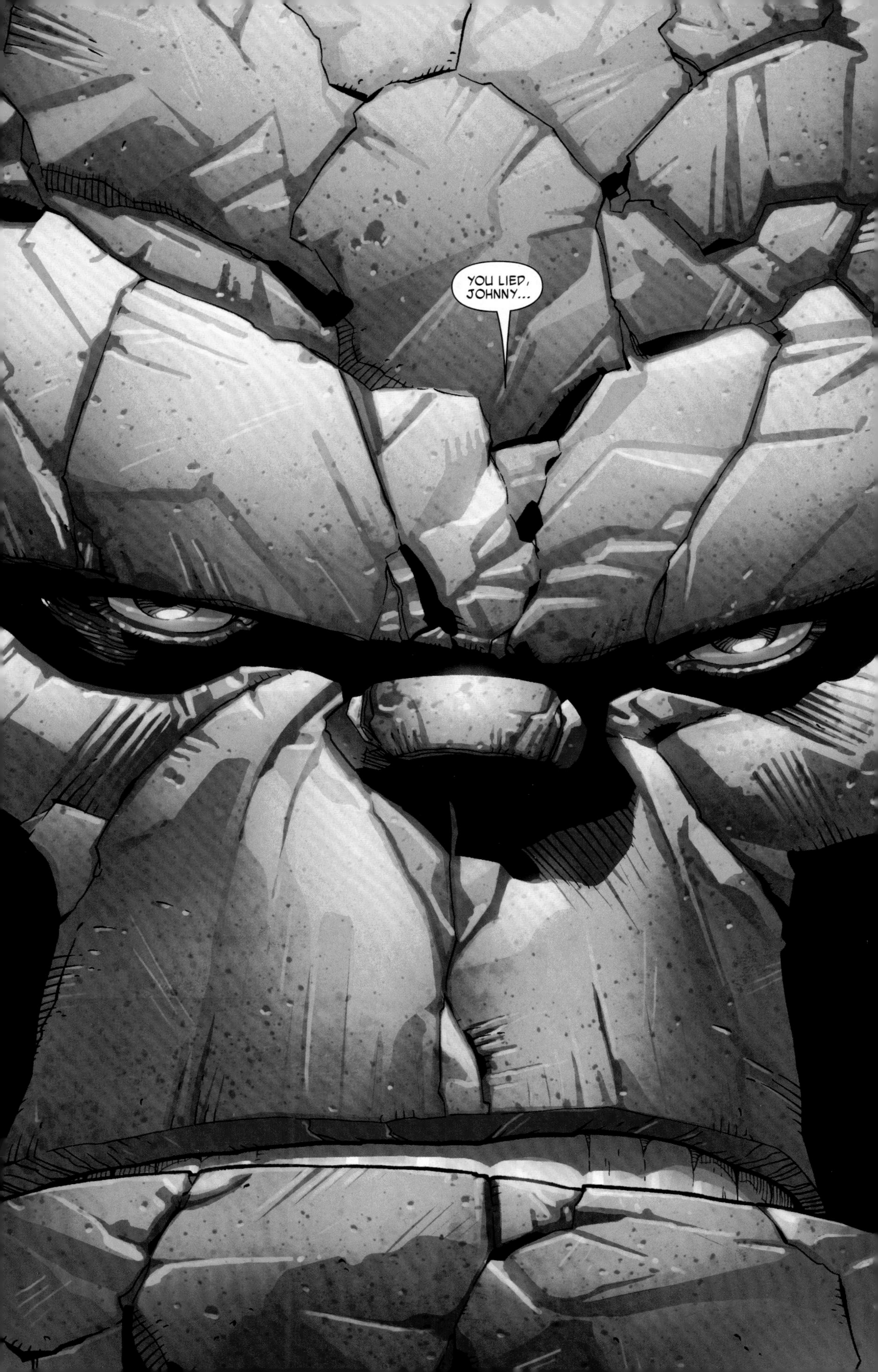
YOU LIED, JOHNNY...

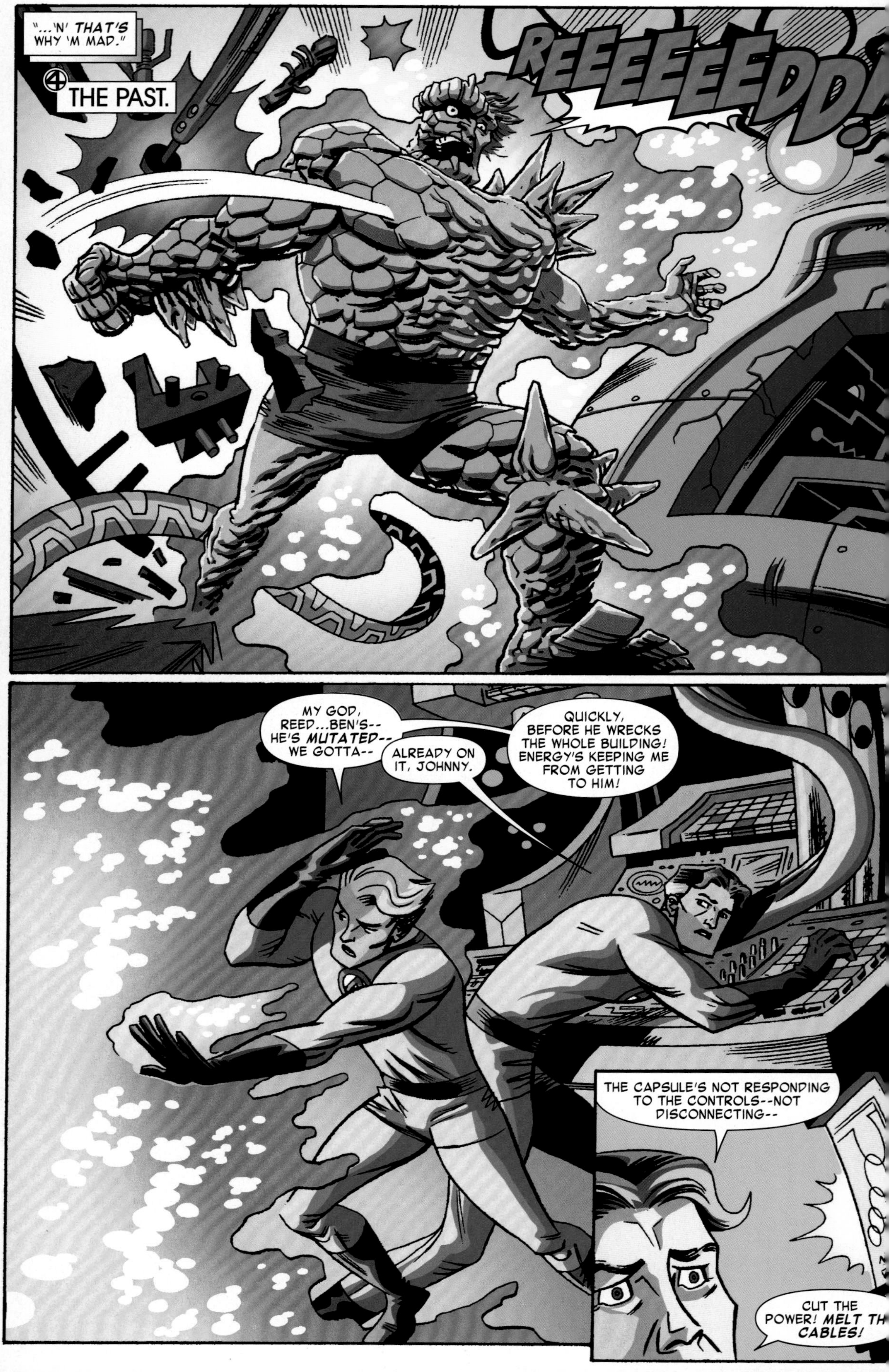

"...'N' THAT'S WHY 'M MAD."
THE PAST.
REEEEEEEDD!
MY GOD, REED...BEN'S-- HE'S MUTATED-- WE GOTTA--
ALREADY ON IT, JOHNNY.
QUICKLY, BEFORE HE WRECKS THE WHOLE BUILDING! ENERGY'S KEEPING ME FROM GETTING TO HIM!
THE CAPSULE'S NOT RESPONDING TO THE CONTROLS--NOT DISCONNECTING--
CUT THE POWER! MELT TH CABLES!

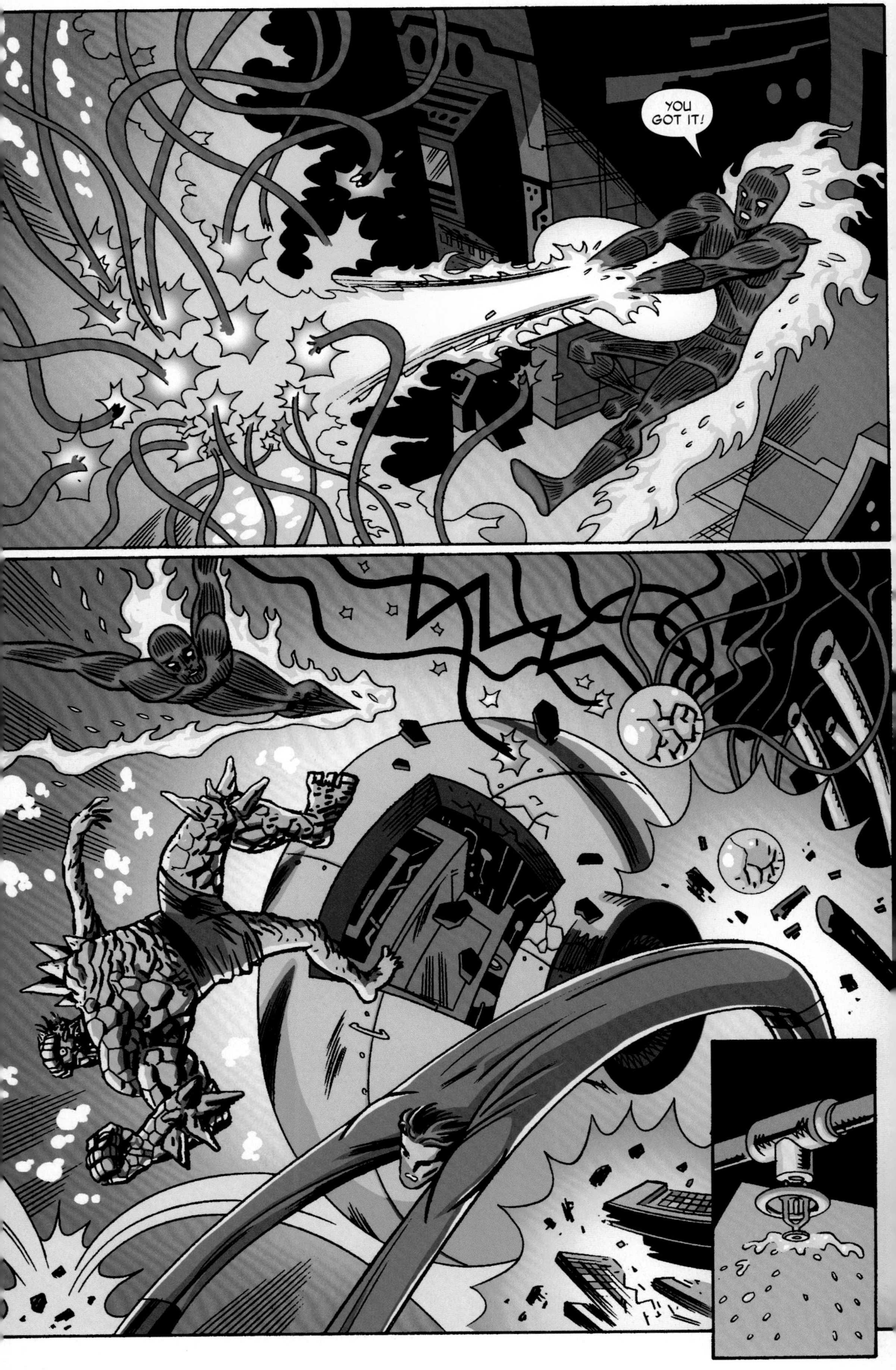
YOU GOT IT!

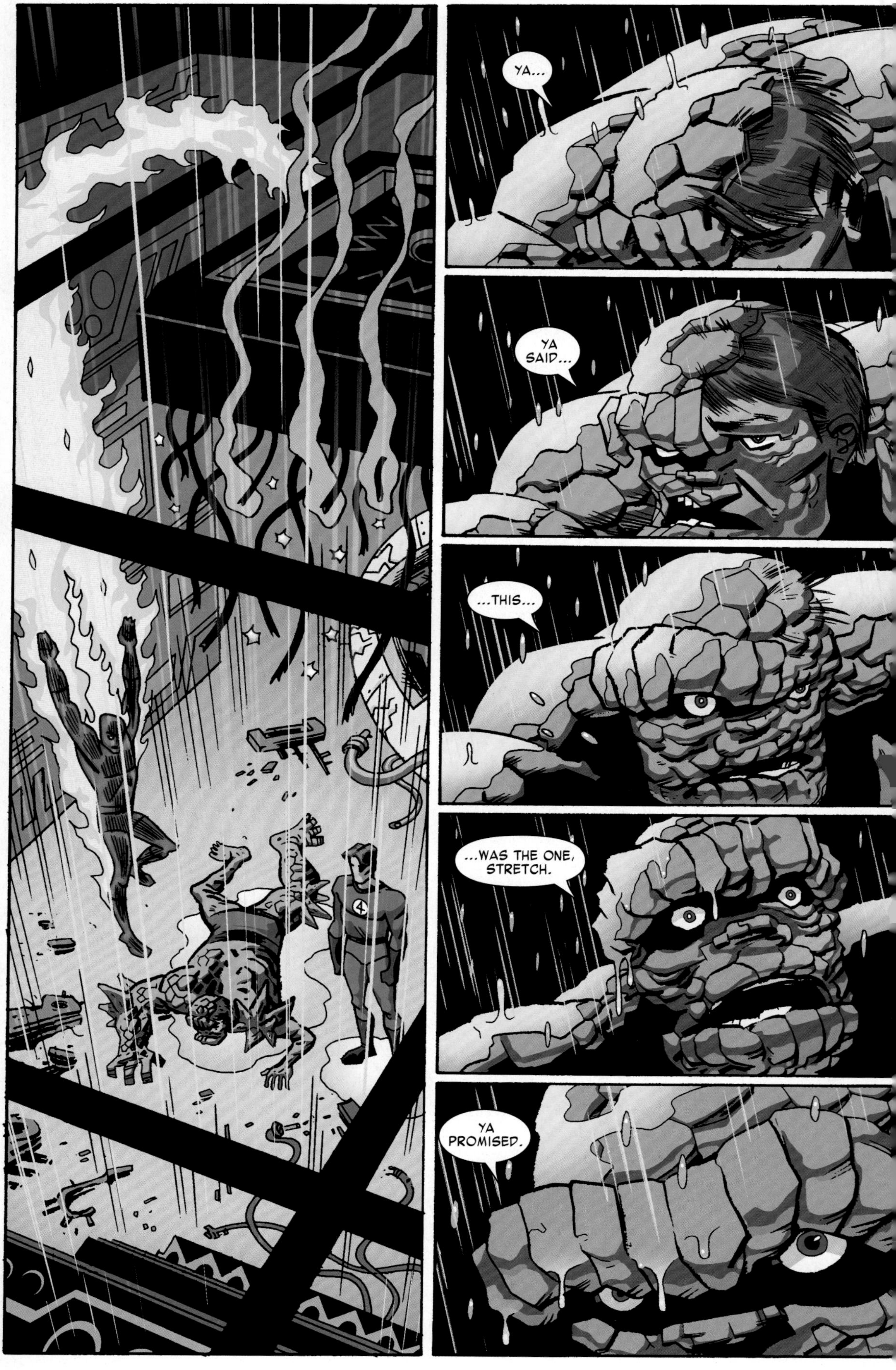

YA...
YA SAID...
...THIS...
...WAS THE ONE, STRETCH.
YA PROMISED.

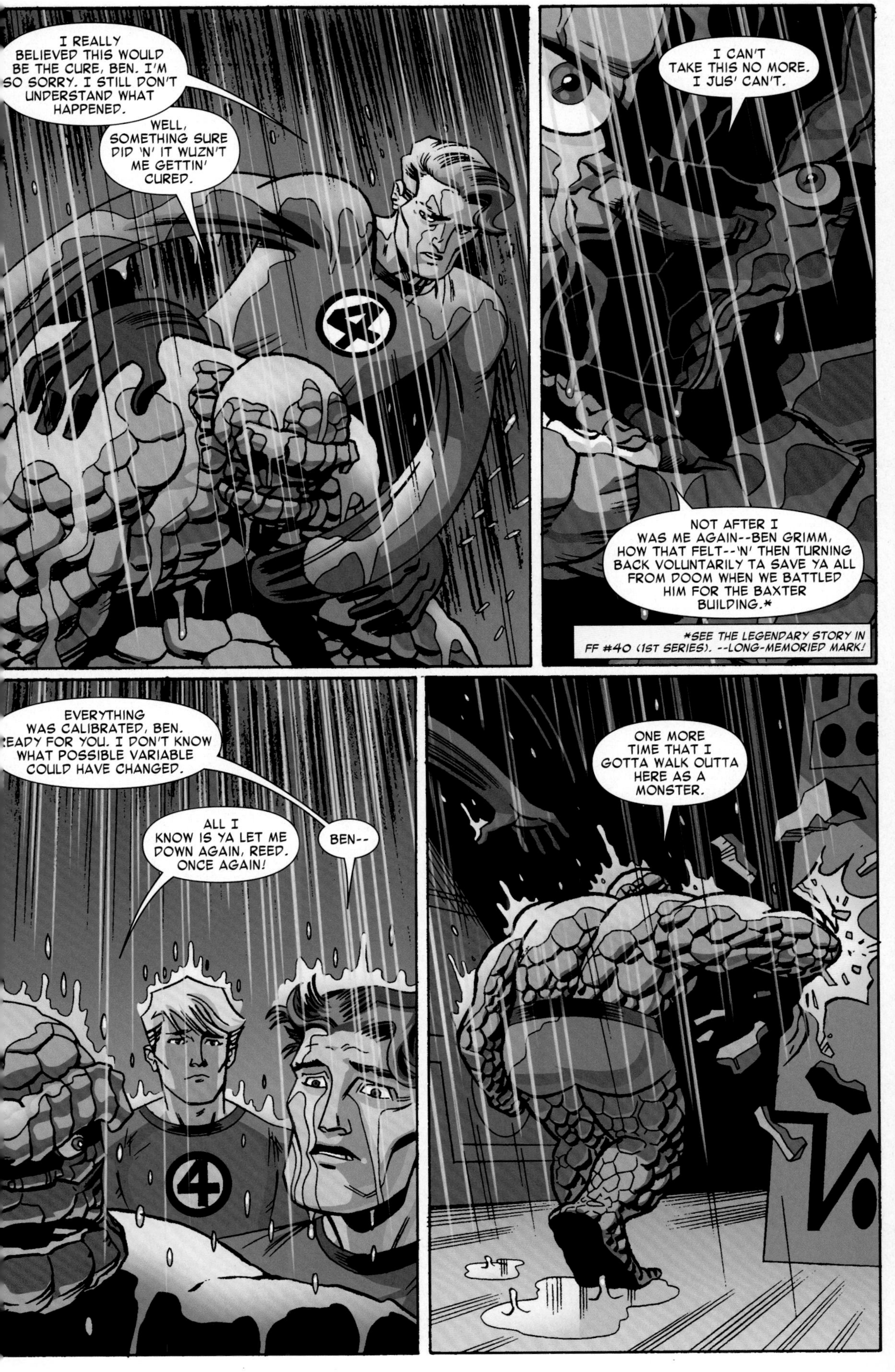
I REALLY BELIEVED THIS WOULD BE THE CURE, BEN. I'M SO SORRY. I STILL DON'T UNDERSTAND WHAT HAPPENED.
WELL, SOMETHING SURE DID 'N' IT WUZN'T ME GETTIN' CURED.
I CAN'T TAKE THIS NO MORE. I JUS' CAN'T.
NOT AFTER I WAS ME AGAIN--BEN GRIMM, HOW THAT FELT--'N' THEN TURNING BACK VOLUNTARILY TA SAVE YA ALL FROM DOOM WHEN WE BATTLED HIM FOR THE BAXTER BUILDING.*
*SEE THE LEGENDARY STORY IN FF #40 (1ST SERIES). --LONG-MEMORIED MARK!
EVERYTHING WAS CALIBRATED, BEN. READY FOR YOU. I DON'T KNOW WHAT POSSIBLE VARIABLE COULD HAVE CHANGED.
ALL I KNOW IS YA LET ME DOWN AGAIN, REED. ONCE AGAIN!
BEN--
ONE MORE TIME THAT I GOTTA WALK OUTTA HERE AS A MONSTER.

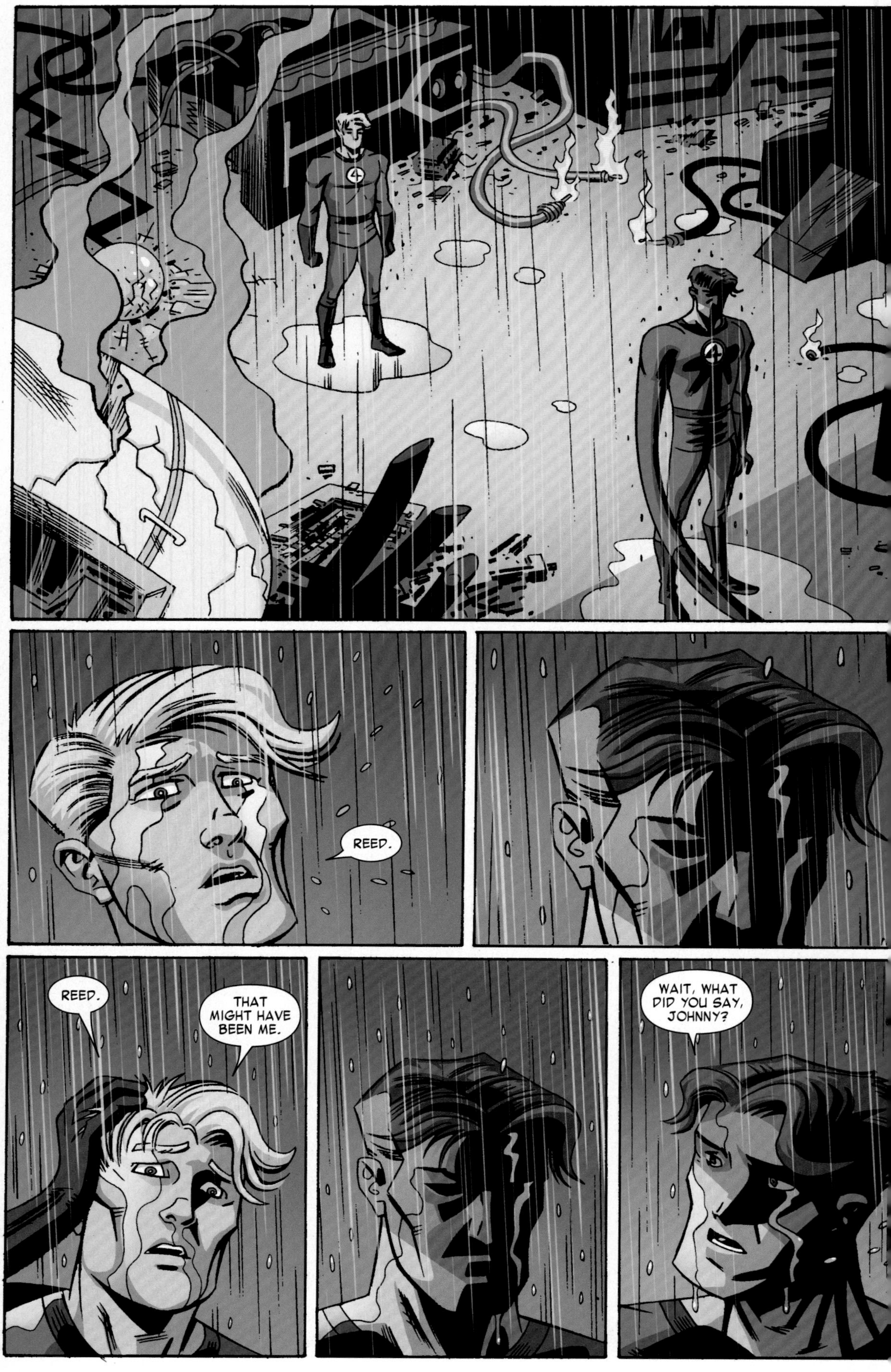
REED.
REED.
THAT MIGHT HAVE BEEN ME.
WAIT, WHAT DID YOU SAY, JOHNNY?

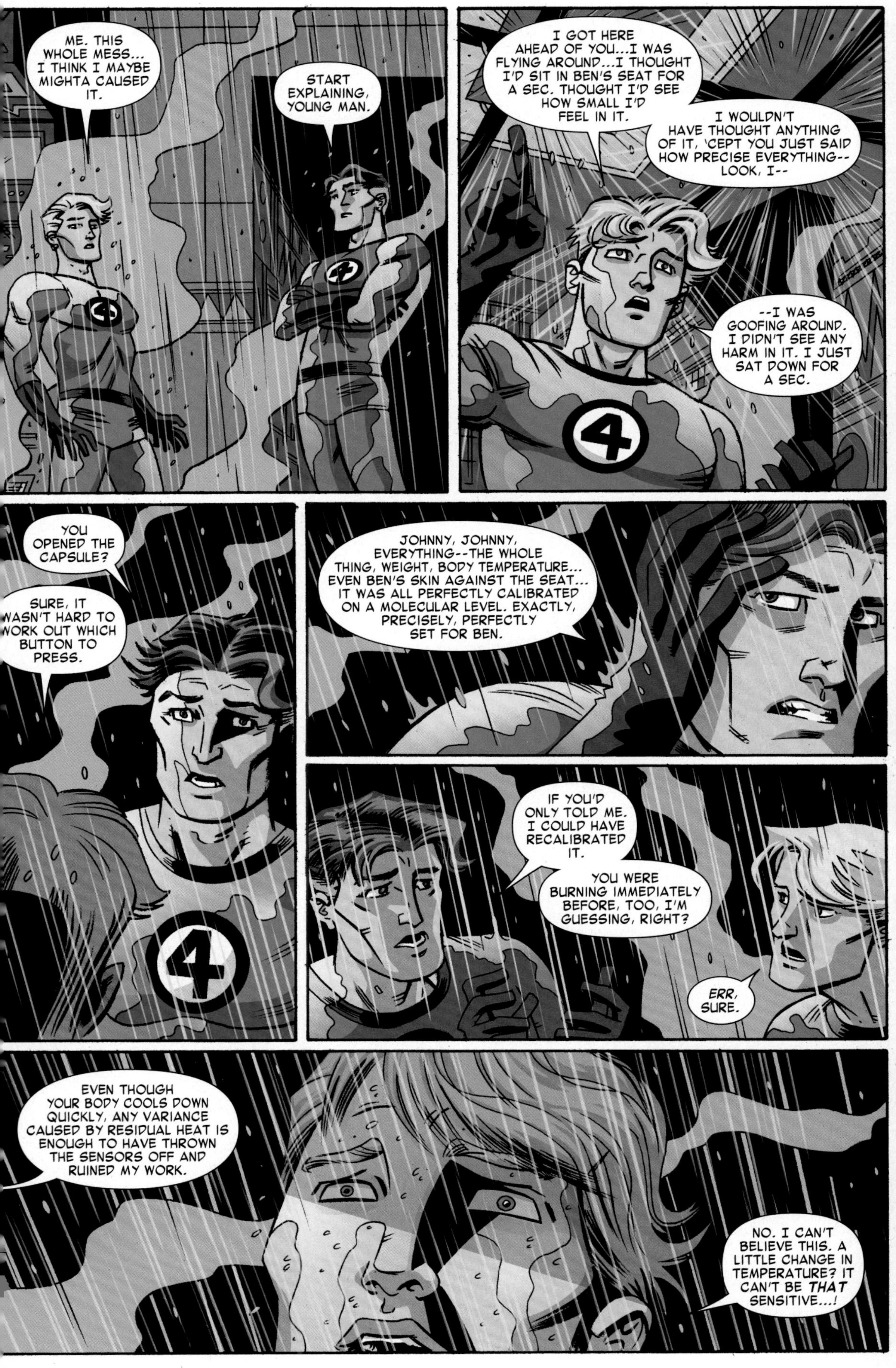
ME. THIS WHOLE MESS... I THINK I MAYBE MIGHTA CAUSED IT.
START EXPLAINING, YOUNG MAN.
I GOT HERE AHEAD OF YOU...I WAS FLYING AROUND...I THOUGHT I'D SIT IN BEN'S SEAT FOR A SEC. THOUGHT I'D SEE HOW SMALL I'D FEEL IN IT.
I WOULDN'T HAVE THOUGHT ANYTHING OF IT, 'CEPT YOU JUST SAID HOW PRECISE EVERYTHING--LOOK, I--
--I WAS GOOFING AROUND. I DIDN'T SEE ANY HARM IN IT. I JUST SAT DOWN FOR A SEC.
YOU OPENED THE CAPSULE?
SURE, IT WASN'T HARD TO WORK OUT WHICH BUTTON TO PRESS.
JOHNNY, JOHNNY, EVERYTHING--THE WHOLE THING, WEIGHT, BODY TEMPERATURE... EVEN BEN'S SKIN AGAINST THE SEAT... IT WAS ALL PERFECTLY CALIBRATED ON A MOLECULAR LEVEL. EXACTLY, PRECISELY, PERFECTLY SET FOR BEN.
IF YOU'D ONLY TOLD ME. I COULD HAVE RECALIBRATED IT.
YOU WERE BURNING IMMEDIATELY BEFORE, TOO, I'M GUESSING, RIGHT?
ERR, SURE.
EVEN THOUGH YOUR BODY COOLS DOWN QUICKLY, ANY VARIANCE CAUSED BY RESIDUAL HEAT IS ENOUGH TO HAVE THROWN THE SENSORS OFF AND RUINED MY WORK.
NO. I CAN'T BELIEVE THIS. A LITTLE CHANGE IN TEMPERATURE? IT CAN'T BE *THAT* SENSITIVE...!

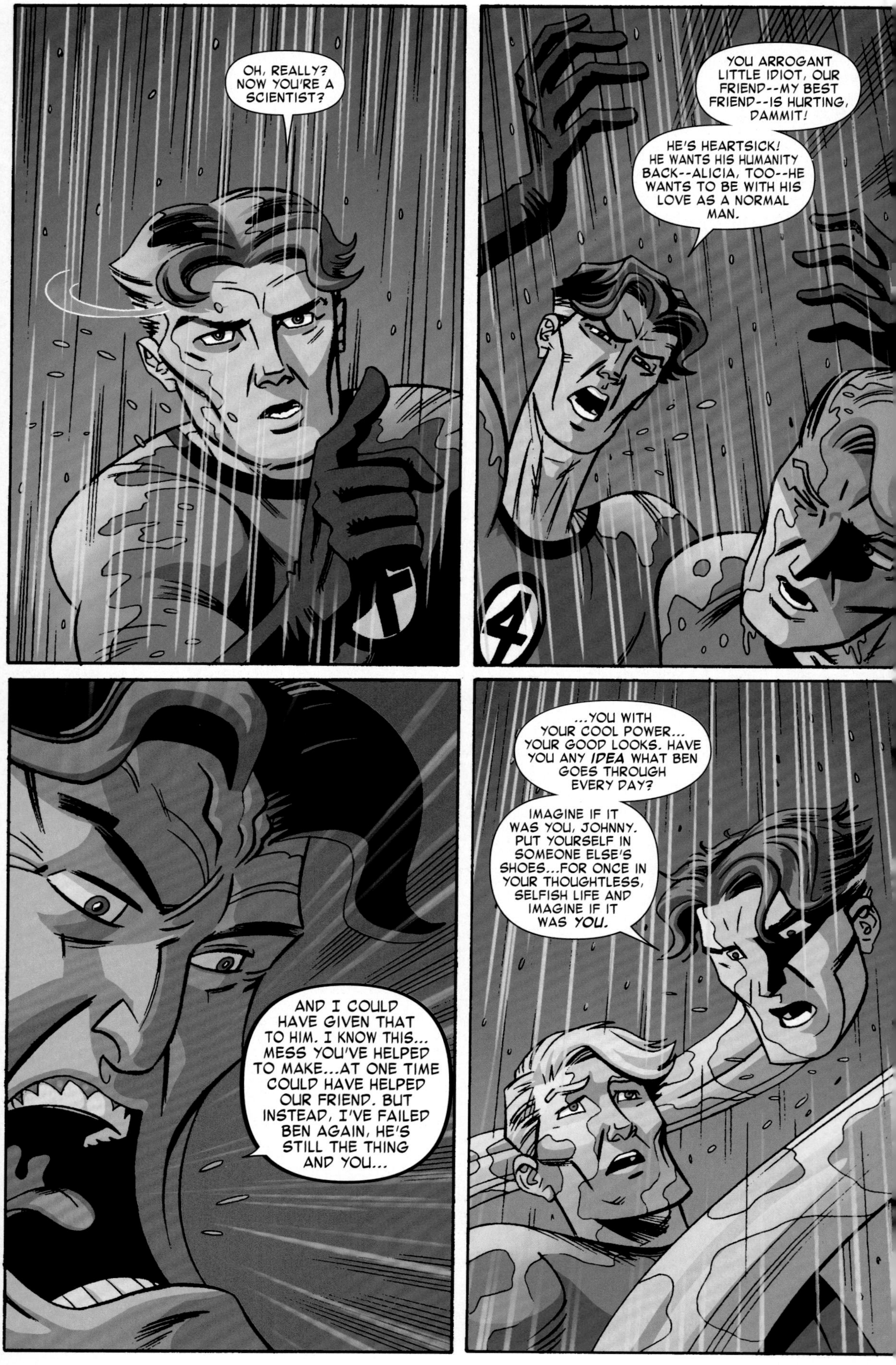
OH, REALLY? NOW YOU'RE A SCIENTIST?
YOU ARROGANT LITTLE IDIOT, OUR FRIEND--MY BEST FRIEND--IS HURTING, DAMMIT!
HE'S HEARTSICK! HE WANTS HIS HUMANITY BACK--ALICIA, TOO--HE WANTS TO BE WITH HIS LOVE AS A NORMAL MAN.
AND I COULD HAVE GIVEN THAT TO HIM. I KNOW THIS... MESS YOU'VE HELPED TO MAKE...AT ONE TIME COULD HAVE HELPED OUR FRIEND. BUT INSTEAD, I'VE FAILED BEN AGAIN, HE'S STILL THE THING AND YOU...
...YOU WITH YOUR COOL POWER... YOUR GOOD LOOKS. HAVE YOU ANY *IDEA* WHAT BEN GOES THROUGH EVERY DAY?
IMAGINE IF IT WAS YOU, JOHNNY. PUT YOURSELF IN SOMEONE ELSE'S SHOES...FOR ONCE IN YOUR THOUGHTLESS, SELFISH LIFE AND IMAGINE IF IT WAS *YOU.*

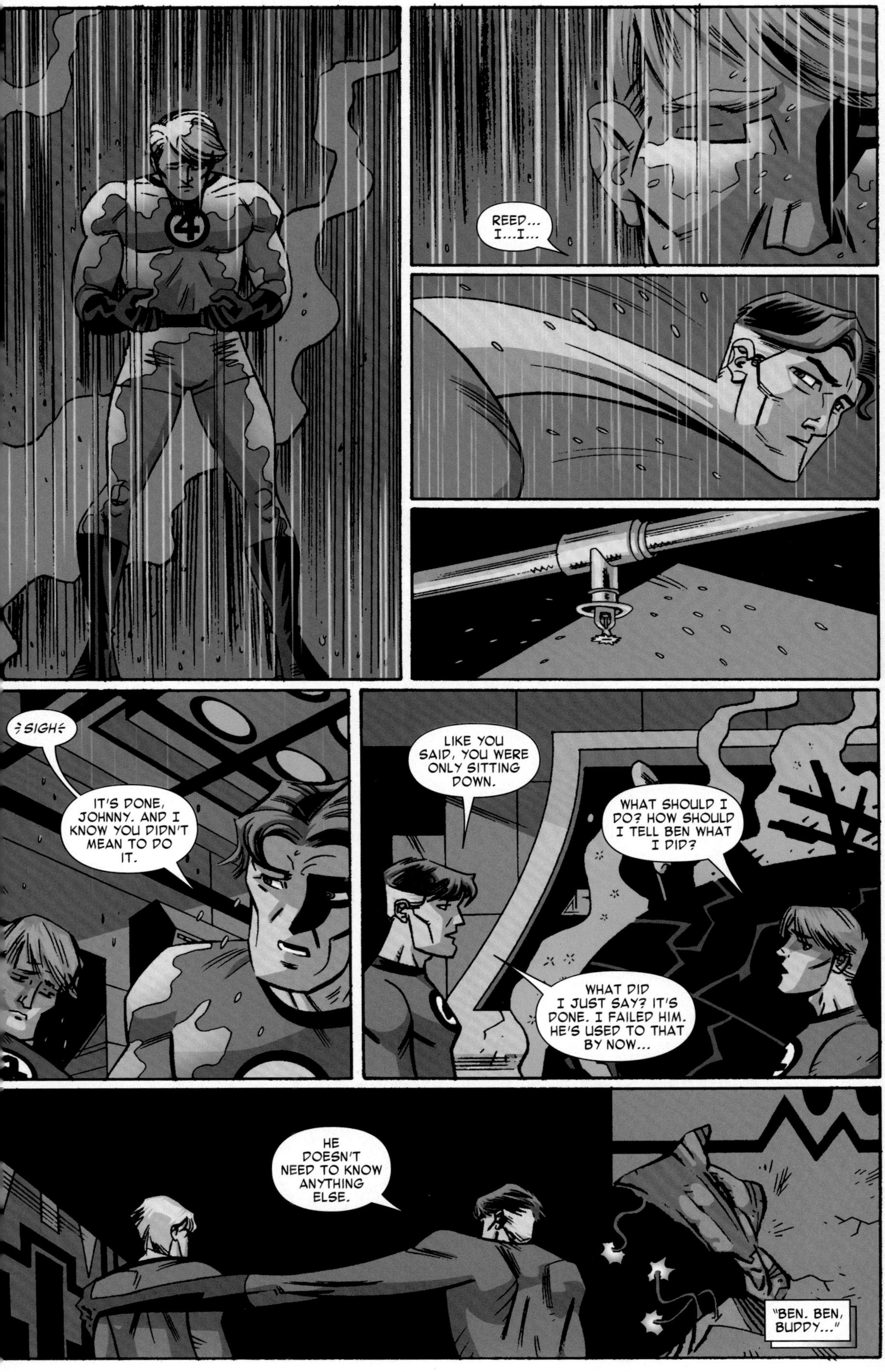
REED... I...I...
⸗SIGH⸗
IT'S DONE, JOHNNY. AND I KNOW YOU DIDN'T MEAN TO DO IT.
LIKE YOU SAID, YOU WERE ONLY SITTING DOWN.
WHAT SHOULD I DO? HOW SHOULD I TELL BEN WHAT I DID?
WHAT DID I JUST SAY? IT'S DONE. I FAILED HIM. HE'S USED TO THAT BY NOW...
HE DOESN'T NEED TO KNOW ANYTHING ELSE.
"BEN. BEN, BUDDY..."

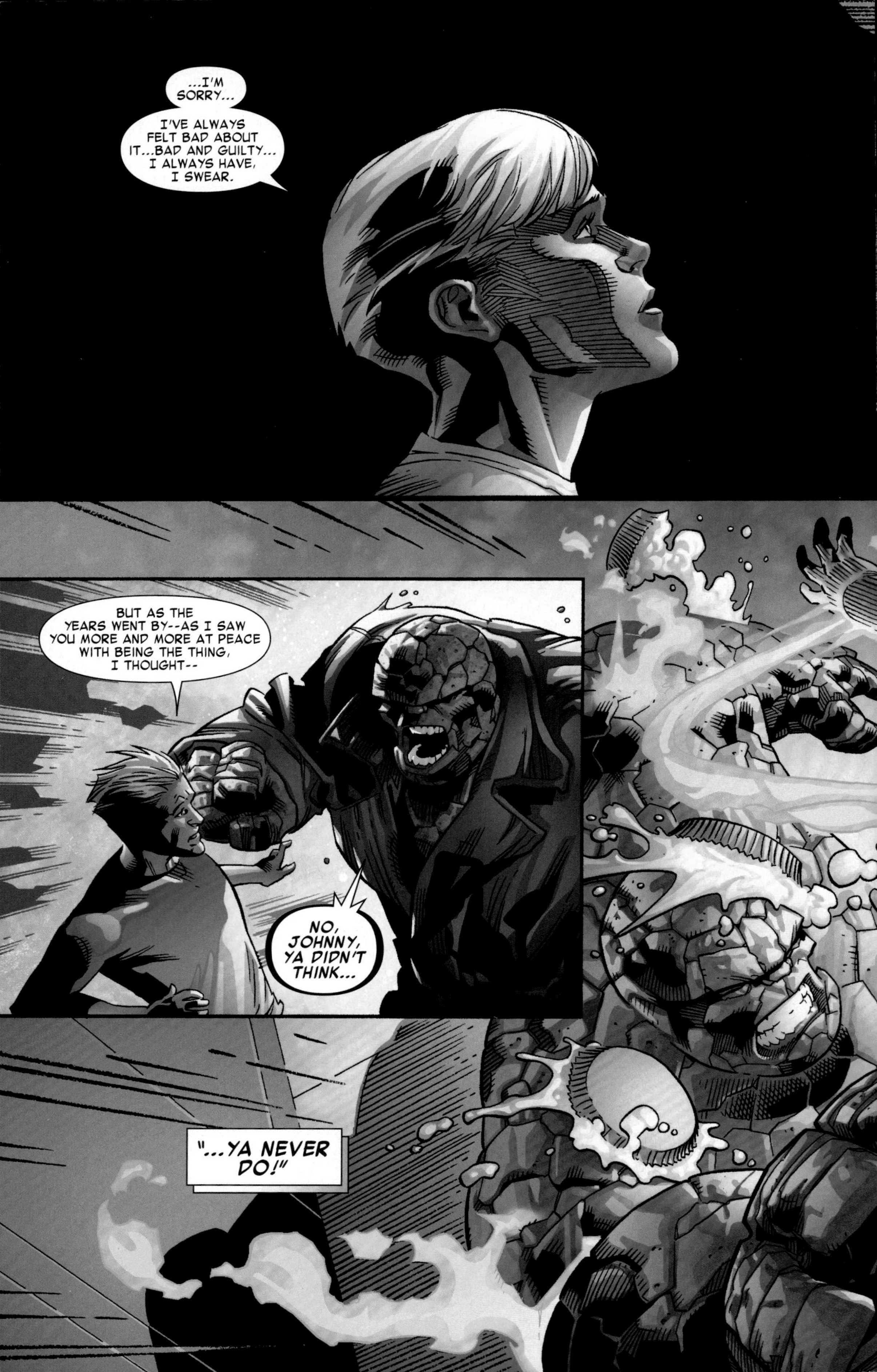
...I'M SORRY...
I'VE ALWAYS FELT BAD ABOUT IT...BAD AND GUILTY... I ALWAYS HAVE, I SWEAR.
BUT AS THE YEARS WENT BY--AS I SAW YOU MORE AND MORE AT PEACE WITH BEING THE THING, I THOUGHT--
NO, JOHNNY, YA DIDN'T THINK...
"...YA NEVER DO!"

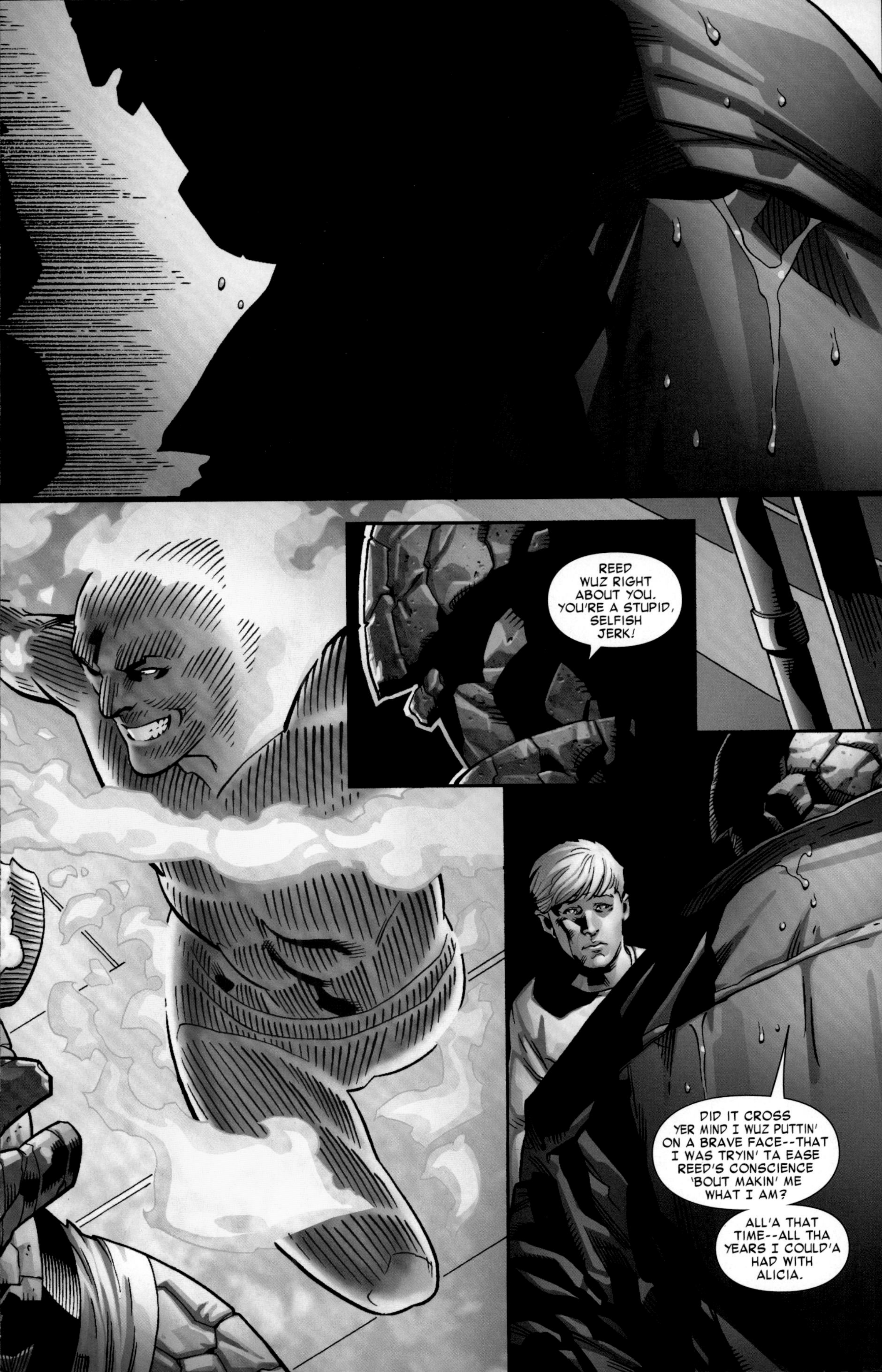
REED WUZ RIGHT ABOUT YOU. YOU'RE A STUPID, SELFISH JERK!
DID IT CROSS YER MIND I WUZ PUTTIN' ON A BRAVE FACE--THAT I WAS TRYIN' TA EASE REED'S CONSCIENCE 'BOUT MAKIN' ME WHAT I AM?
ALL'A THAT TIME--ALL THA YEARS I COULD'A HAD WITH ALICIA.

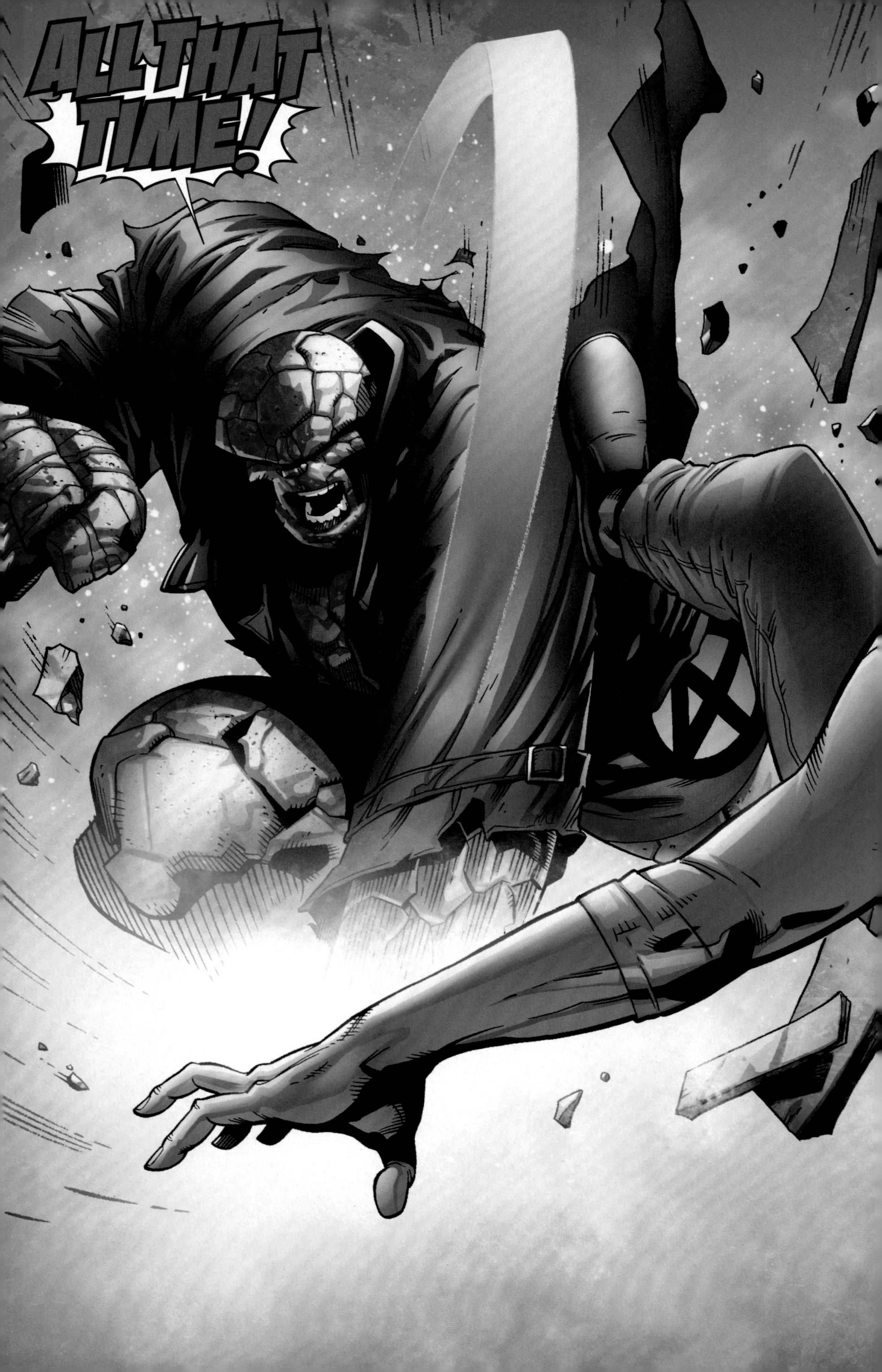
ALL THAT TIME!

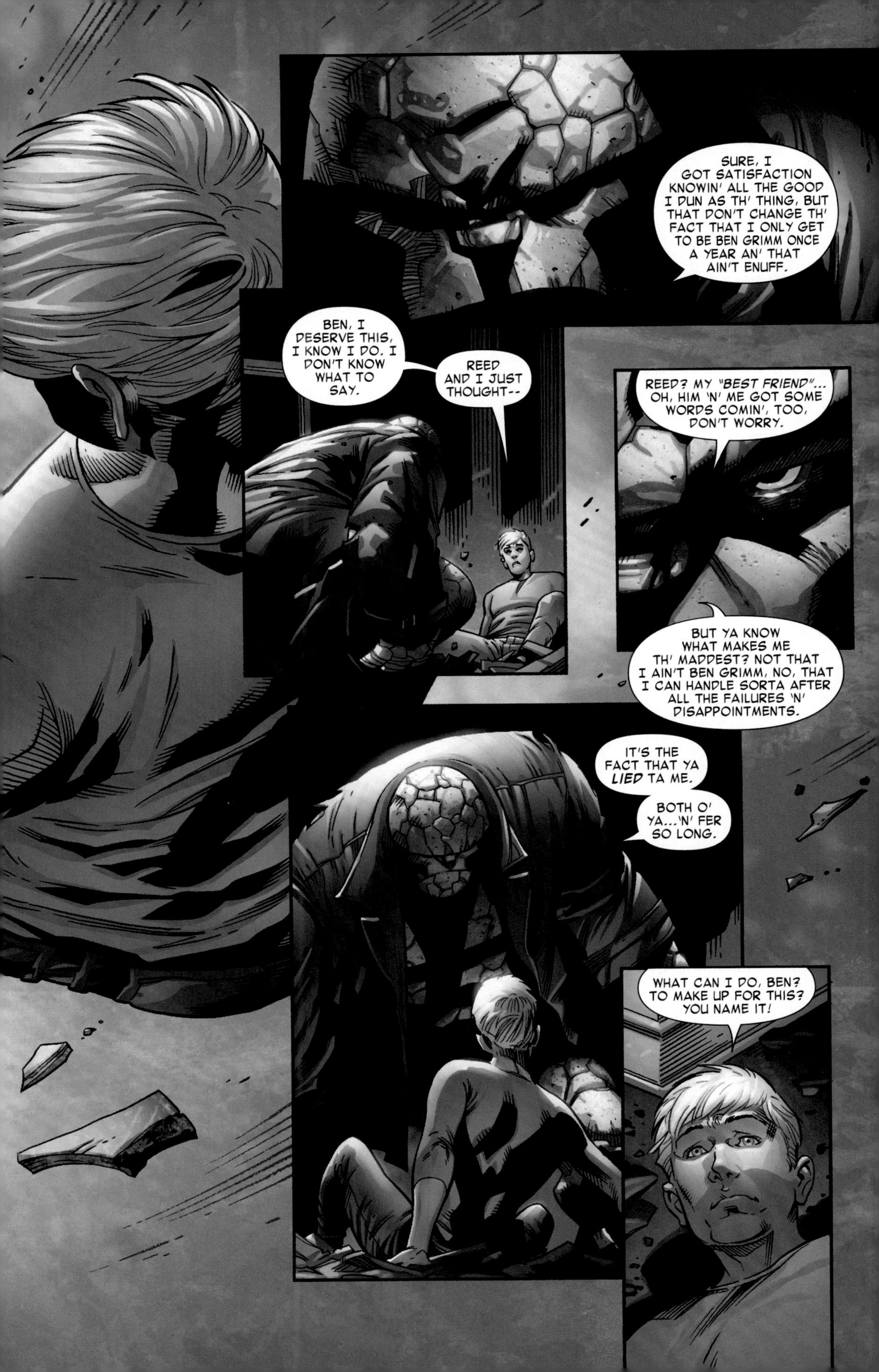
SURE, I GOT SATISFACTION KNOWIN' ALL THE GOOD I DUN AS TH' THING, BUT THAT DON'T CHANGE TH' FACT THAT I ONLY GET TO BE BEN GRIMM ONCE A YEAR AN' THAT AIN'T ENUFF.
BEN, I DESERVE THIS, I KNOW I DO. I DON'T KNOW WHAT TO SAY.
REED AND I JUST THOUGHT--
REED? MY "BEST FRIEND"... OH, HIM 'N' ME GOT SOME WORDS COMIN', TOO, DON'T WORRY.
BUT YA KNOW WHAT MAKES ME TH' MADDEST? NOT THAT I AIN'T BEN GRIMM, NO, THAT I CAN HANDLE SORTA AFTER ALL THE FAILURES 'N' DISAPPOINTMENTS.
IT'S THE FACT THAT YA LIED TA ME.
BOTH O' YA...'N' FER SO LONG.
WHAT CAN I DO, BEN? TO MAKE UP FOR THIS? YOU NAME IT!

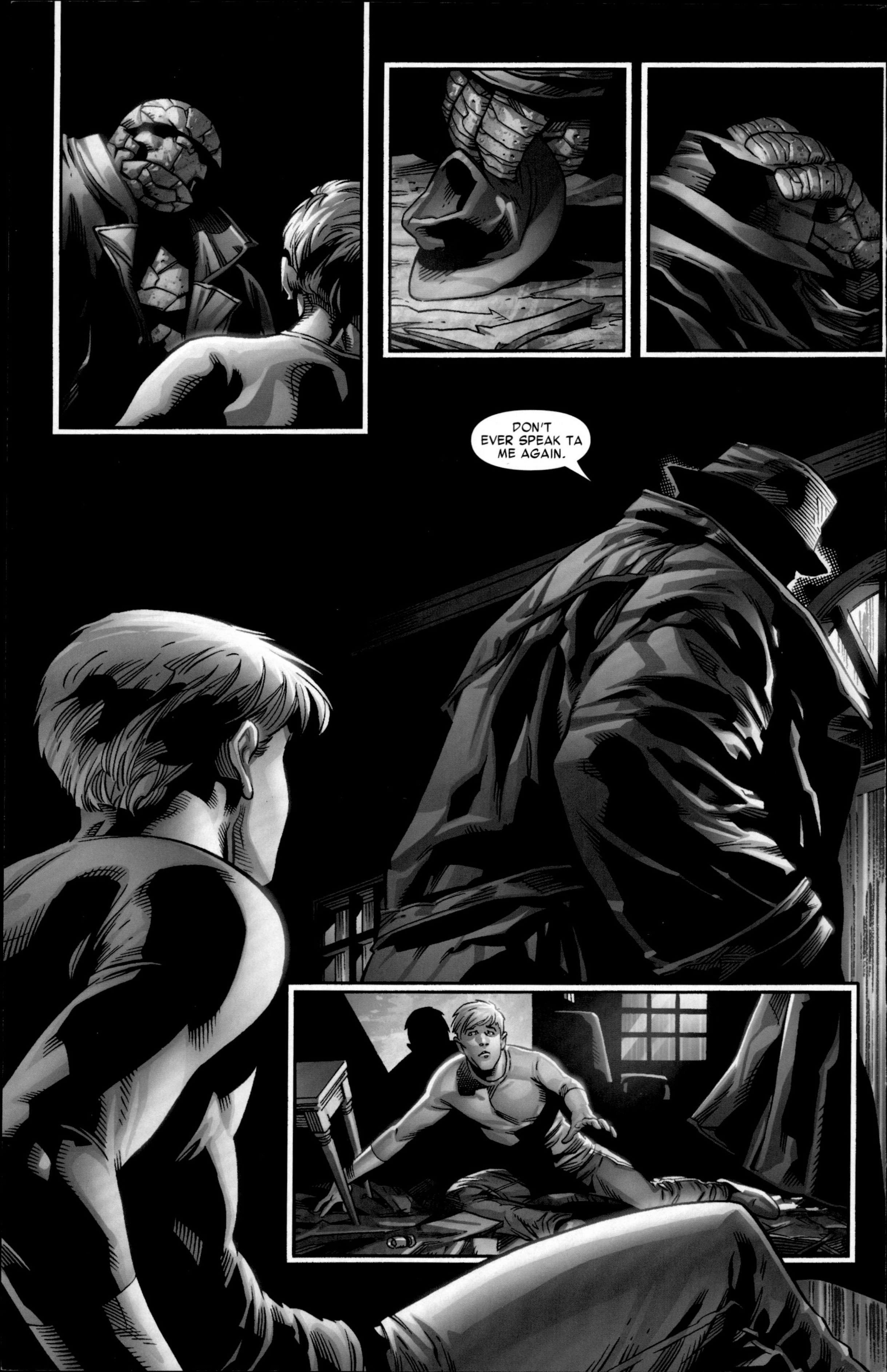
DON'T EVER SPEAK TA ME AGAIN.

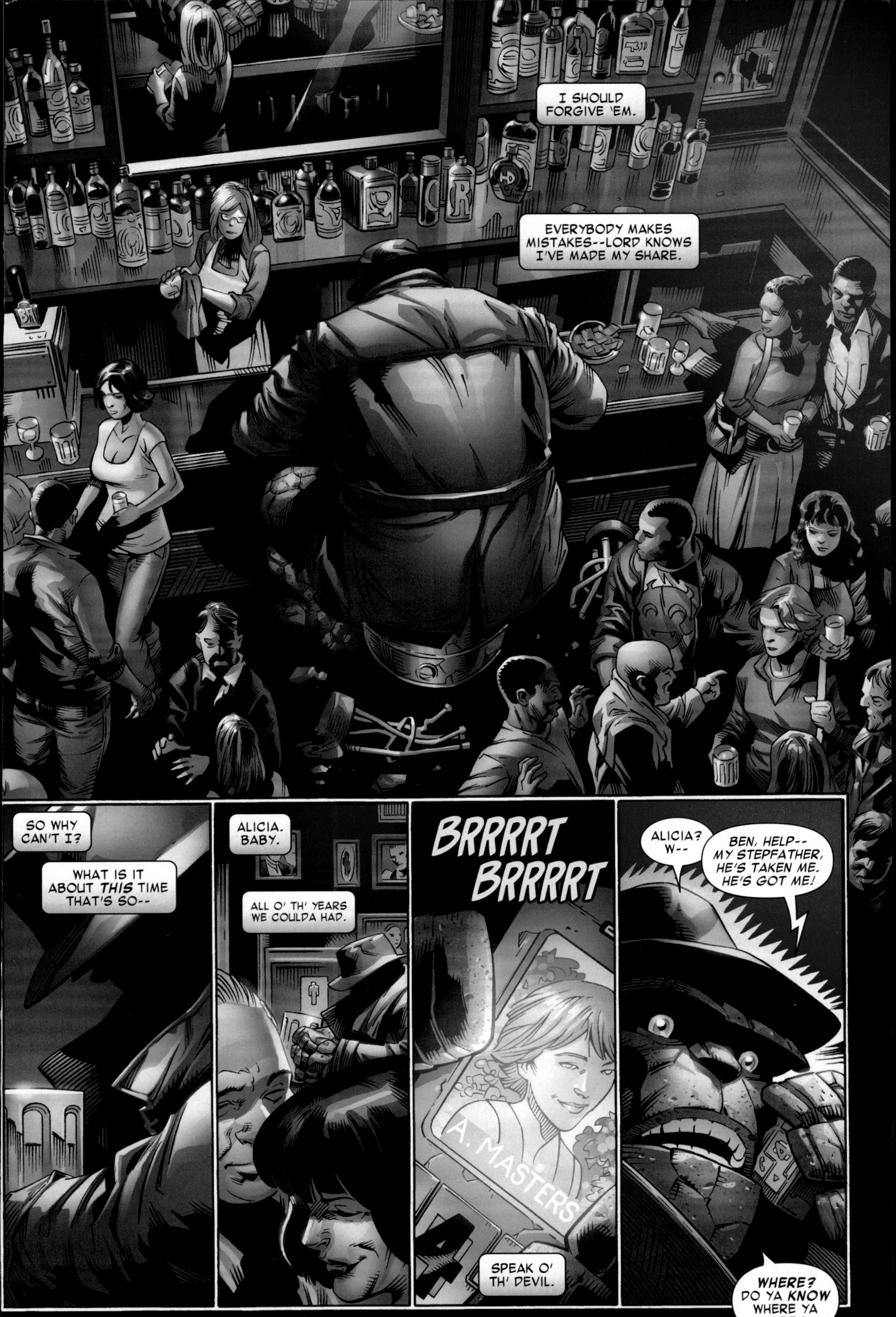
I SHOULD FORGIVE 'EM.
EVERYBODY MAKES MISTAKES--LORD KNOWS I'VE MADE MY SHARE.
SO WHY CAN'T I?
WHAT IS IT ABOUT THIS TIME THAT'S SO--
ALICIA. BABY.
ALL O' TH' YEARS WE COULDA HAD.
BRRRRT BRRRRT
A. MASTERS
SPEAK O' TH' DEVIL.
ALICIA? W--
BEN, HELP-- MY STEPFATHER, HE'S TAKEN ME. HE'S GOT ME!
WHERE? DO YA KNOW WHERE YA ARE?

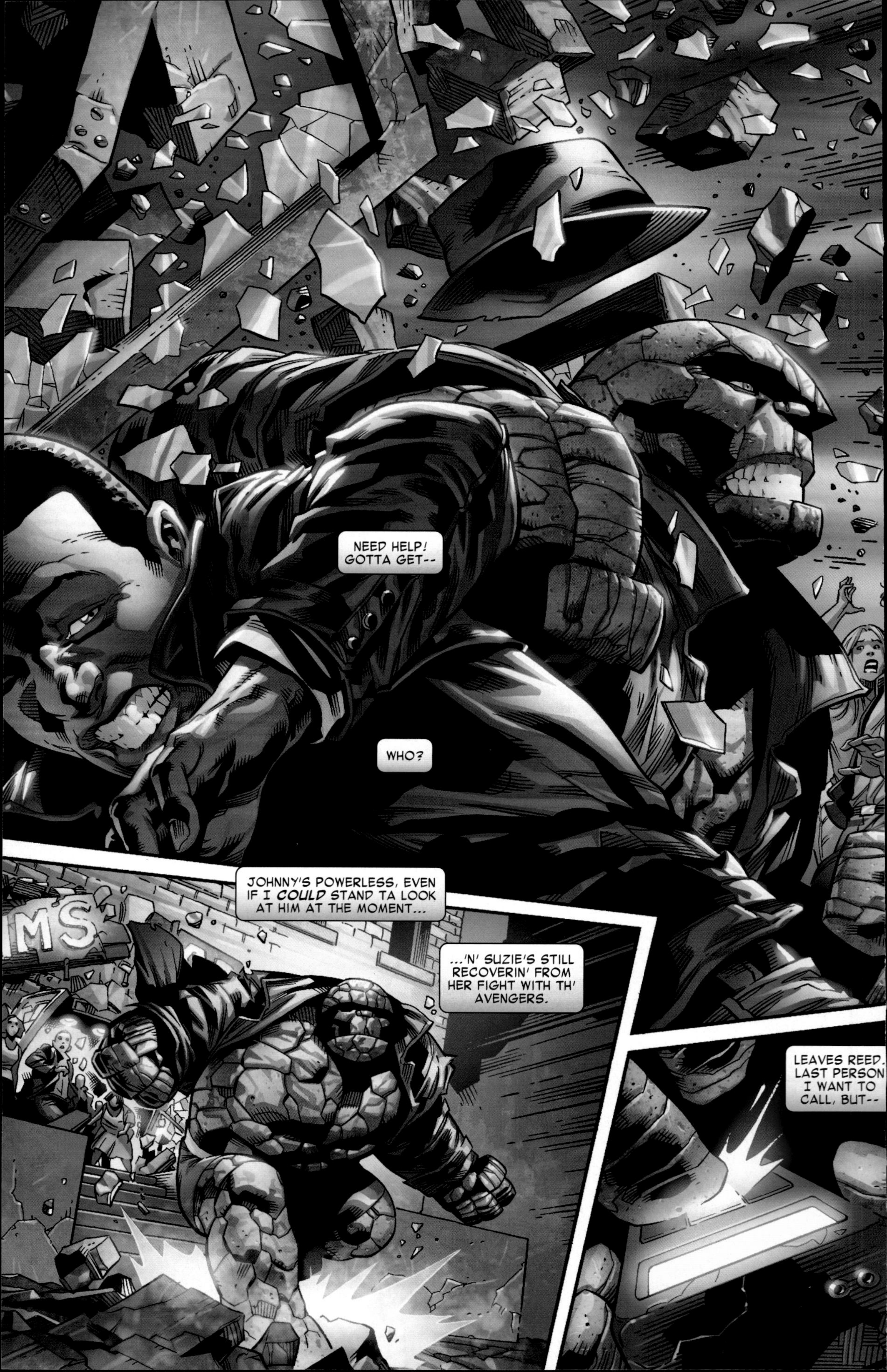
NEED HELP! GOTTA GET--
WHO?
JOHNNY'S POWERLESS, EVEN IF I COULD STAND TA LOOK AT HIM AT THE MOMENT...
...'N' SUZIE'S STILL RECOVERIN' FROM HER FIGHT WITH TH' AVENGERS.
LEAVES REED. LAST PERSON I WANT TO CALL, BUT--

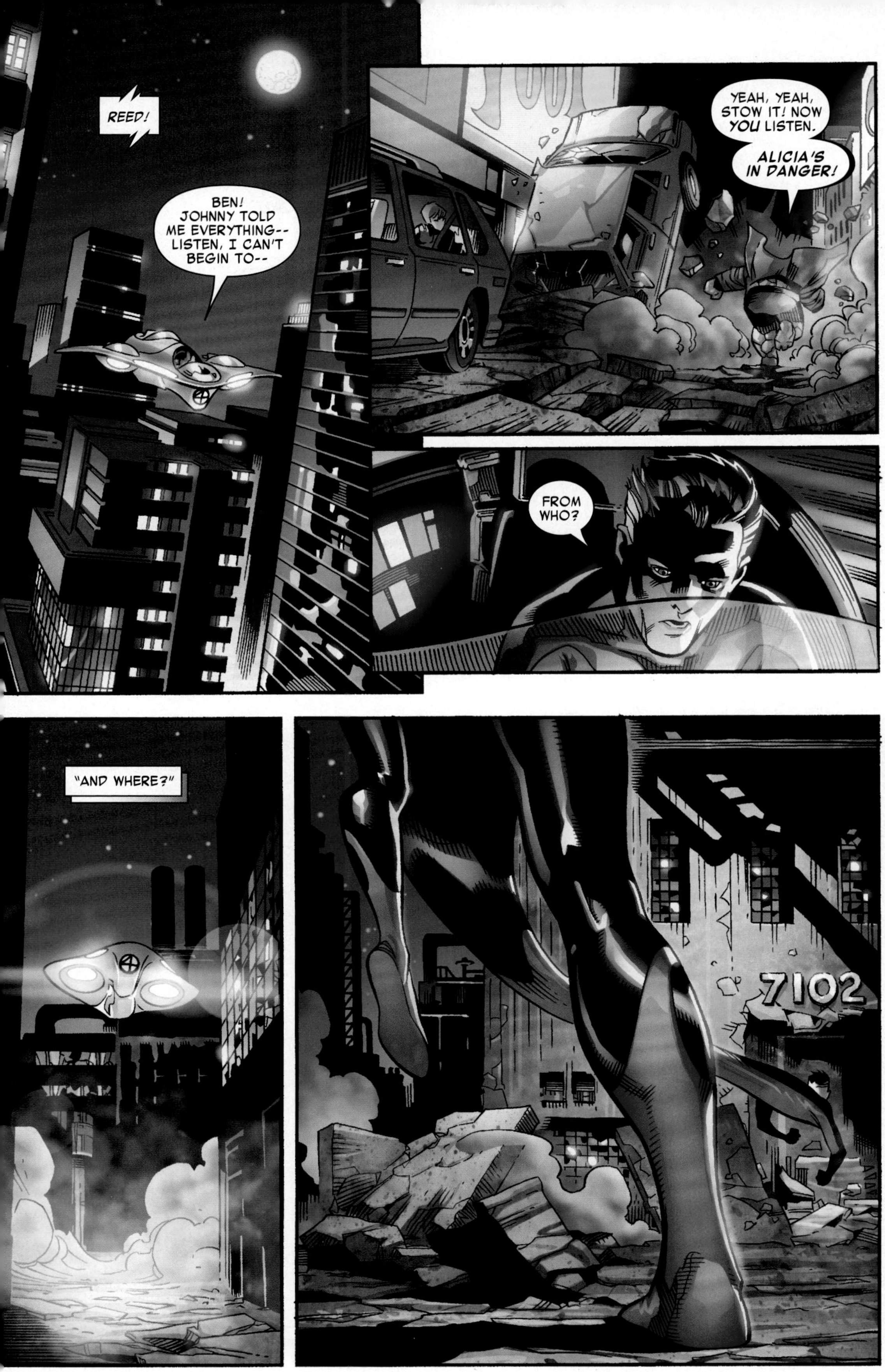
REED!
BEN! JOHNNY TOLD ME EVERYTHING-- LISTEN, I CAN'T BEGIN TO--
YEAH, YEAH, STOW IT! NOW YOU LISTEN.
ALICIA'S IN DANGER!
FROM WHO?
"AND WHERE?"
7102

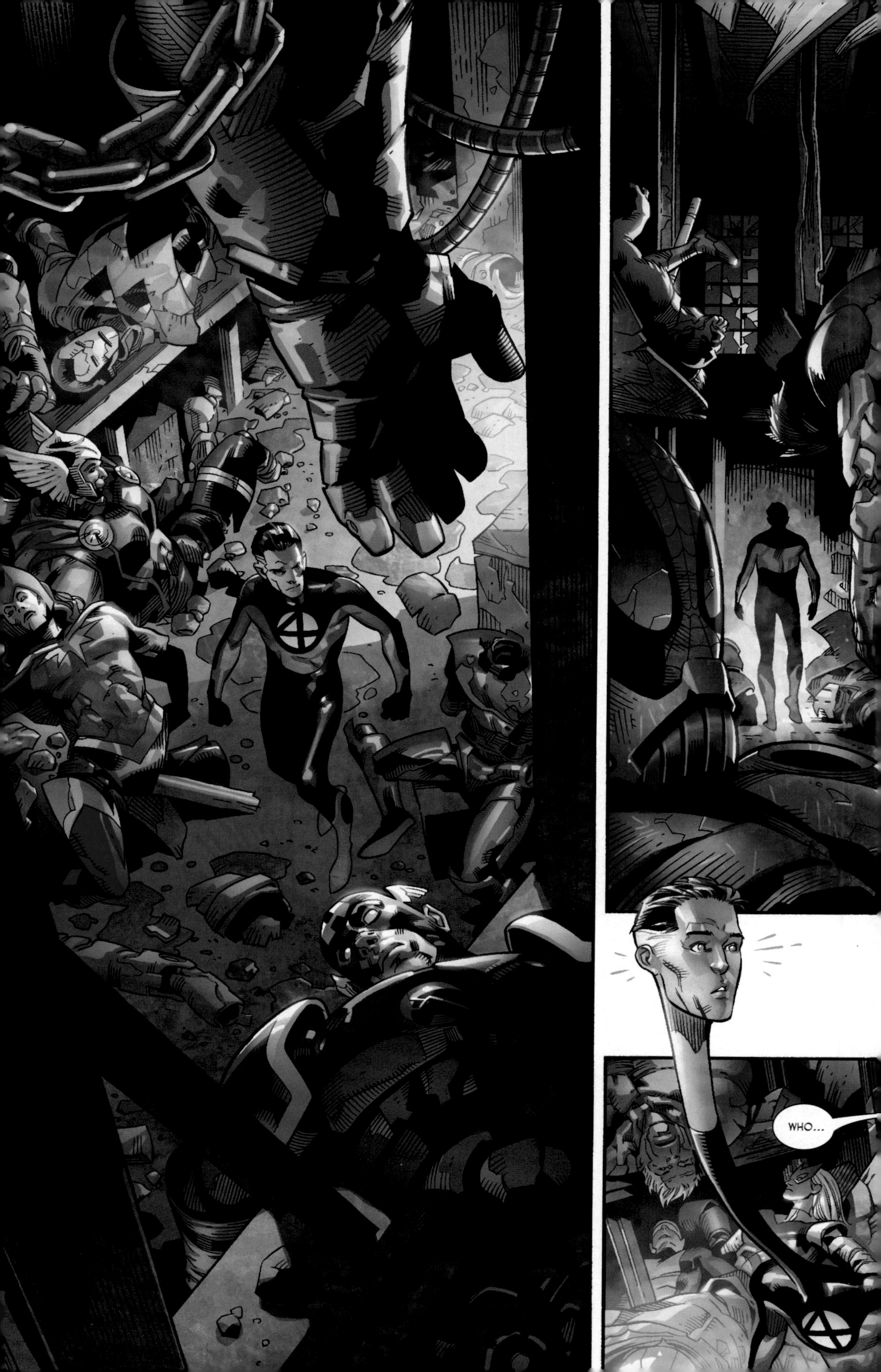
WHO...

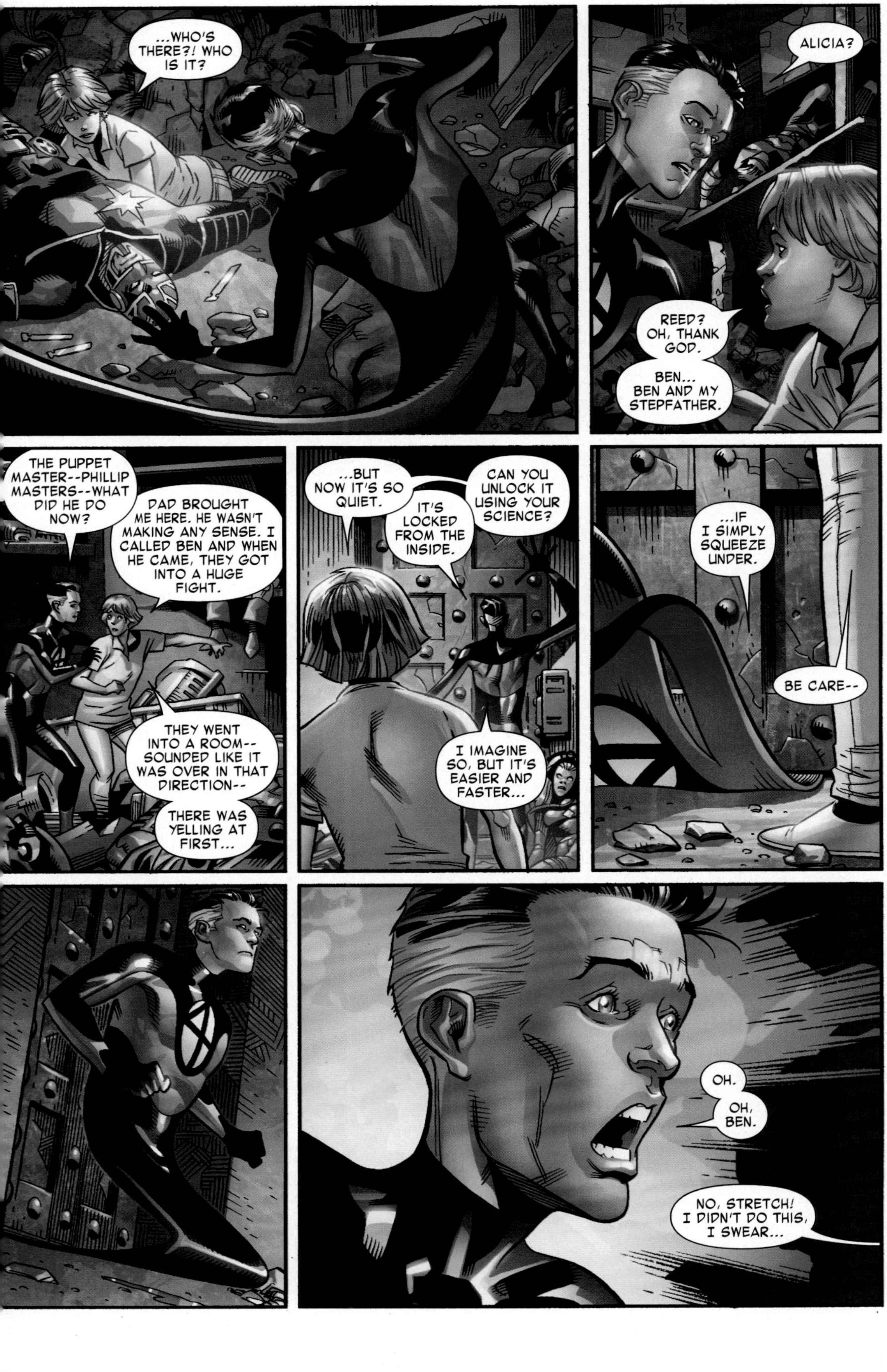
...WHO'S THERE?! WHO IS IT?
ALICIA?
REED? OH, THANK GOD.
BEN... BEN AND MY STEPFATHER.
THE PUPPET MASTER--PHILLIP MASTERS--WHAT DID HE DO NOW?
DAD BROUGHT ME HERE. HE WASN'T MAKING ANY SENSE. I CALLED BEN AND WHEN HE CAME, THEY GOT INTO A HUGE FIGHT.
THEY WENT INTO A ROOM--SOUNDED LIKE IT WAS OVER IN THAT DIRECTION--
THERE WAS YELLING AT FIRST...
...BUT NOW IT'S SO QUIET.
IT'S LOCKED FROM THE INSIDE.
CAN YOU UNLOCK IT USING YOUR SCIENCE?
I IMAGINE SO, BUT IT'S EASIER AND FASTER...
...IF I SIMPLY SQUEEZE UNDER.
BE CARE--
OH.
OH, BEN.
NO, STRETCH! I DIDN'T DO THIS, I SWEAR...

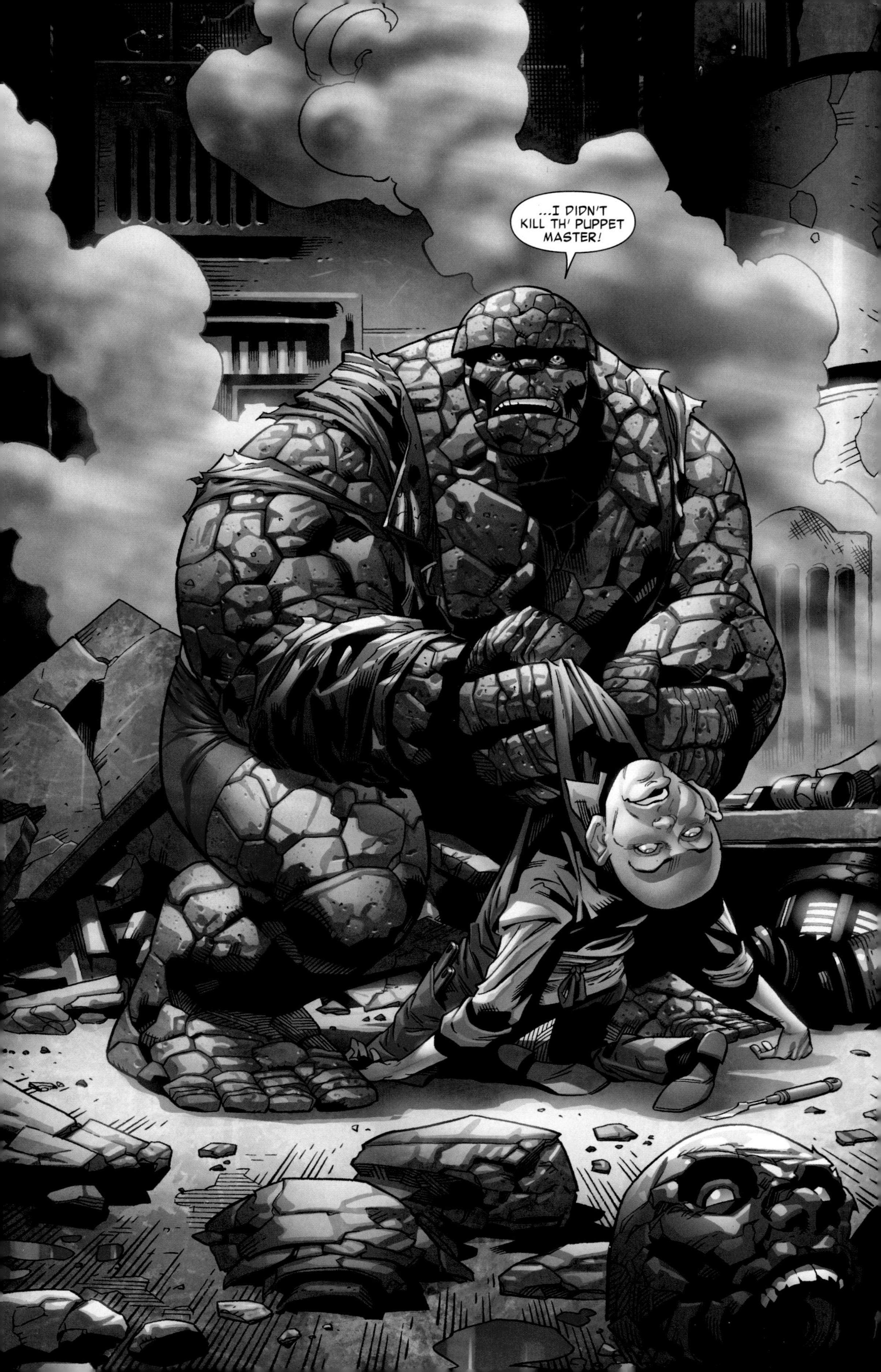
...I DIDN'T KILL TH' PUPPET MASTER!

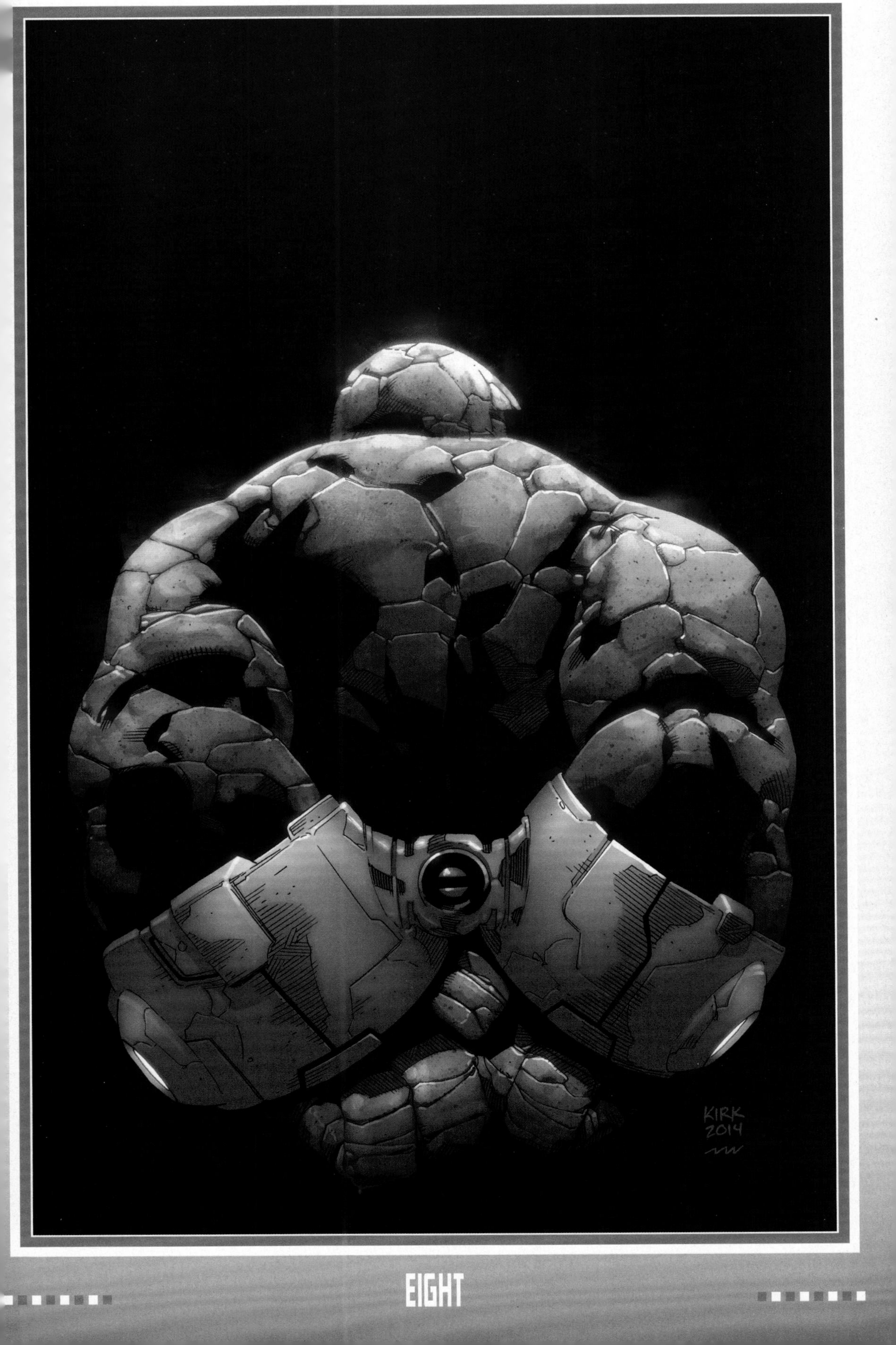
KIRK
2014

EIGHT

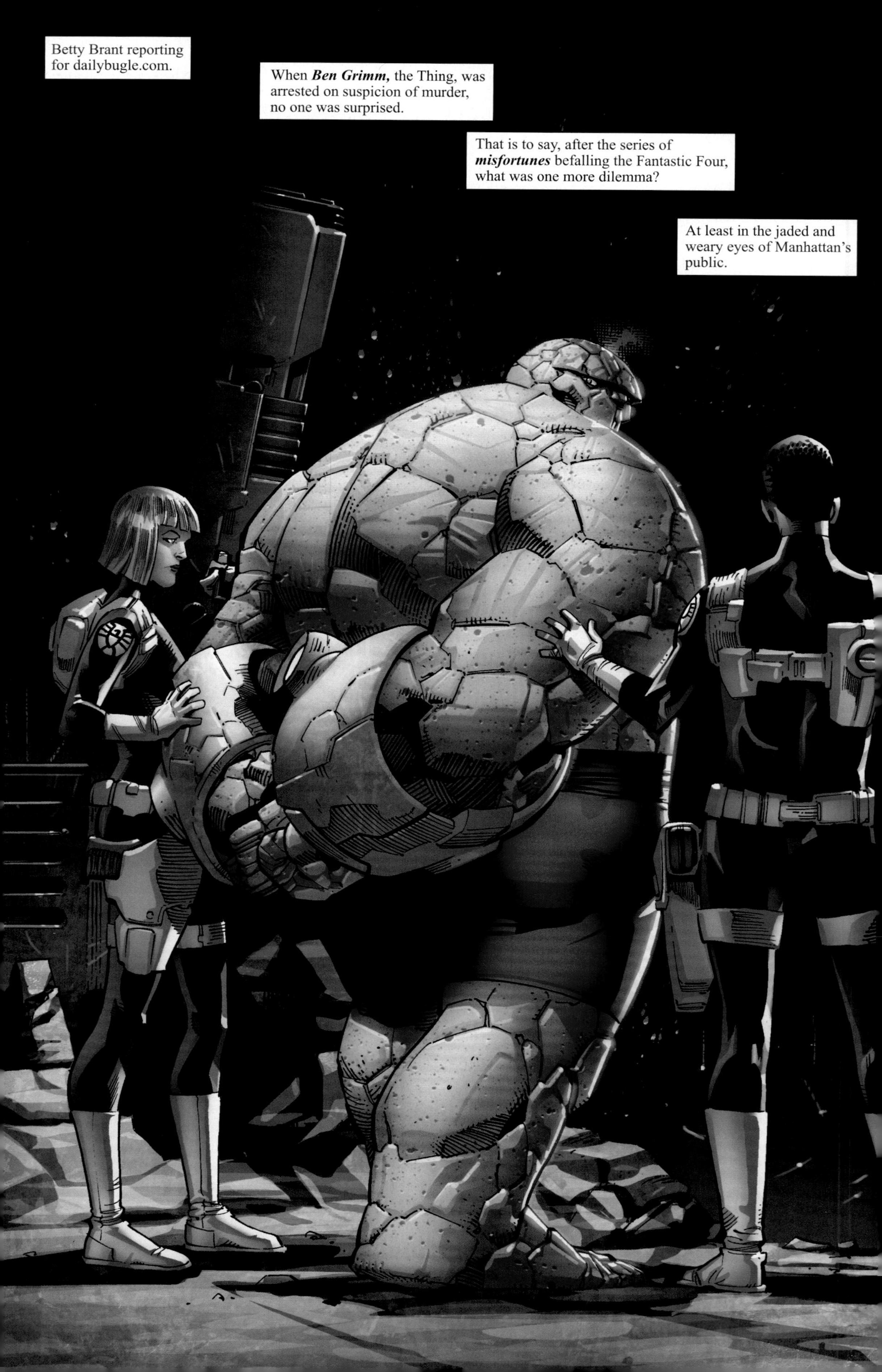
Betty Brant reporting for dailybugle.com.
When ***Ben Grimm,*** the Thing, was arrested on suspicion of murder, no one was surprised.
That is to say, after the series of ***misfortunes*** befalling the Fantastic Four, what was one more dilemma?
At least in the jaded and weary eyes of Manhattan's public.

But there it was, nevertheless-- Grimm had been discovered looming over the **dead body** of Phillip Masters, **the Puppet Master**...

...and with a tragically iron-clad witness to the event.

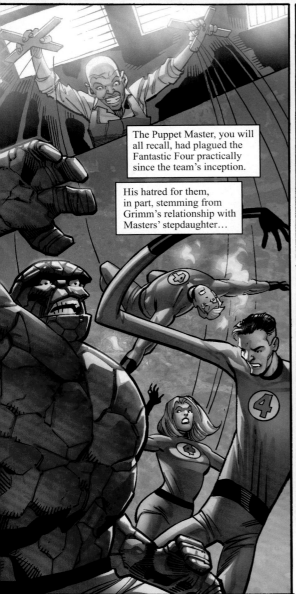

The Puppet Master, you will all recall, had plagued the Fantastic Four practically since the team's inception.

His hatred for them, in part, stemming from Grimm's relationship with Masters' stepdaughter...

...famed sculptor **Alicia Masters**...

...who by all accounts was there when the terrible act occurred. Although, being **blind,** Ms. Masters was unable to act as a reliable witness either for or against Grimm's claims of his own innocence.

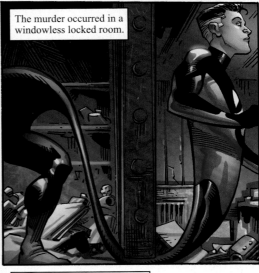

The murder occurred in a windowless locked room.

Reed Richards, Mr. Fantastic, upon arriving at the scene...

...was himself barely able to slip under the door of its sole entry-point...

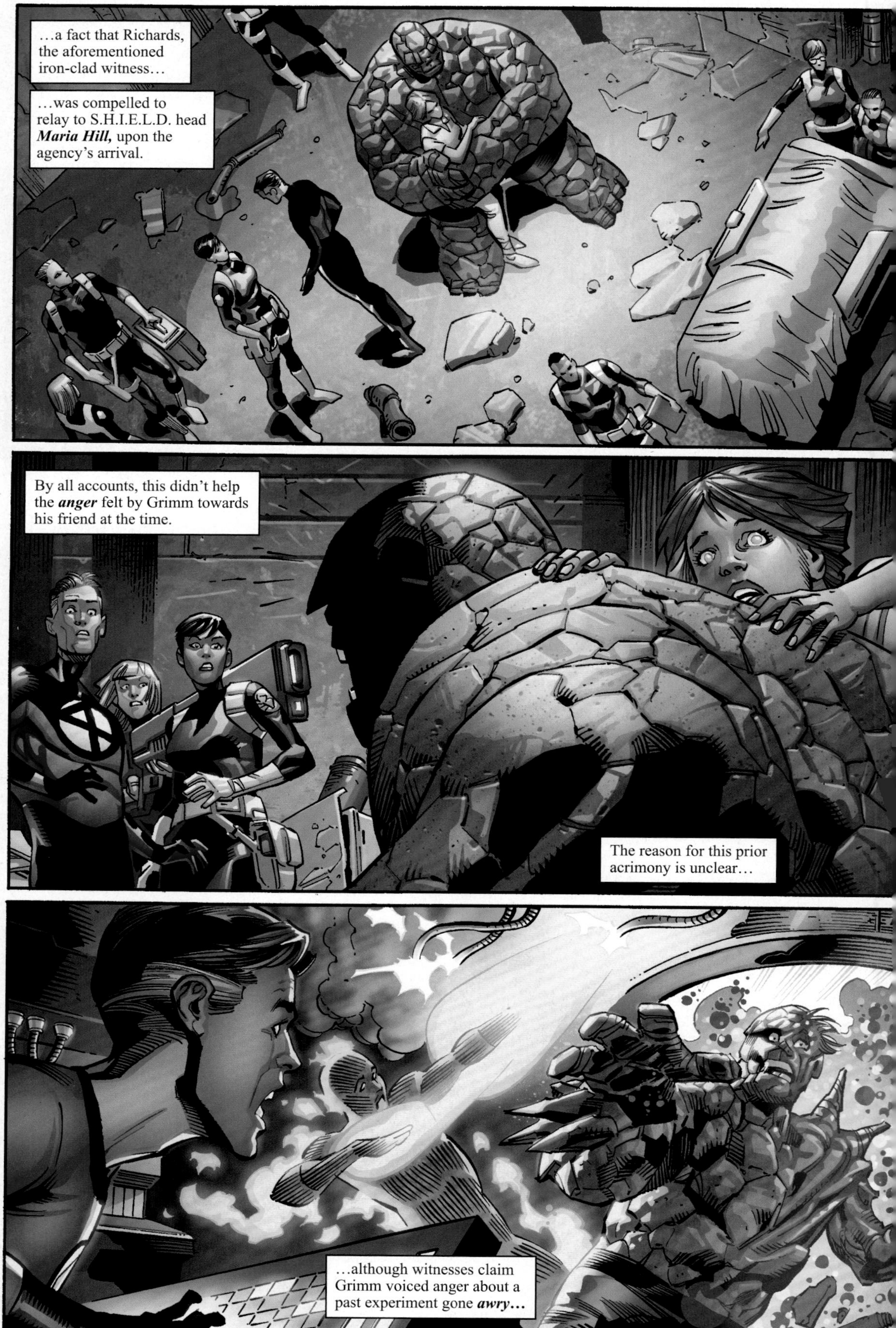
…a fact that Richards, the aforementioned iron-clad witness…
…was compelled to relay to S.H.I.E.L.D. head ***Maria Hill,*** upon the agency's arrival.
By all accounts, this didn't help the ***anger*** felt by Grimm towards his friend at the time.
The reason for this prior acrimony is unclear…
…although witnesses claim Grimm voiced anger about a past experiment gone ***awry…***

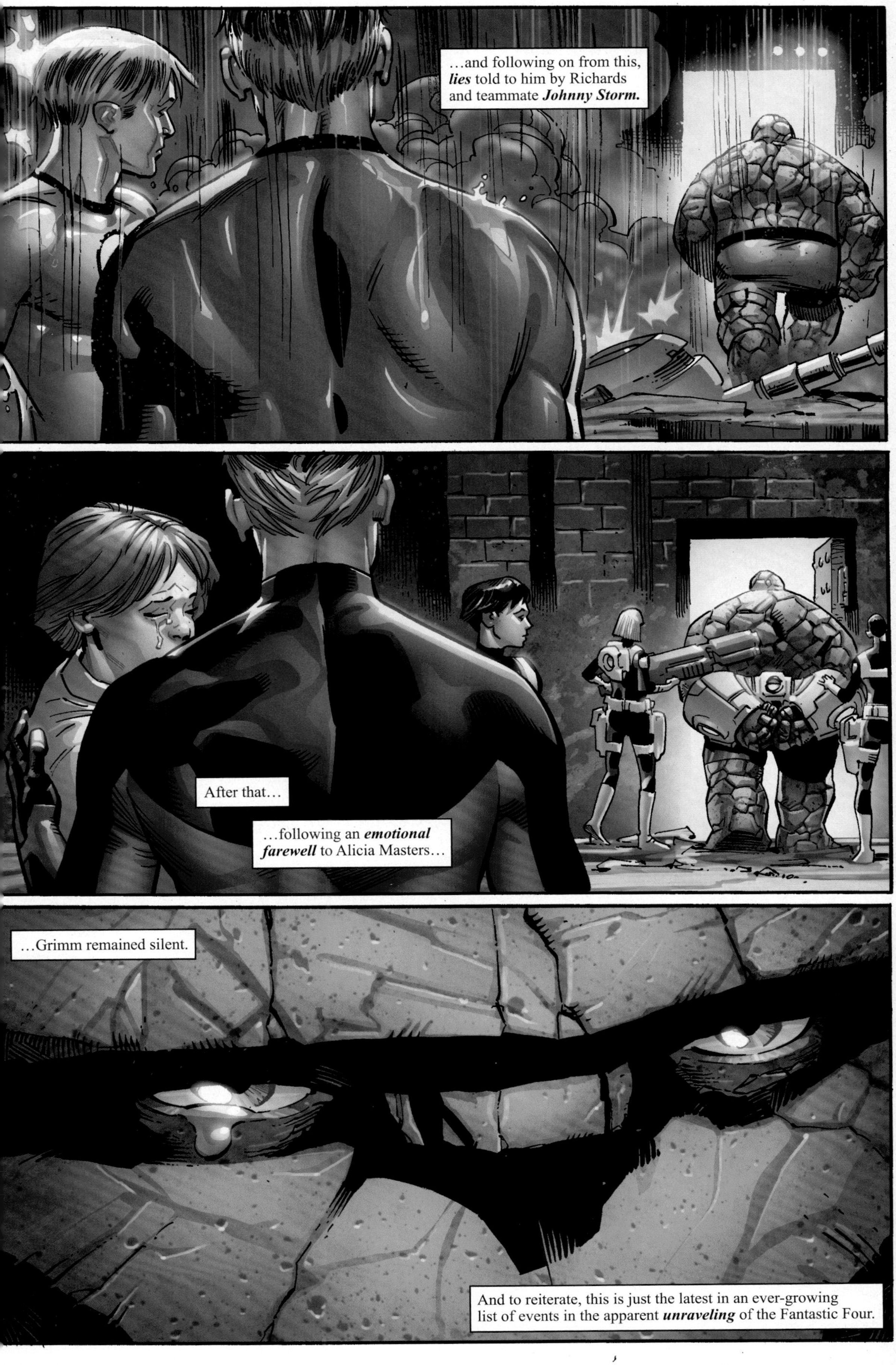
...and following on from this, ***lies*** told to him by Richards and teammate ***Johnny Storm.***
After that...
...following an ***emotional farewell*** to Alicia Masters...
...Grimm remained silent.
And to reiterate, this is just the latest in an ever-growing list of events in the apparent ***unraveling*** of the Fantastic Four.

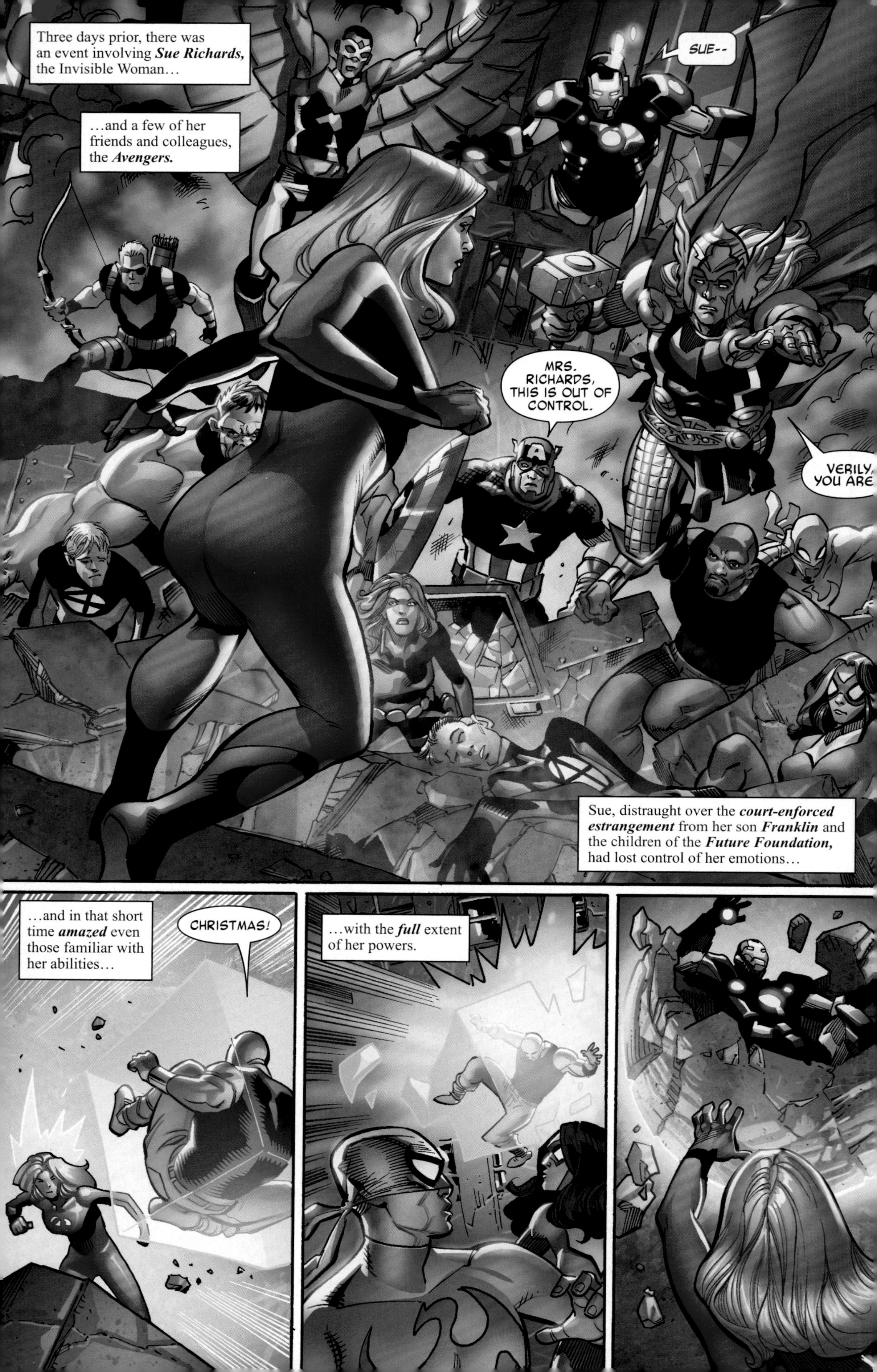
Three days prior, there was an event involving *Sue Richards,* the Invisible Woman…
…and a few of her friends and colleagues, the *Avengers.*
SUE--
MRS. RICHARDS, THIS IS OUT OF CONTROL.
VERILY, YOU ARE
Sue, distraught over the *court-enforced estrangement* from her son *Franklin* and the children of the *Future Foundation,* had lost control of her emotions…
…and in that short time *amazed* even those familiar with her abilities…
CHRISTMAS!
…with the *full* extent of her powers.

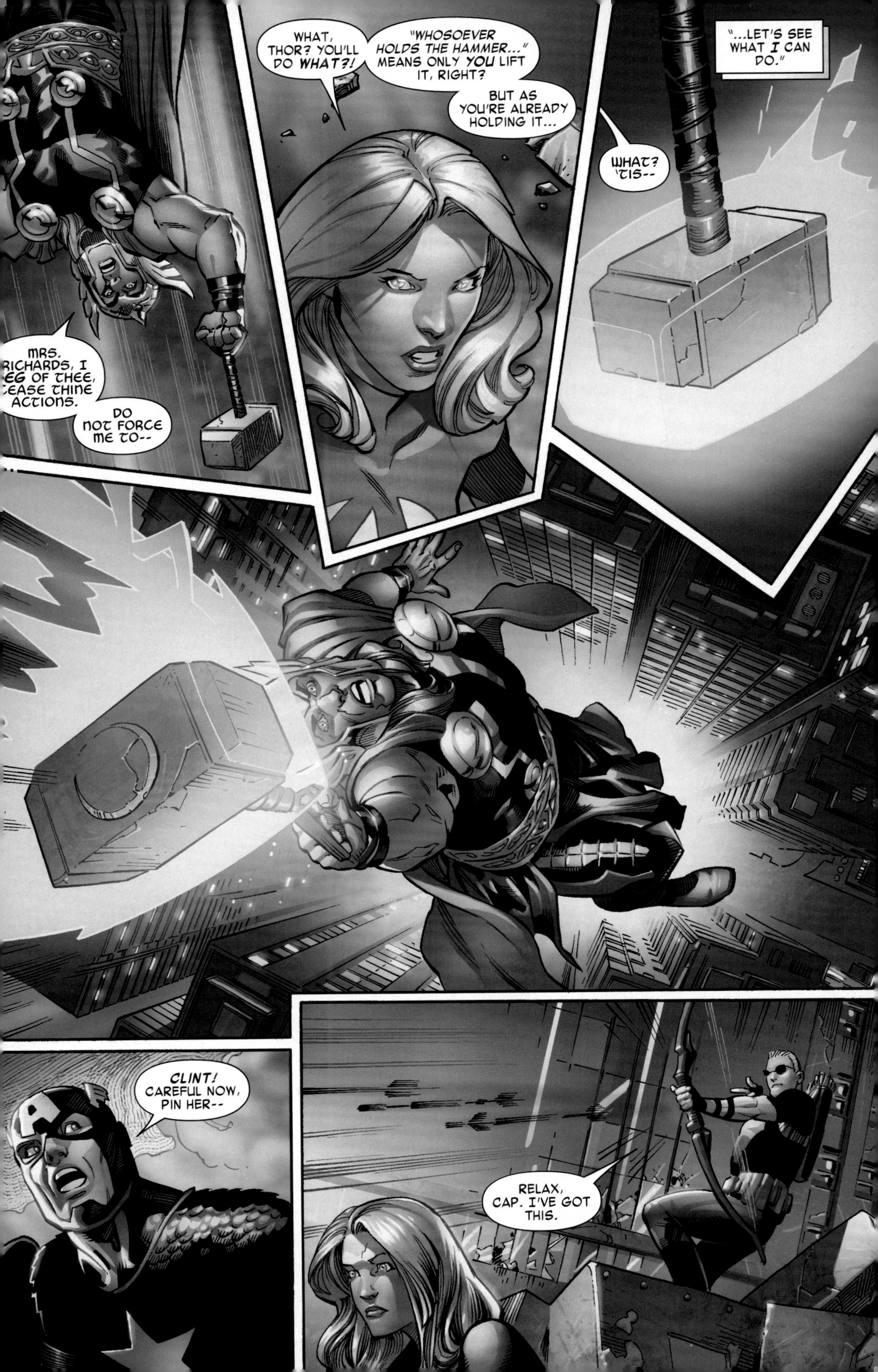
MRS. RICHARDS, I BEG OF THEE, CEASE THINE ACTIONS.
DO NOT FORCE ME TO--
WHAT, THOR? YOU'LL DO WHAT?!
"WHOSOEVER HOLDS THE HAMMER..." MEANS ONLY YOU LIFT IT, RIGHT?
BUT AS YOU'RE ALREADY HOLDING IT...
"...LET'S SEE WHAT I CAN DO."
WHAT? 'TIS--
CLINT! CAREFUL NOW, PIN HER--
RELAX, CAP. I'VE GOT THIS.

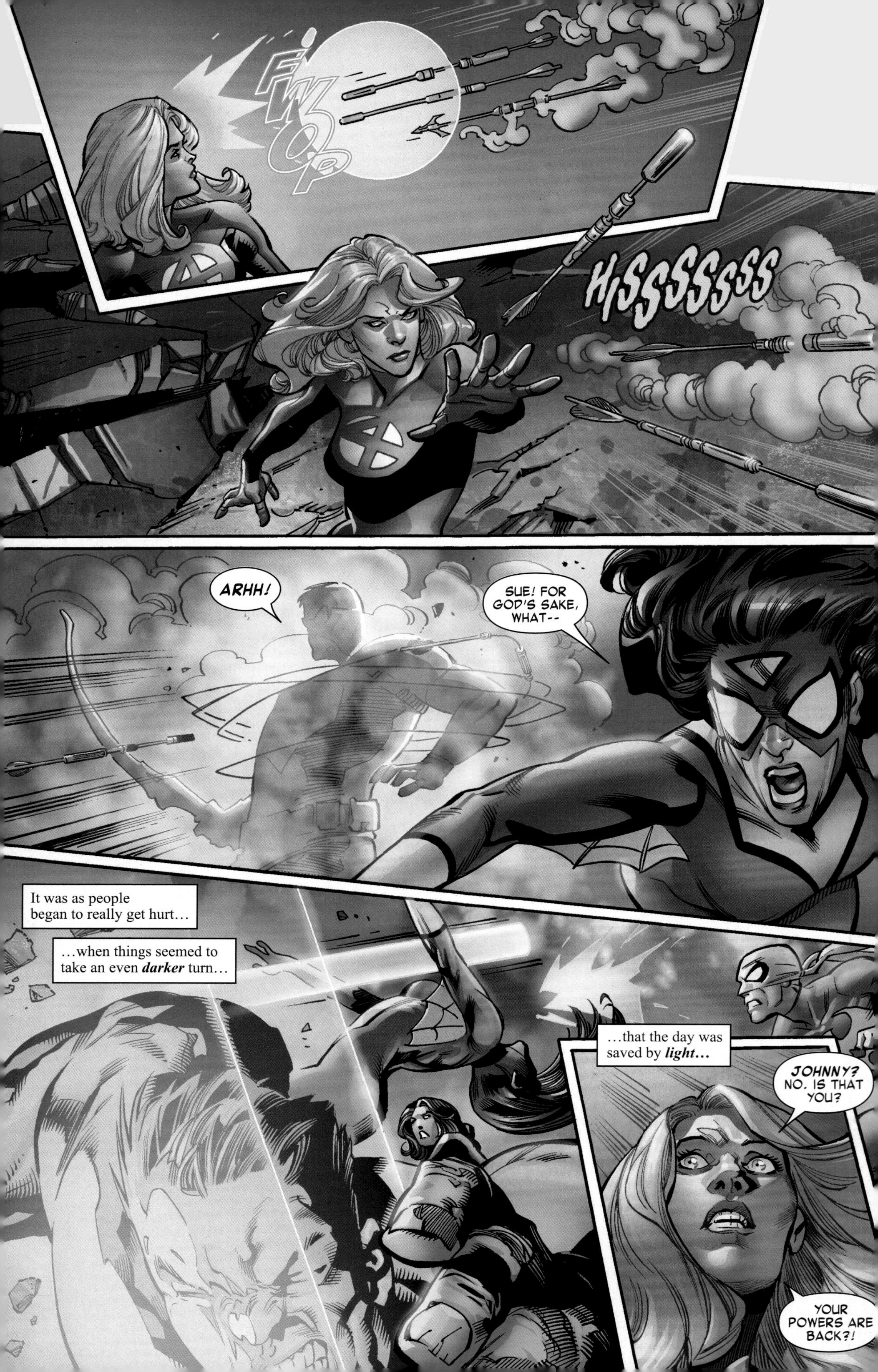
FWOOP
HISSSSSSSS
ARHH!
SUE! FOR GOD'S SAKE, WHAT--
It was as people began to really get hurt…
…when things seemed to take an even darker turn…
…that the day was saved by light…
JOHNNY? NO. IS THAT YOU?
YOUR POWERS ARE BACK?!

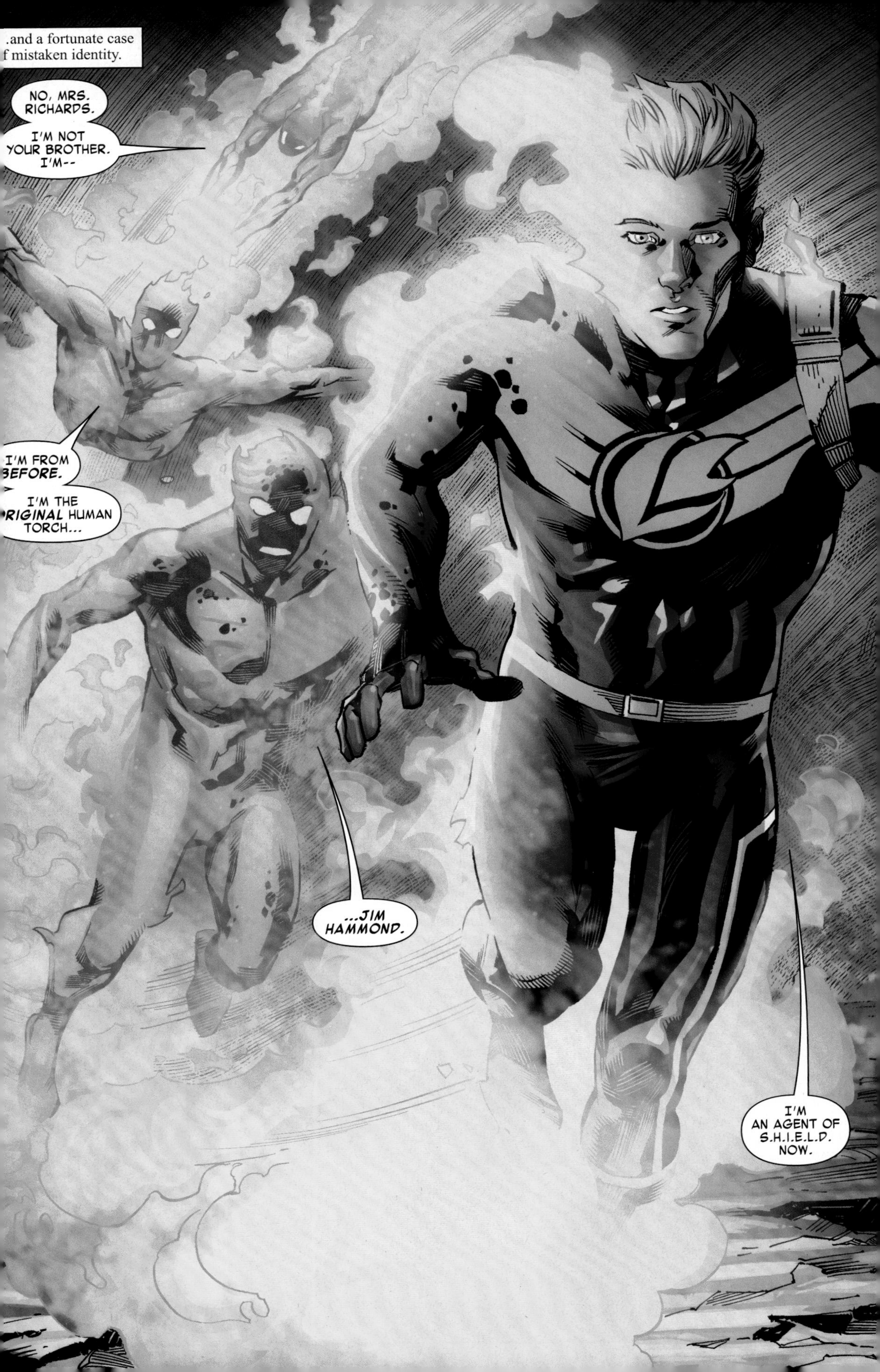
.and a fortunate case
f mistaken identity.
NO, MRS. RICHARDS.
I'M NOT YOUR BROTHER. I'M--
I'M FROM BEFORE.
I'M THE RIGINAL HUMAN TORCH...
...JIM HAMMOND.
I'M AN AGENT OF S.H.I.E.L.D. NOW.

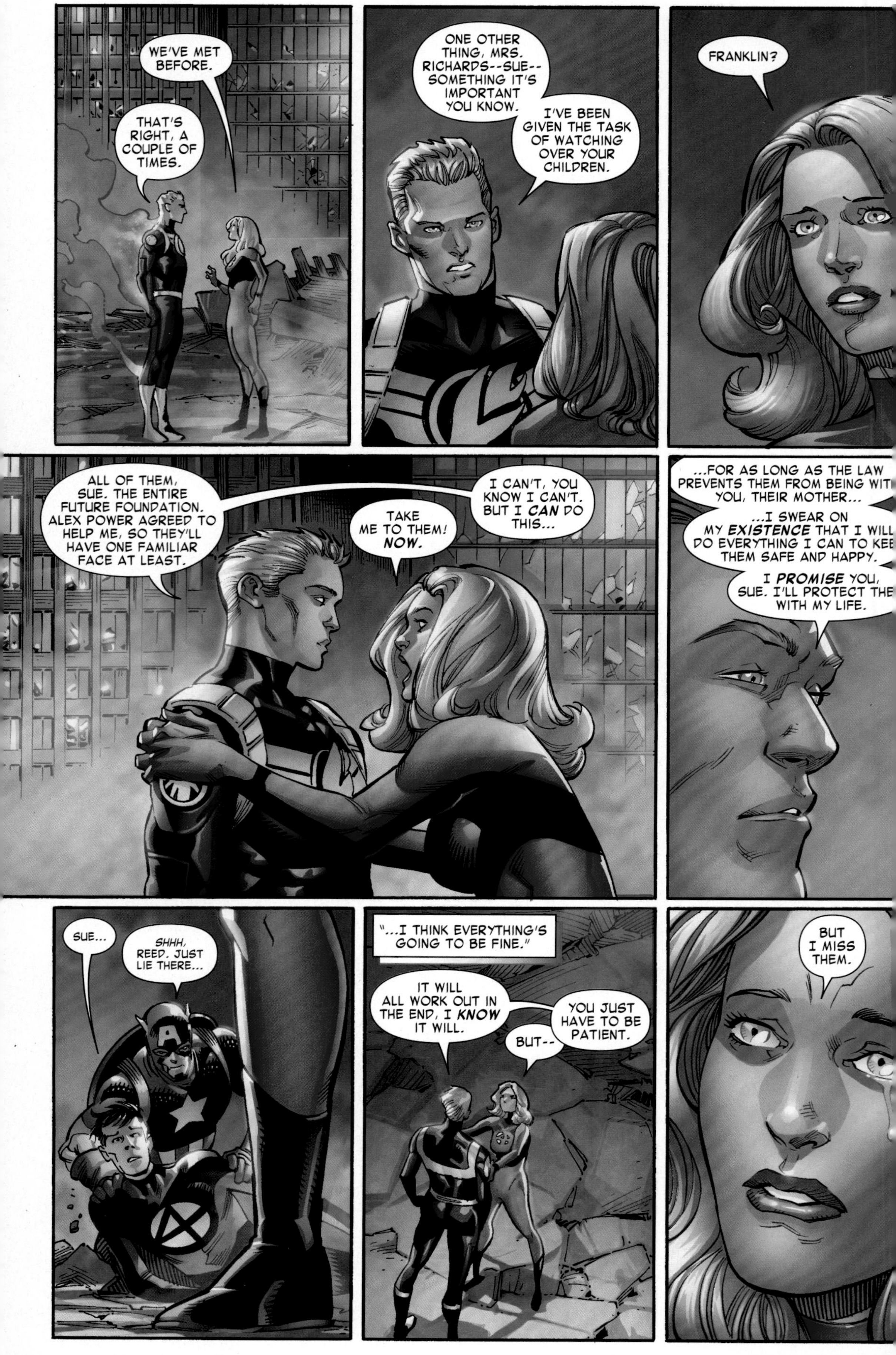

WE'VE MET BEFORE.
THAT'S RIGHT, A COUPLE OF TIMES.
ONE OTHER THING, MRS. RICHARDS--SUE--SOMETHING IT'S IMPORTANT YOU KNOW.
I'VE BEEN GIVEN THE TASK OF WATCHING OVER YOUR CHILDREN.
FRANKLIN?
ALL OF THEM, SUE. THE ENTIRE FUTURE FOUNDATION. ALEX POWER AGREED TO HELP ME, SO THEY'LL HAVE ONE FAMILIAR FACE AT LEAST.
TAKE ME TO THEM! NOW.
I CAN'T, YOU KNOW I CAN'T. BUT I CAN DO THIS...
...FOR AS LONG AS THE LAW PREVENTS THEM FROM BEING WIT YOU, THEIR MOTHER...
...I SWEAR ON MY EXISTENCE THAT I WILL DO EVERYTHING I CAN TO KEE THEM SAFE AND HAPPY.
I PROMISE YOU, SUE. I'LL PROTECT THE WITH MY LIFE.
SUE...
SHHH, REED. JUST LIE THERE...
"...I THINK EVERYTHING'S GOING TO BE FINE."
IT WILL ALL WORK OUT IN THE END, I KNOW IT WILL.
YOU JUST HAVE TO BE PATIENT.
BUT--
BUT I MISS THEM.

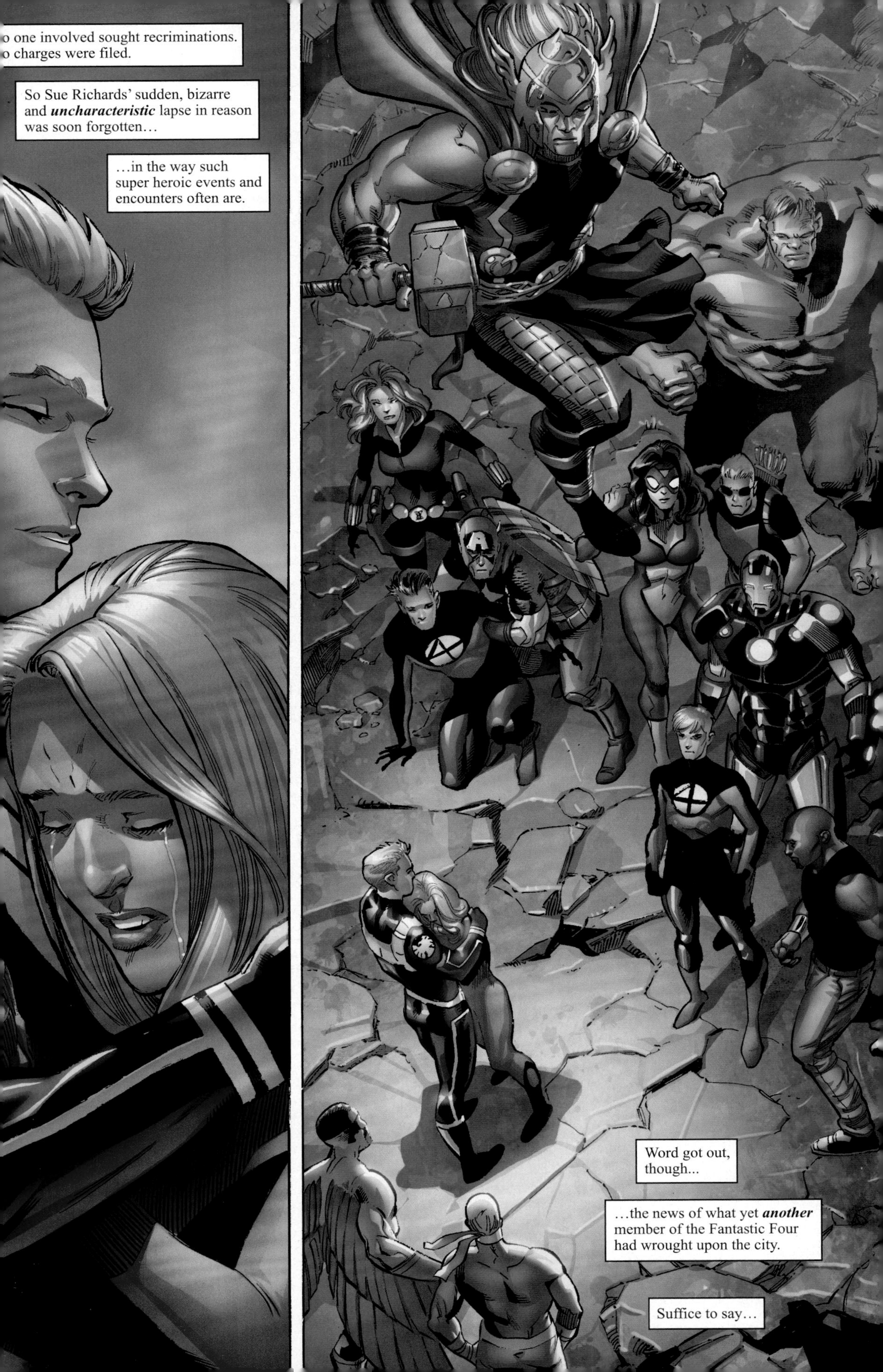
o one involved sought recriminations. o charges were filed.
So Sue Richards' sudden, bizarre and ***uncharacteristic*** lapse in reason was soon forgotten…
…in the way such super heroic events and encounters often are.
Word got out, though...
…the news of what yet ***another*** member of the Fantastic Four had wrought upon the city.
Suffice to say…

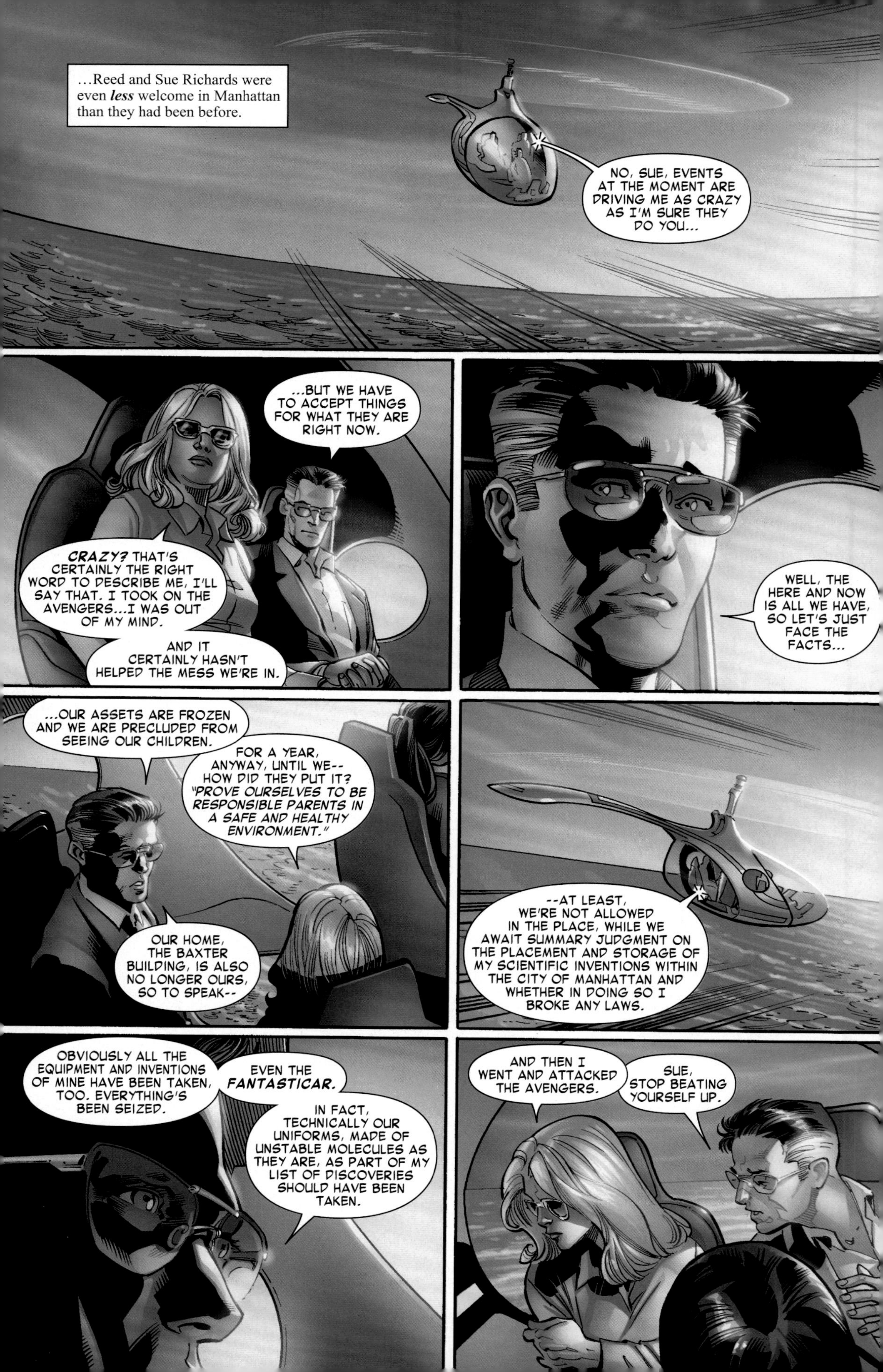
...Reed and Sue Richards were even *less* welcome in Manhattan than they had been before.
NO, SUE, EVENTS AT THE MOMENT ARE DRIVING ME AS CRAZY AS I'M SURE THEY DO YOU...
...BUT WE HAVE TO ACCEPT THINGS FOR WHAT THEY ARE RIGHT NOW.
CRAZY? THAT'S CERTAINLY THE RIGHT WORD TO DESCRIBE ME, I'LL SAY THAT. I TOOK ON THE AVENGERS...I WAS OUT OF MY MIND.
AND IT CERTAINLY HASN'T HELPED THE MESS WE'RE IN.
WELL, THE HERE AND NOW IS ALL WE HAVE, SO LET'S JUST FACE THE FACTS...
...OUR ASSETS ARE FROZEN AND WE ARE PRECLUDED FROM SEEING OUR CHILDREN.
FOR A YEAR, ANYWAY, UNTIL WE--HOW DID THEY PUT IT? "PROVE OURSELVES TO BE RESPONSIBLE PARENTS IN A SAFE AND HEALTHY ENVIRONMENT."
OUR HOME, THE BAXTER BUILDING, IS ALSO NO LONGER OURS, SO TO SPEAK--
--AT LEAST, WE'RE NOT ALLOWED IN THE PLACE, WHILE WE AWAIT SUMMARY JUDGMENT ON THE PLACEMENT AND STORAGE OF MY SCIENTIFIC INVENTIONS WITHIN THE CITY OF MANHATTAN AND WHETHER IN DOING SO I BROKE ANY LAWS.
OBVIOUSLY ALL THE EQUIPMENT AND INVENTIONS OF MINE HAVE BEEN TAKEN, TOO. EVERYTHING'S BEEN SEIZED.
EVEN THE FANTASTICAR.
IN FACT, TECHNICALLY OUR UNIFORMS, MADE OF UNSTABLE MOLECULES AS THEY ARE, AS PART OF MY LIST OF DISCOVERIES SHOULD HAVE BEEN TAKEN.
AND THEN I WENT AND ATTACKED THE AVENGERS.
SUE, STOP BEATING YOURSELF UP.

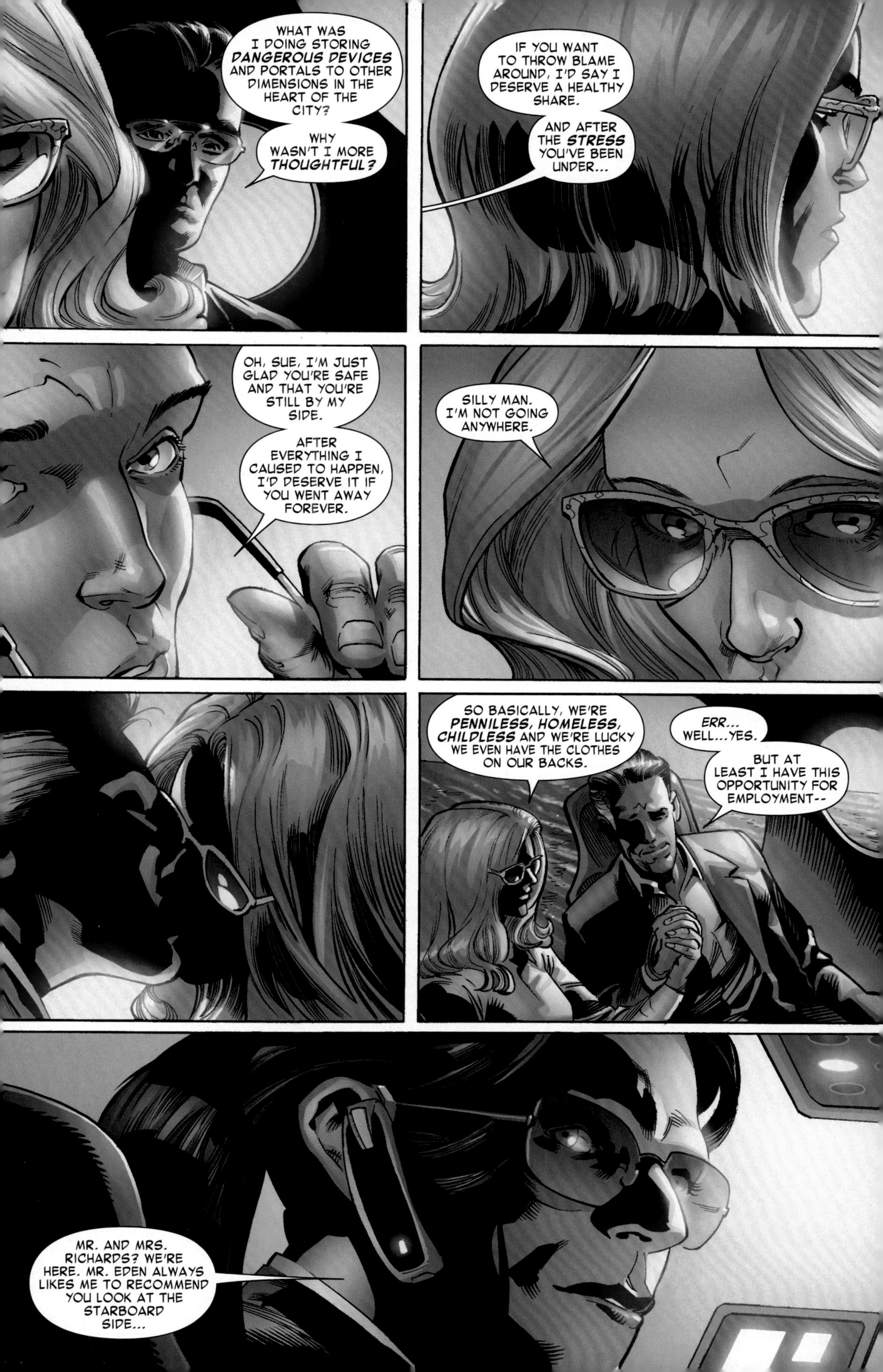
WHAT WAS I DOING STORING DANGEROUS DEVICES AND PORTALS TO OTHER DIMENSIONS IN THE HEART OF THE CITY?
WHY WASN'T I MORE THOUGHTFUL?
IF YOU WANT TO THROW BLAME AROUND, I'D SAY I DESERVE A HEALTHY SHARE.
AND AFTER THE STRESS YOU'VE BEEN UNDER...
OH, SUE, I'M JUST GLAD YOU'RE SAFE AND THAT YOU'RE STILL BY MY SIDE.
AFTER EVERYTHING I CAUSED TO HAPPEN, I'D DESERVE IT IF YOU WENT AWAY FOREVER.
SILLY MAN. I'M NOT GOING ANYWHERE.
SO BASICALLY, WE'RE PENNILESS, HOMELESS, CHILDLESS AND WE'RE LUCKY WE EVEN HAVE THE CLOTHES ON OUR BACKS.
ERR... WELL...YES.
BUT AT LEAST I HAVE THIS OPPORTUNITY FOR EMPLOYMENT--
MR. AND MRS. RICHARDS? WE'RE HERE. MR. EDEN ALWAYS LIKES ME TO RECOMMEND YOU LOOK AT THE STARBOARD SIDE...

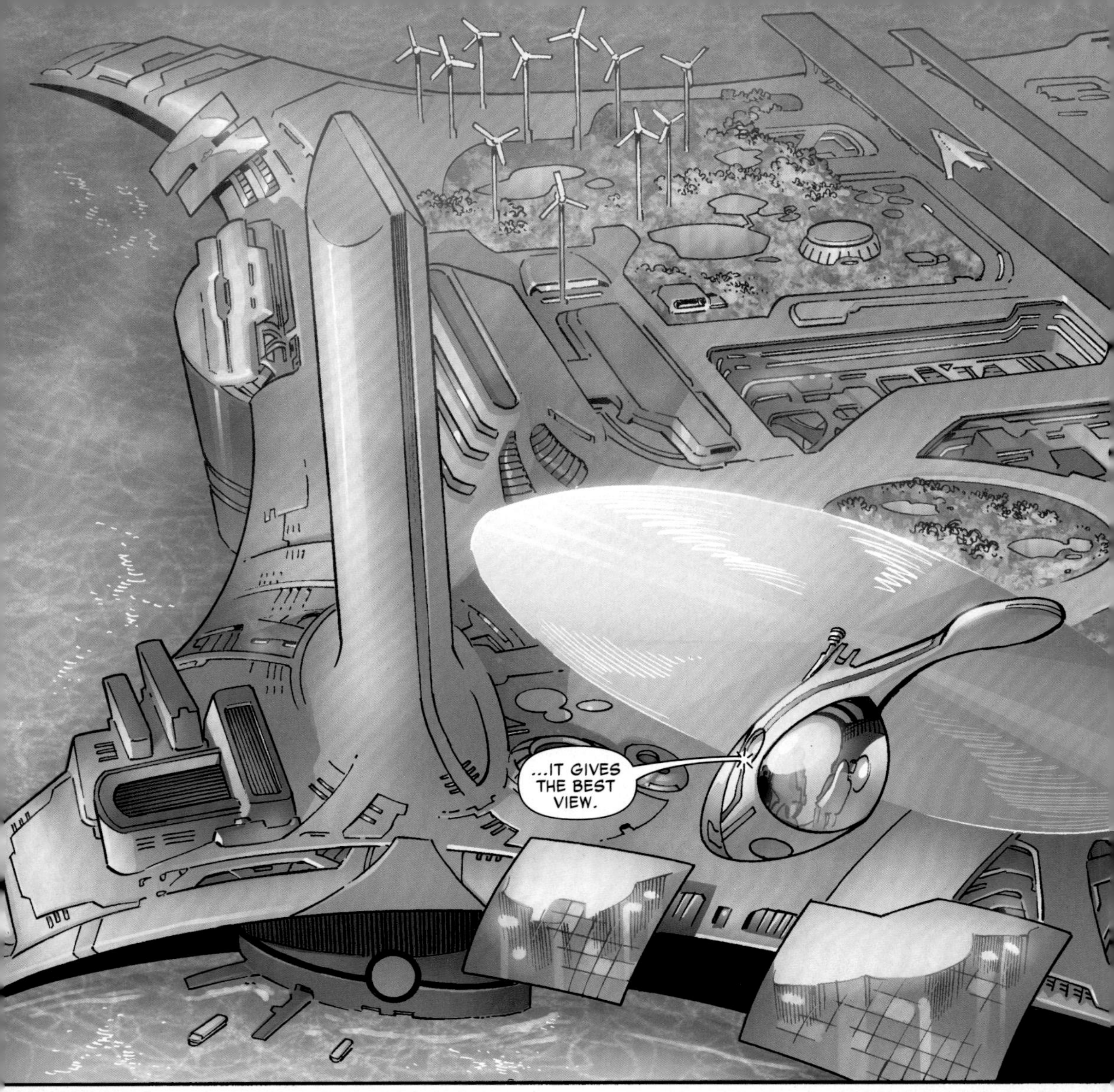
...IT GIVES THE BEST VIEW.

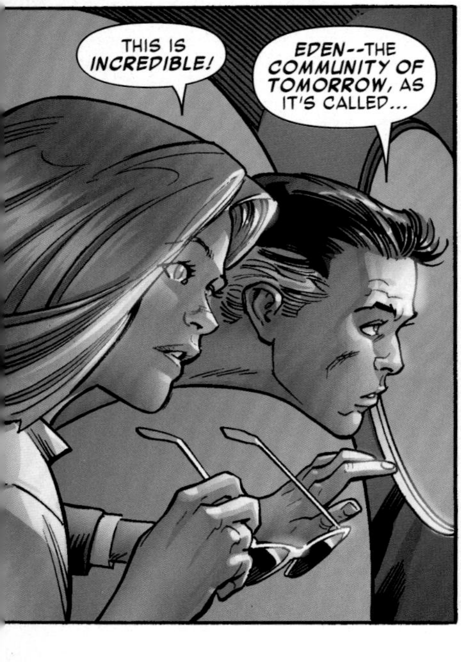
THIS IS INCREDIBLE!
EDEN--THE COMMUNITY OF TOMORROW, AS IT'S CALLED...

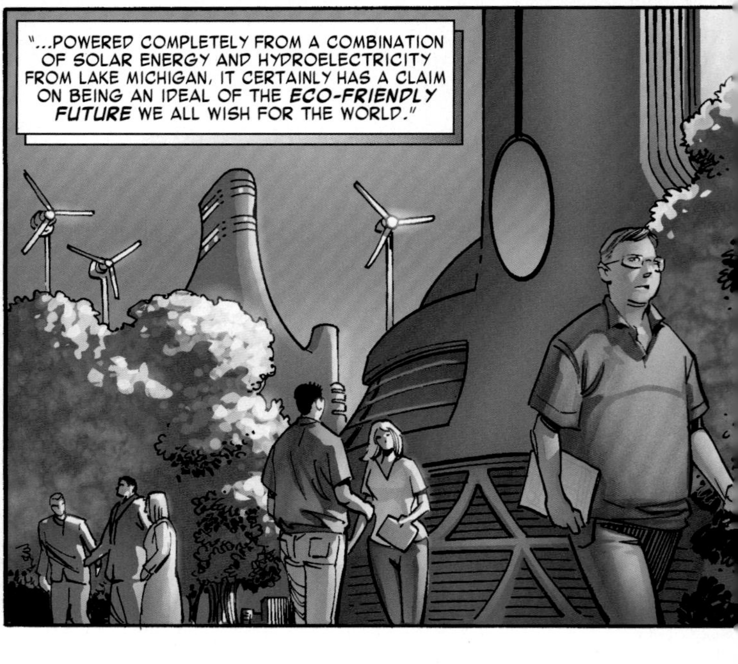
"...POWERED COMPLETELY FROM A COMBINATION OF SOLAR ENERGY AND HYDROELECTRICITY FROM LAKE MICHIGAN, IT CERTAINLY HAS A CLAIM ON BEING AN IDEAL OF THE ECO-FRIENDLY FUTURE WE ALL WISH FOR THE WORLD."

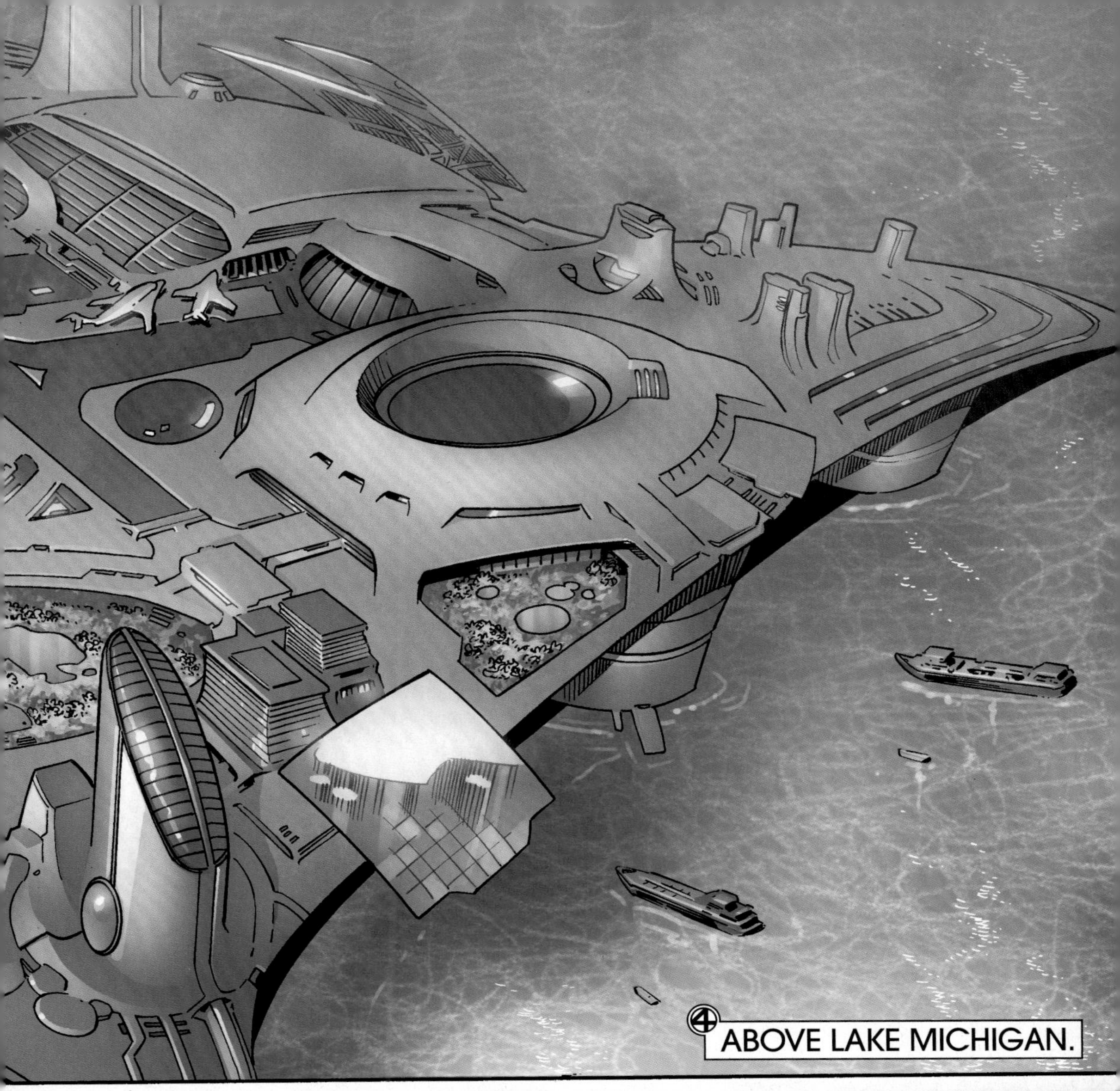
ABOVE LAKE MICHIGAN.

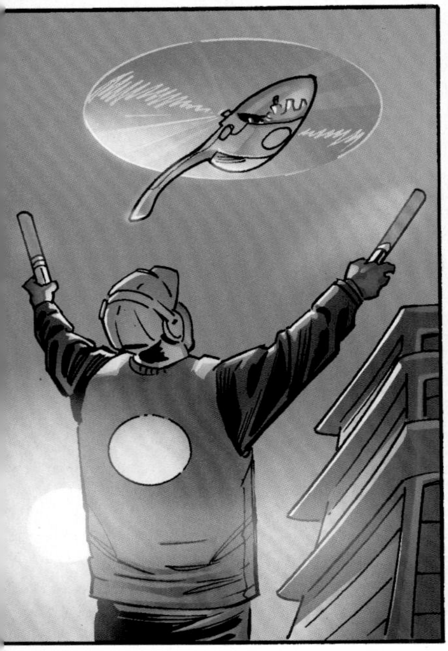

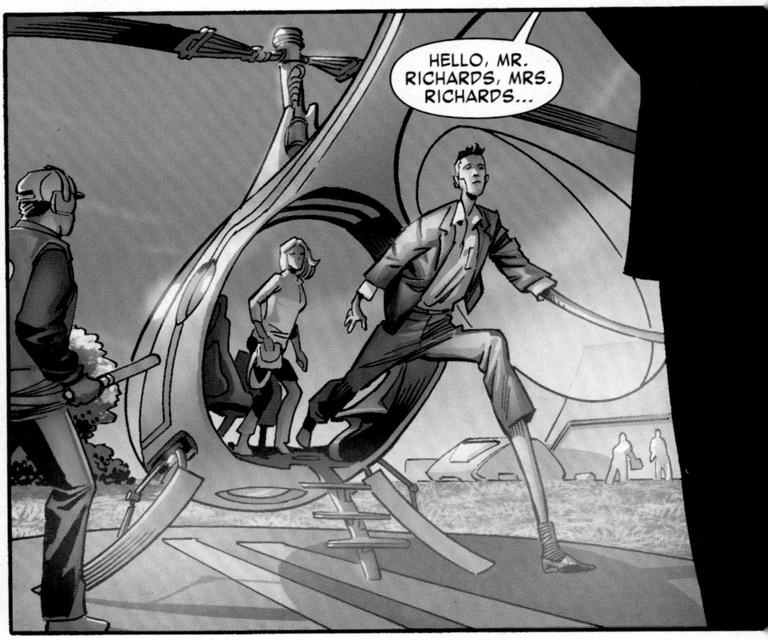
HELLO, MR. RICHARDS, MRS. RICHARDS...

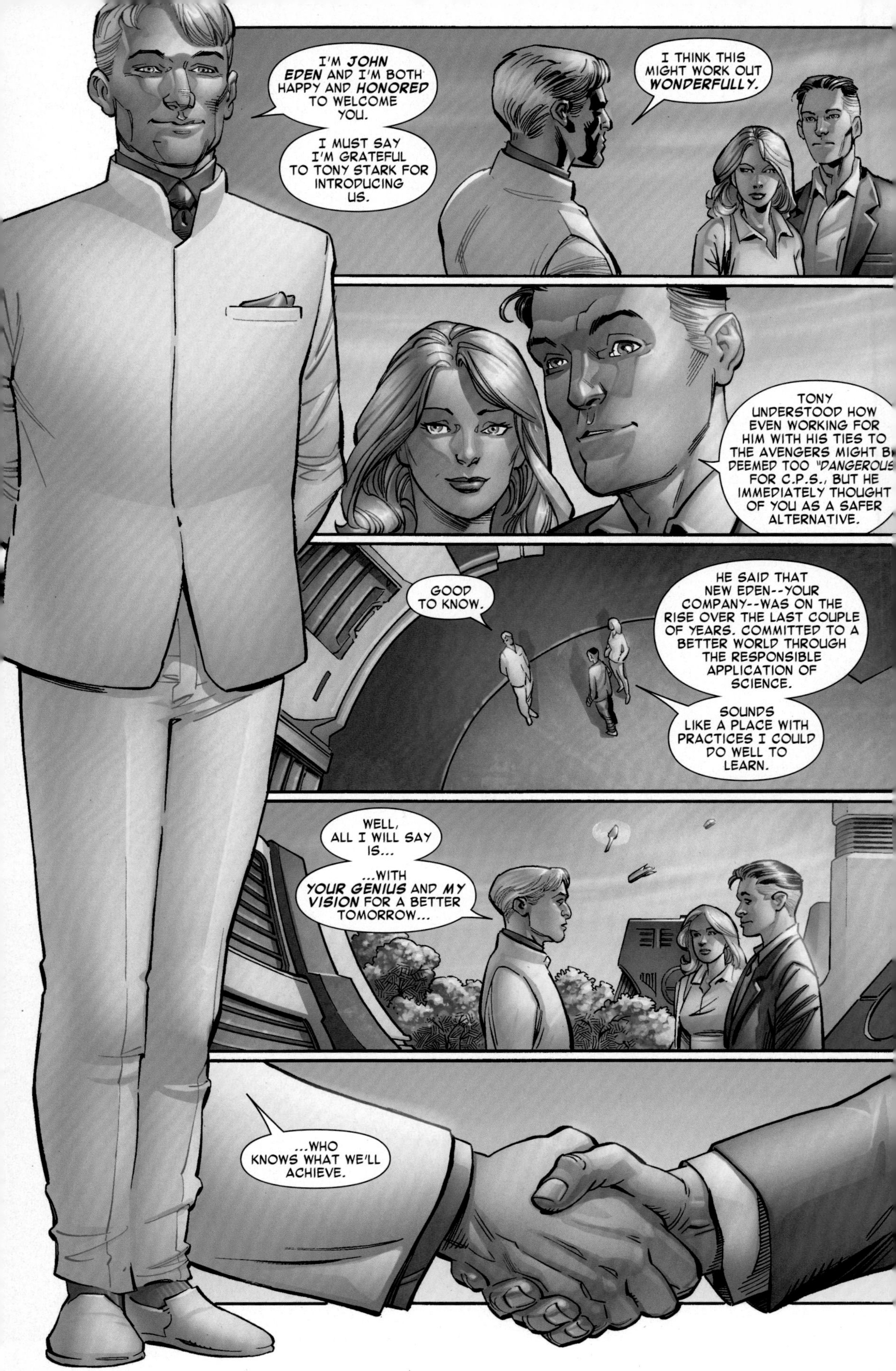
I'M JOHN EDEN AND I'M BOTH HAPPY AND HONORED TO WELCOME YOU.
I MUST SAY I'M GRATEFUL TO TONY STARK FOR INTRODUCING US.
I THINK THIS MIGHT WORK OUT WONDERFULLY.
TONY UNDERSTOOD HOW EVEN WORKING FOR HIM WITH HIS TIES TO THE AVENGERS MIGHT BE DEEMED TOO "DANGEROUS" FOR C.P.S., BUT HE IMMEDIATELY THOUGHT OF YOU AS A SAFER ALTERNATIVE.
GOOD TO KNOW.
HE SAID THAT NEW EDEN--YOUR COMPANY--WAS ON THE RISE OVER THE LAST COUPLE OF YEARS. COMMITTED TO A BETTER WORLD THROUGH THE RESPONSIBLE APPLICATION OF SCIENCE.
SOUNDS LIKE A PLACE WITH PRACTICES I COULD DO WELL TO LEARN.
WELL, ALL I WILL SAY IS...
...WITH YOUR GENIUS AND MY VISION FOR A BETTER TOMORROW...
...WHO KNOWS WHAT WE'LL ACHIEVE.

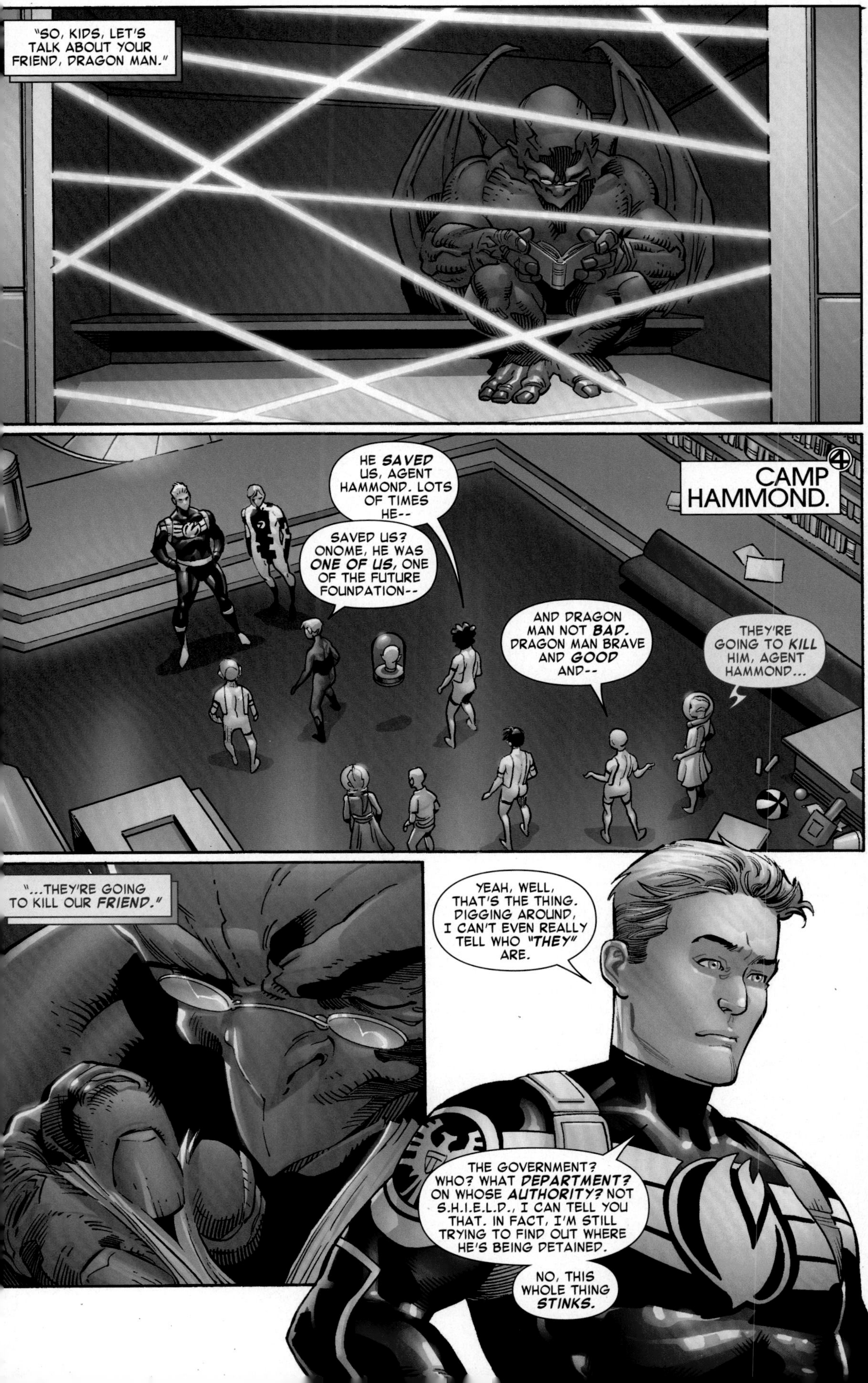

"SO, KIDS, LET'S TALK ABOUT YOUR FRIEND, DRAGON MAN."
CAMP HAMMOND.
HE SAVED US, AGENT HAMMOND. LOTS OF TIMES HE--
SAVED US? ONOME, HE WAS ONE OF US, ONE OF THE FUTURE FOUNDATION--
AND DRAGON MAN NOT BAD. DRAGON MAN BRAVE AND GOOD AND--
THEY'RE GOING TO KILL HIM, AGENT HAMMOND...
"...THEY'RE GOING TO KILL OUR FRIEND."
YEAH, WELL, THAT'S THE THING. DIGGING AROUND, I CAN'T EVEN REALLY TELL WHO "THEY" ARE.
THE GOVERNMENT? WHO? WHAT DEPARTMENT? ON WHOSE AUTHORITY? NOT S.H.I.E.L.D., I CAN TELL YOU THAT. IN FACT, I'M STILL TRYING TO FIND OUT WHERE HE'S BEING DETAINED.
NO, THIS WHOLE THING STINKS.

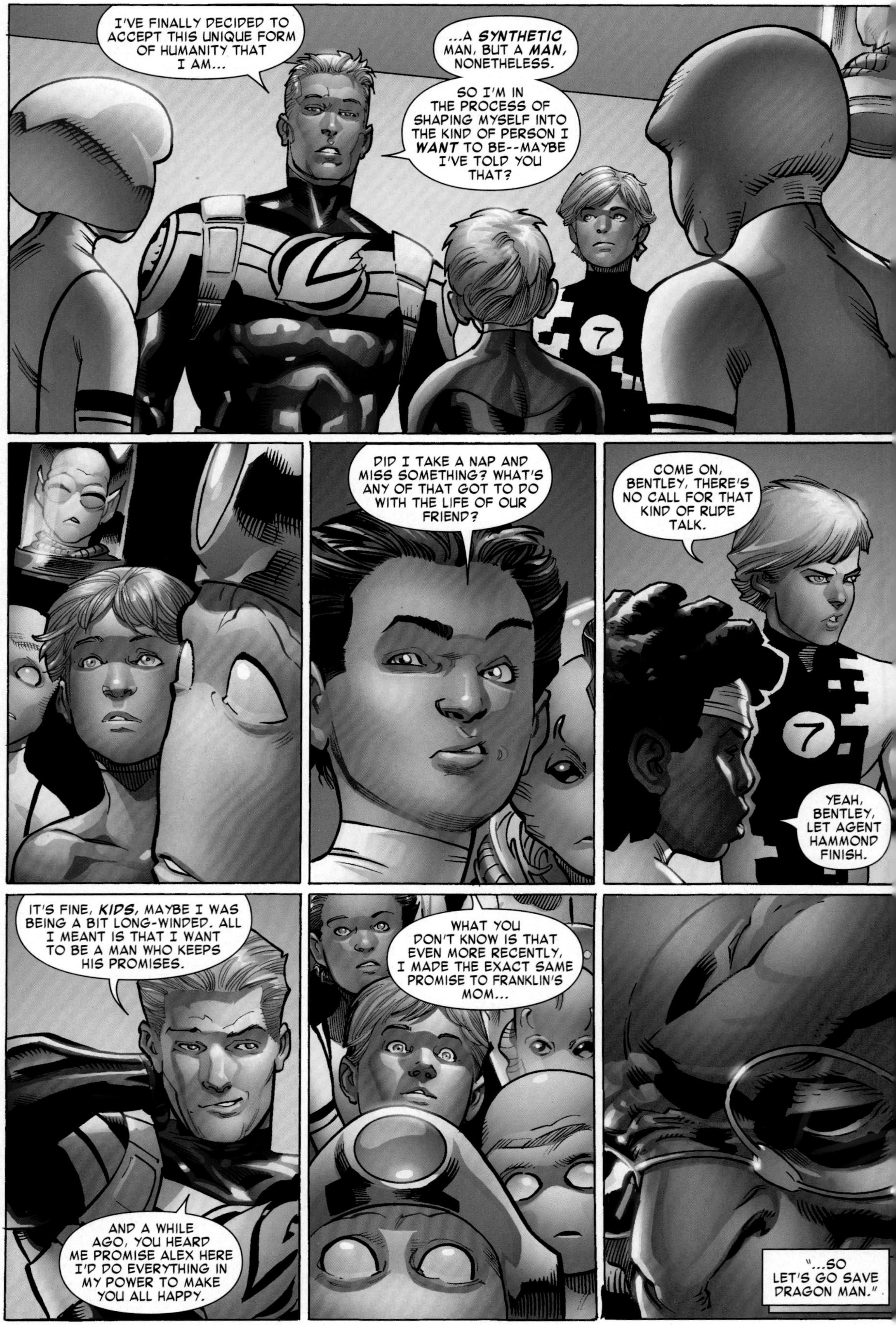
I'VE FINALLY DECIDED TO ACCEPT THIS UNIQUE FORM OF HUMANITY THAT I AM...
...A SYNTHETIC MAN, BUT A MAN, NONETHELESS.
SO I'M IN THE PROCESS OF SHAPING MYSELF INTO THE KIND OF PERSON I WANT TO BE--MAYBE I'VE TOLD YOU THAT?
DID I TAKE A NAP AND MISS SOMETHING? WHAT'S ANY OF THAT GOT TO DO WITH THE LIFE OF OUR FRIEND?
COME ON, BENTLEY, THERE'S NO CALL FOR THAT KIND OF RUDE TALK.
YEAH, BENTLEY, LET AGENT HAMMOND FINISH.
IT'S FINE, KIDS, MAYBE I WAS BEING A BIT LONG-WINDED. ALL I MEANT IS THAT I WANT TO BE A MAN WHO KEEPS HIS PROMISES.
AND A WHILE AGO, YOU HEARD ME PROMISE ALEX HERE I'D DO EVERYTHING IN MY POWER TO MAKE YOU ALL HAPPY.
WHAT YOU DON'T KNOW IS THAT EVEN MORE RECENTLY, I MADE THE EXACT SAME PROMISE TO FRANKLIN'S MOM...
"...SO LET'S GO SAVE DRAGON MAN."

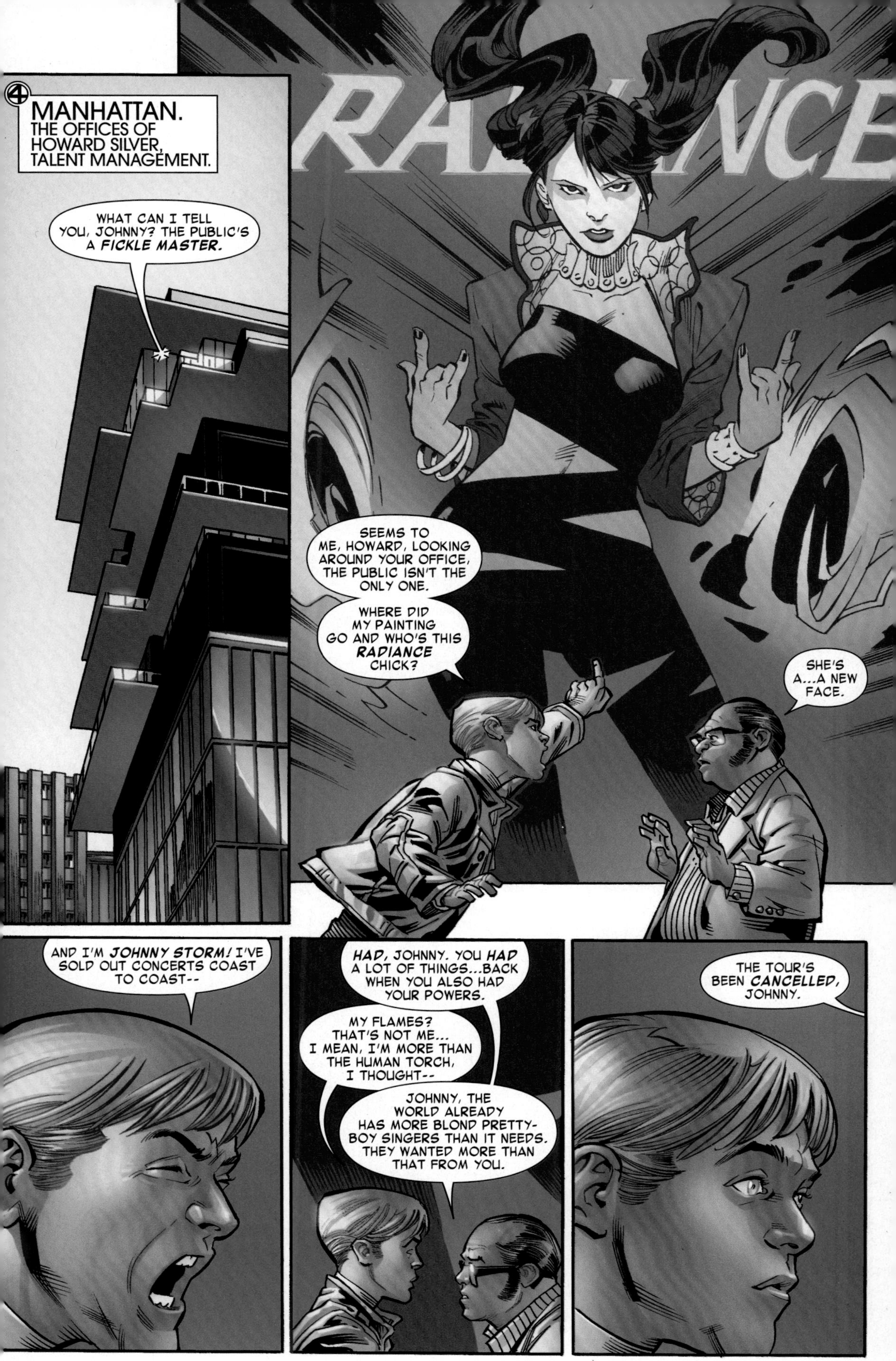

MANHATTAN. THE OFFICES OF HOWARD SILVER, TALENT MANAGEMENT.
WHAT CAN I TELL YOU, JOHNNY? THE PUBLIC'S A FICKLE MASTER.
RADIANCE
SEEMS TO ME, HOWARD, LOOKING AROUND YOUR OFFICE, THE PUBLIC ISN'T THE ONLY ONE.
WHERE DID MY PAINTING GO AND WHO'S THIS RADIANCE CHICK?
SHE'S A...A NEW FACE.
AND I'M JOHNNY STORM! I'VE SOLD OUT CONCERTS COAST TO COAST--
HAD, JOHNNY. YOU HAD A LOT OF THINGS...BACK WHEN YOU ALSO HAD YOUR POWERS.
MY FLAMES? THAT'S NOT ME... I MEAN, I'M MORE THAN THE HUMAN TORCH, I THOUGHT--
JOHNNY, THE WORLD ALREADY HAS MORE BLOND PRETTY-BOY SINGERS THAN IT NEEDS. THEY WANTED MORE THAN THAT FROM YOU.
THE TOUR'S BEEN CANCELLED, JOHNNY.

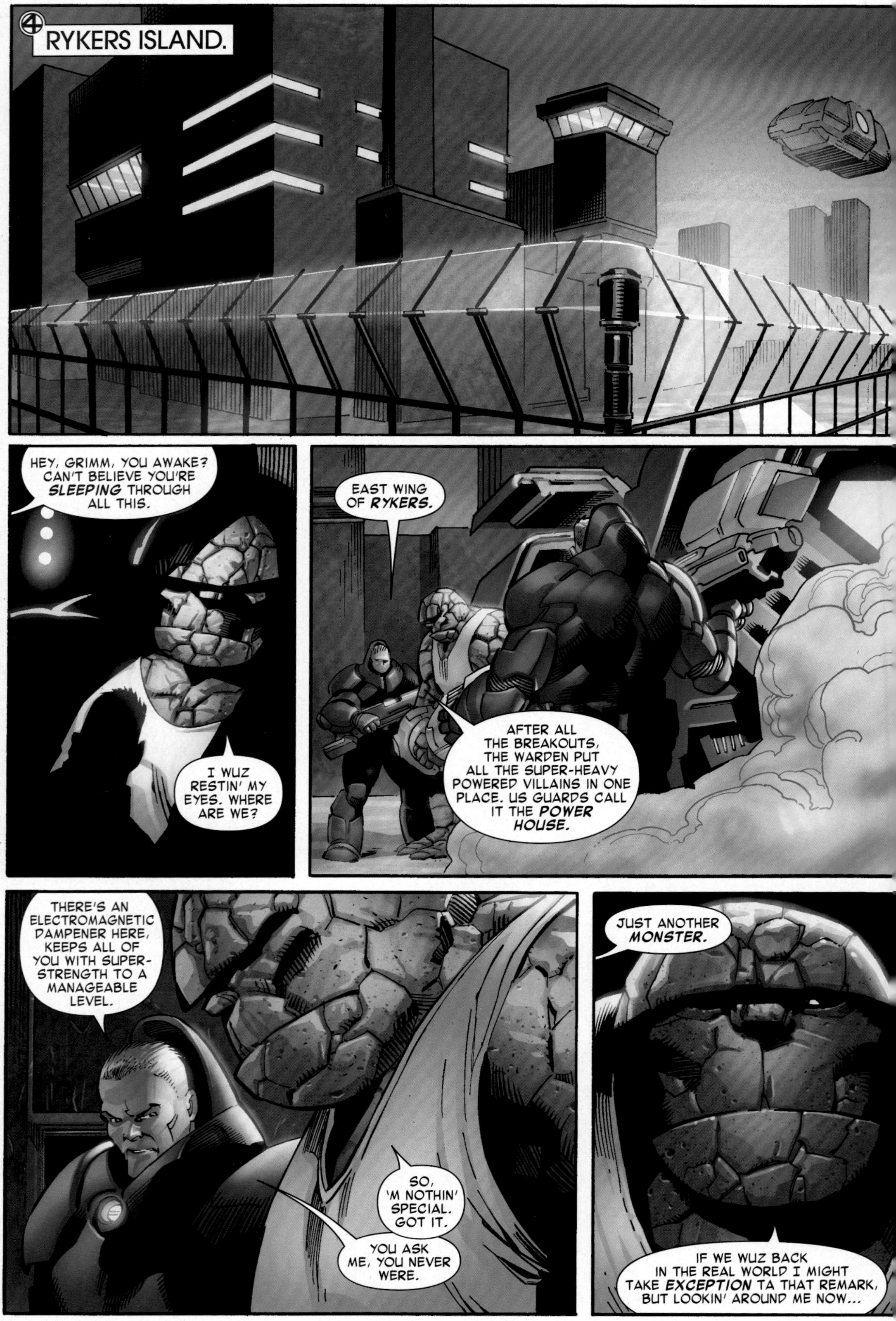
RYKERS ISLAND.
HEY, GRIMM, YOU AWAKE? CAN'T BELIEVE YOU'RE SLEEPING THROUGH ALL THIS.
I WUZ RESTIN' MY EYES. WHERE ARE WE?
EAST WING OF RYKERS.
AFTER ALL THE BREAKOUTS, THE WARDEN PUT ALL THE SUPER-HEAVY POWERED VILLAINS IN ONE PLACE. US GUARDS CALL IT THE POWER HOUSE.
THERE'S AN ELECTROMAGNETIC DAMPENER HERE, KEEPS ALL OF YOU WITH SUPER-STRENGTH TO A MANAGEABLE LEVEL.
SO, 'M NOTHIN' SPECIAL. GOT IT.
YOU ASK ME, YOU NEVER WERE.
JUST ANOTHER MONSTER.
IF WE WUZ BACK IN THE REAL WORLD I MIGHT TAKE EXCEPTION TA THAT REMARK, BUT LOOKIN' AROUND ME NOW...

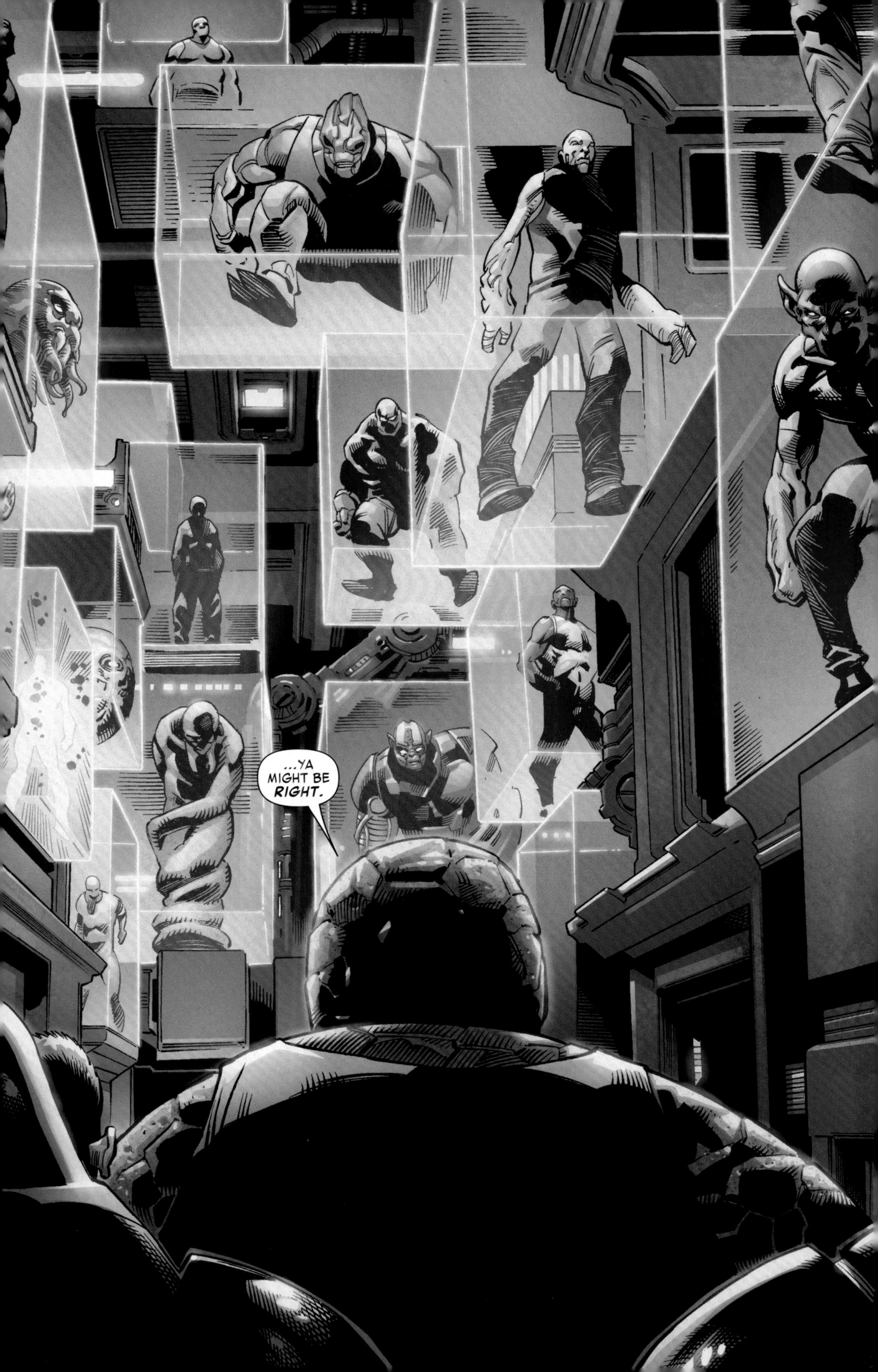
...YA MIGHT BE RIGHT.

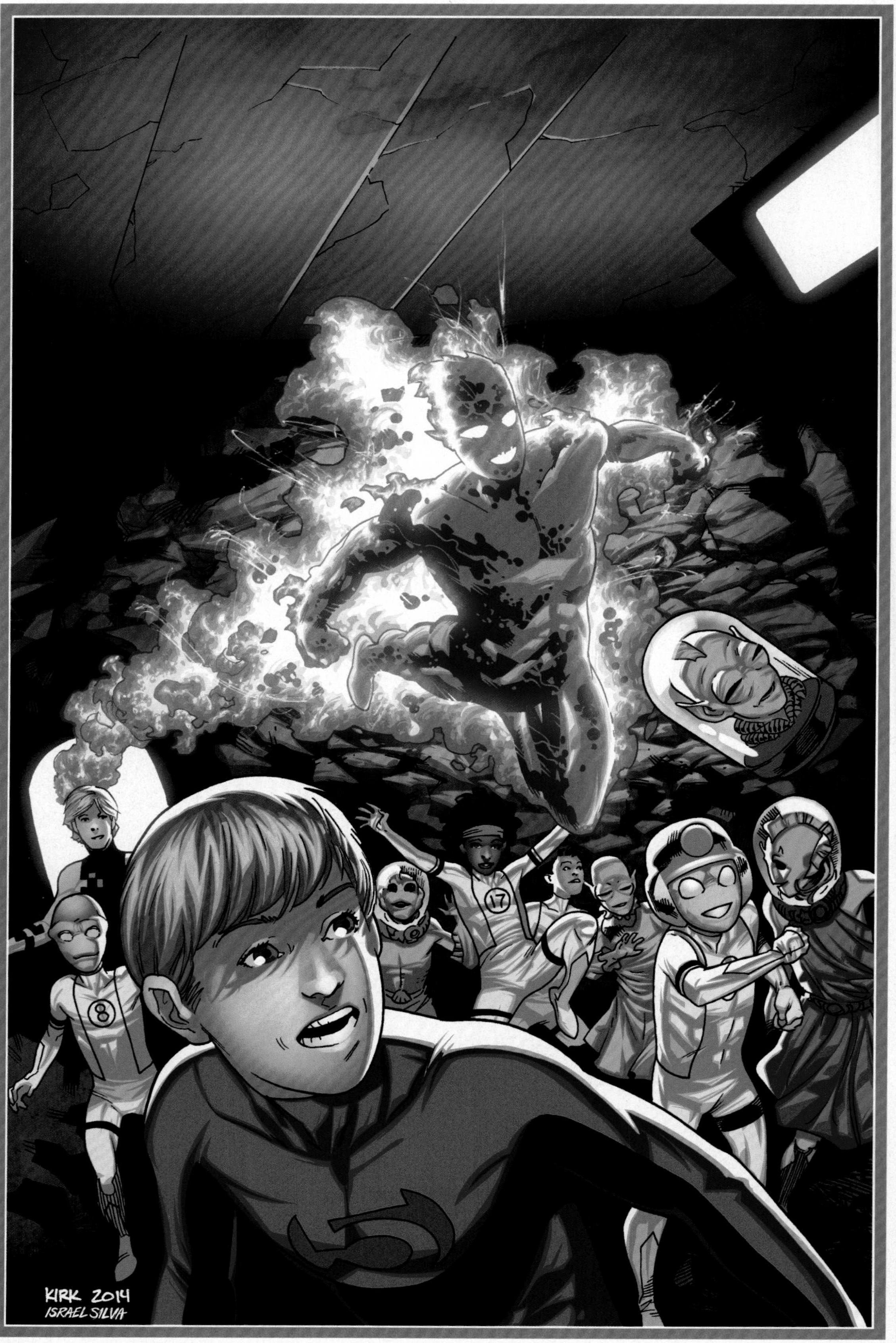
KIRK 2014
ISRAEL SILVA

NINE

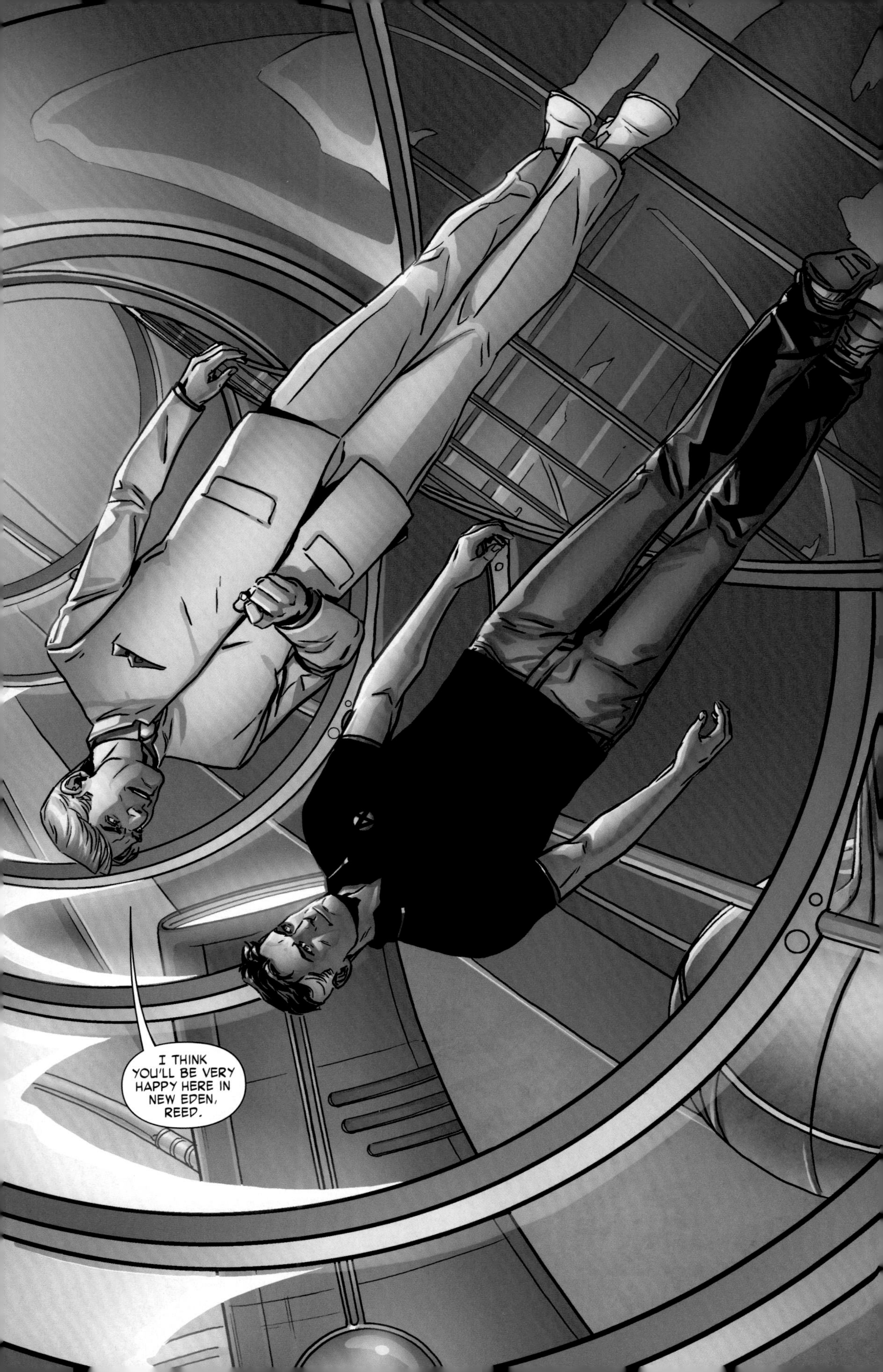
I THINK YOU'LL BE VERY HAPPY HERE IN NEW EDEN, REED.

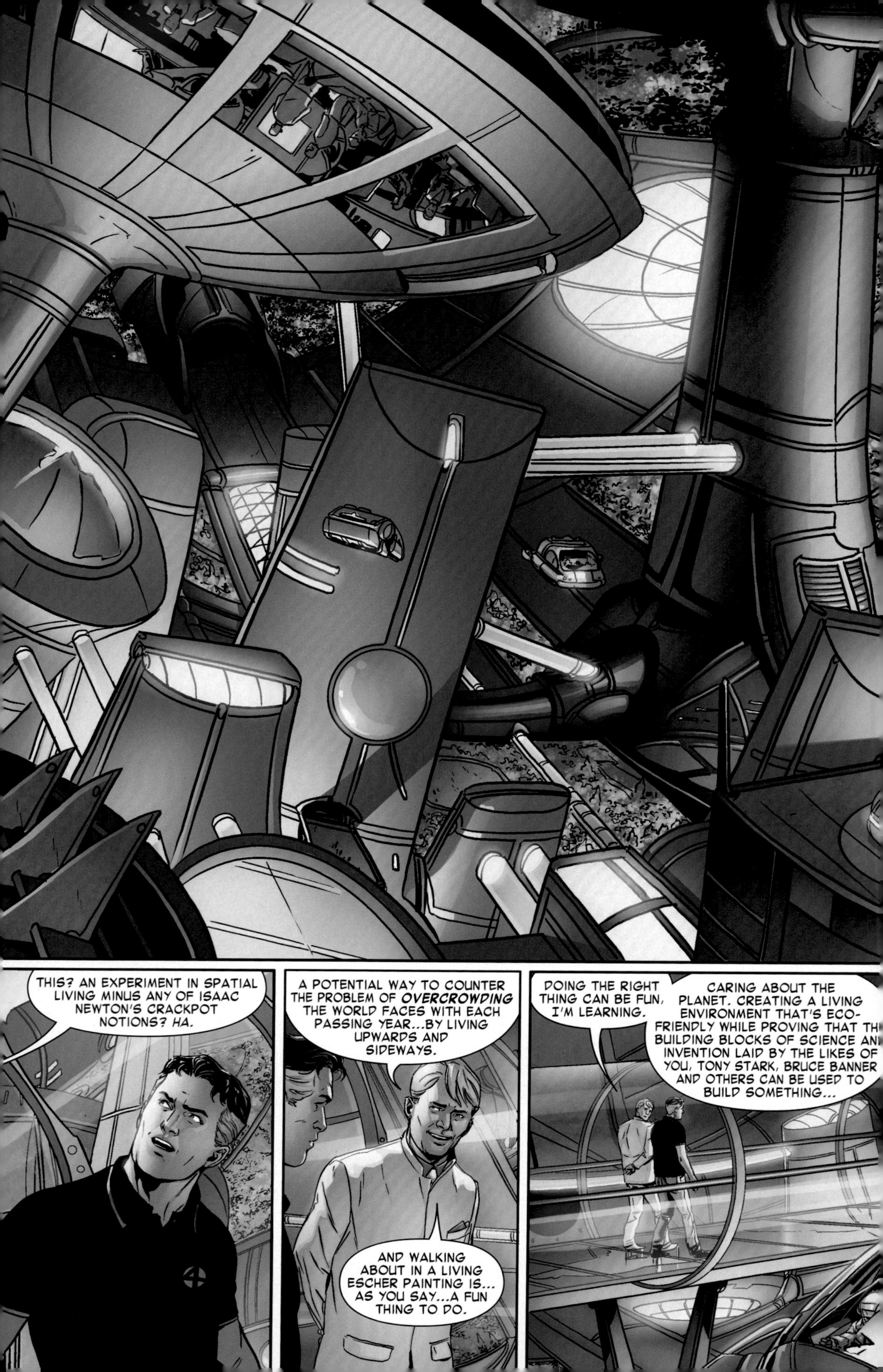
THIS? AN EXPERIMENT IN SPATIAL LIVING MINUS ANY OF ISAAC NEWTON'S CRACKPOT NOTIONS? *HA.*
A POTENTIAL WAY TO COUNTER THE PROBLEM OF ***OVERCROWDING*** THE WORLD FACES WITH EACH PASSING YEAR...BY LIVING UPWARDS AND SIDEWAYS.
AND WALKING ABOUT IN A LIVING ESCHER PAINTING IS... AS YOU SAY...A FUN THING TO DO.
DOING THE RIGHT THING CAN BE FUN, I'M LEARNING.
CARING ABOUT THE PLANET. CREATING A LIVING ENVIRONMENT THAT'S ECO-FRIENDLY WHILE PROVING THAT TH BUILDING BLOCKS OF SCIENCE AN INVENTION LAID BY THE LIKES OF YOU, TONY STARK, BRUCE BANNER AND OTHERS CAN BE USED TO BUILD SOMETHING...

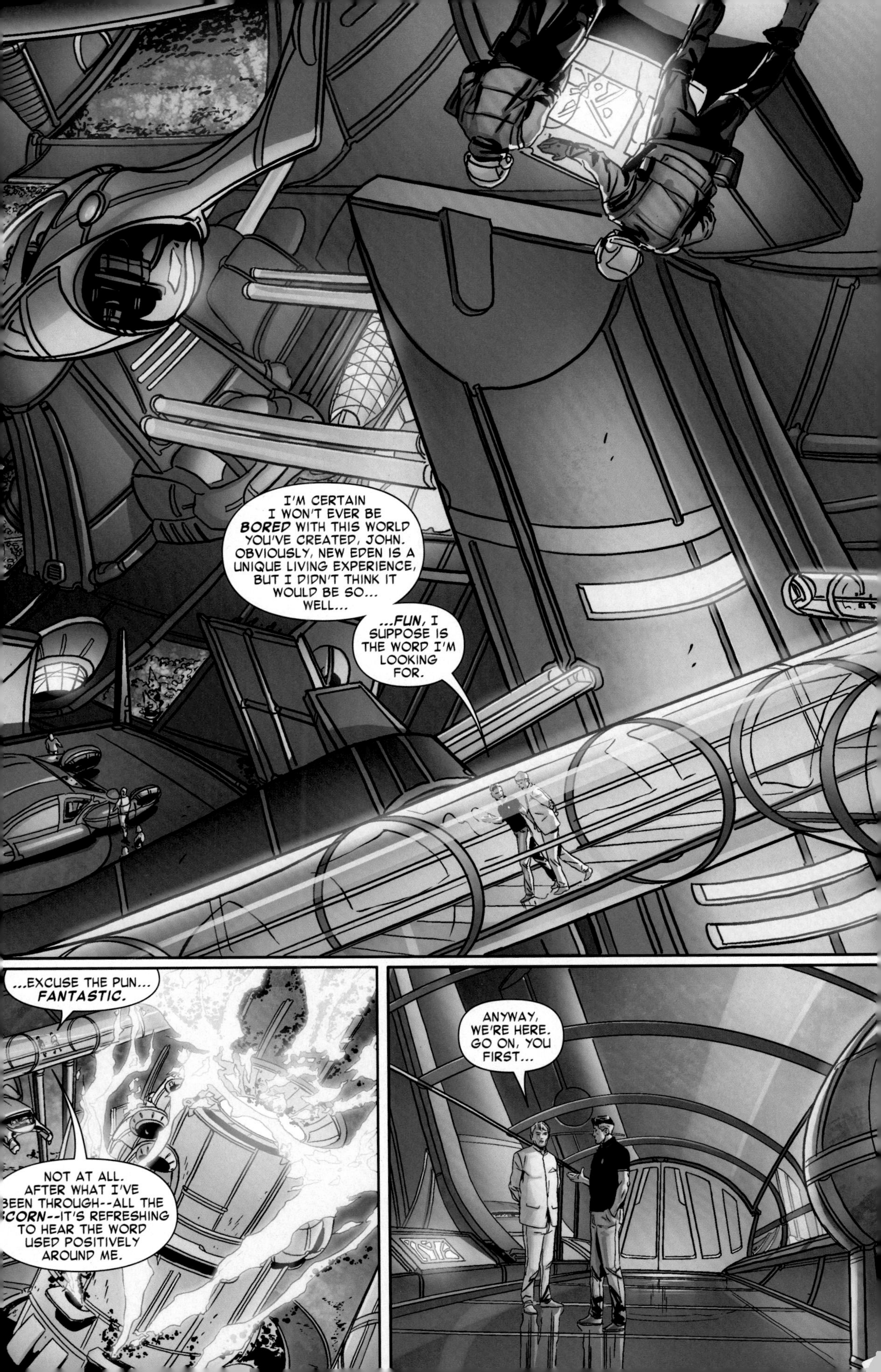
I'M CERTAIN I WON'T EVER BE BORED WITH THIS WORLD YOU'VE CREATED, JOHN. OBVIOUSLY, NEW EDEN IS A UNIQUE LIVING EXPERIENCE, BUT I DIDN'T THINK IT WOULD BE SO... WELL...
...FUN, I SUPPOSE IS THE WORD I'M LOOKING FOR.
...EXCUSE THE PUN... FANTASTIC.
NOT AT ALL. AFTER WHAT I'VE BEEN THROUGH--ALL THE SCORN--IT'S REFRESHING TO HEAR THE WORD USED POSITIVELY AROUND ME.
ANYWAY, WE'RE HERE. GO ON, YOU FIRST...

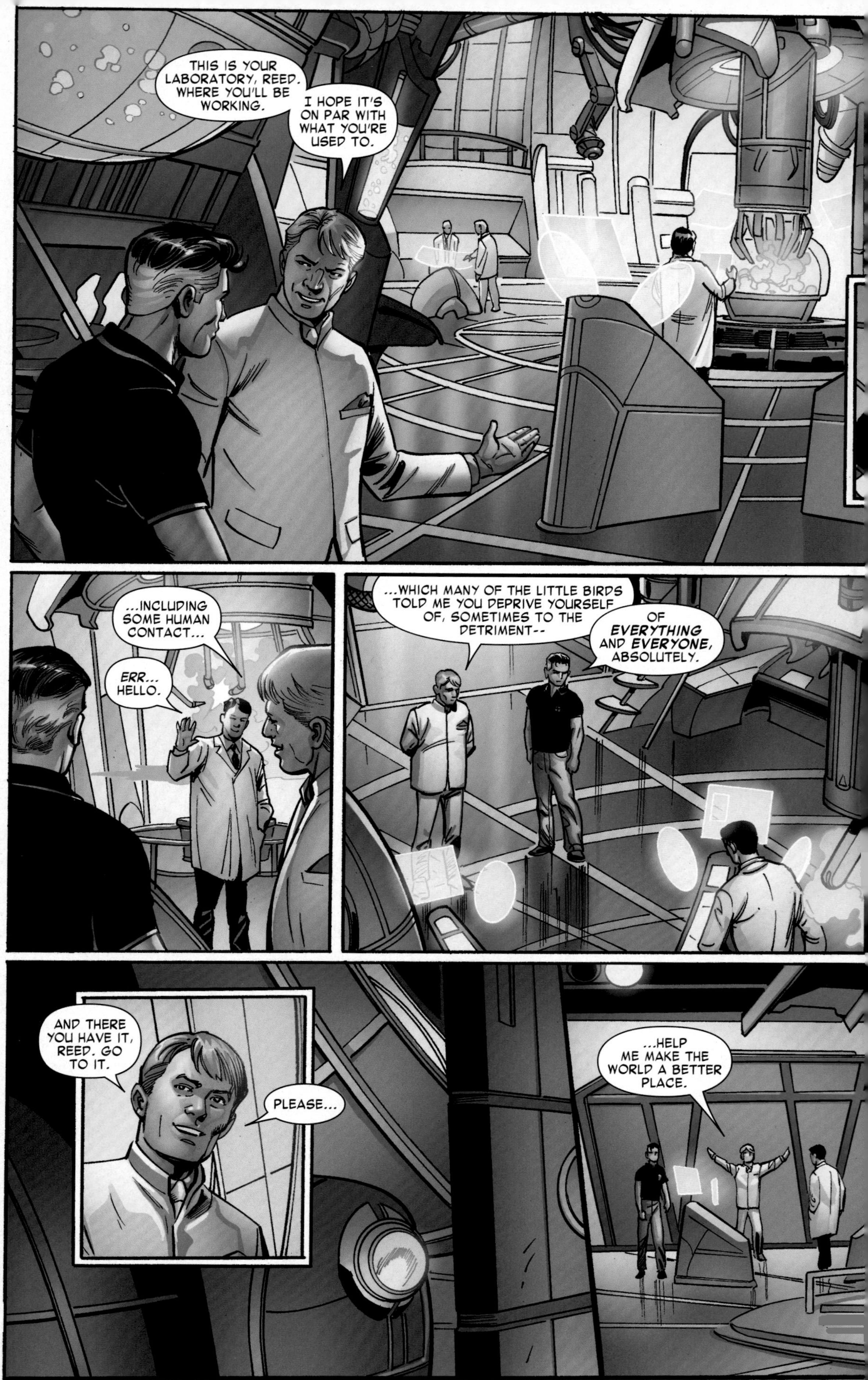
THIS IS YOUR LABORATORY, REED. WHERE YOU'LL BE WORKING.
I HOPE IT'S ON PAR WITH WHAT YOU'RE USED TO.
...INCLUDING SOME HUMAN CONTACT...
ERR... HELLO.
...WHICH MANY OF THE LITTLE BIRDS TOLD ME YOU DEPRIVE YOURSELF OF, SOMETIMES TO THE DETRIMENT--
OF EVERYTHING AND EVERYONE, ABSOLUTELY.
AND THERE YOU HAVE IT, REED. GO TO IT.
PLEASE...
...HELP ME MAKE THE WORLD A BETTER PLACE.

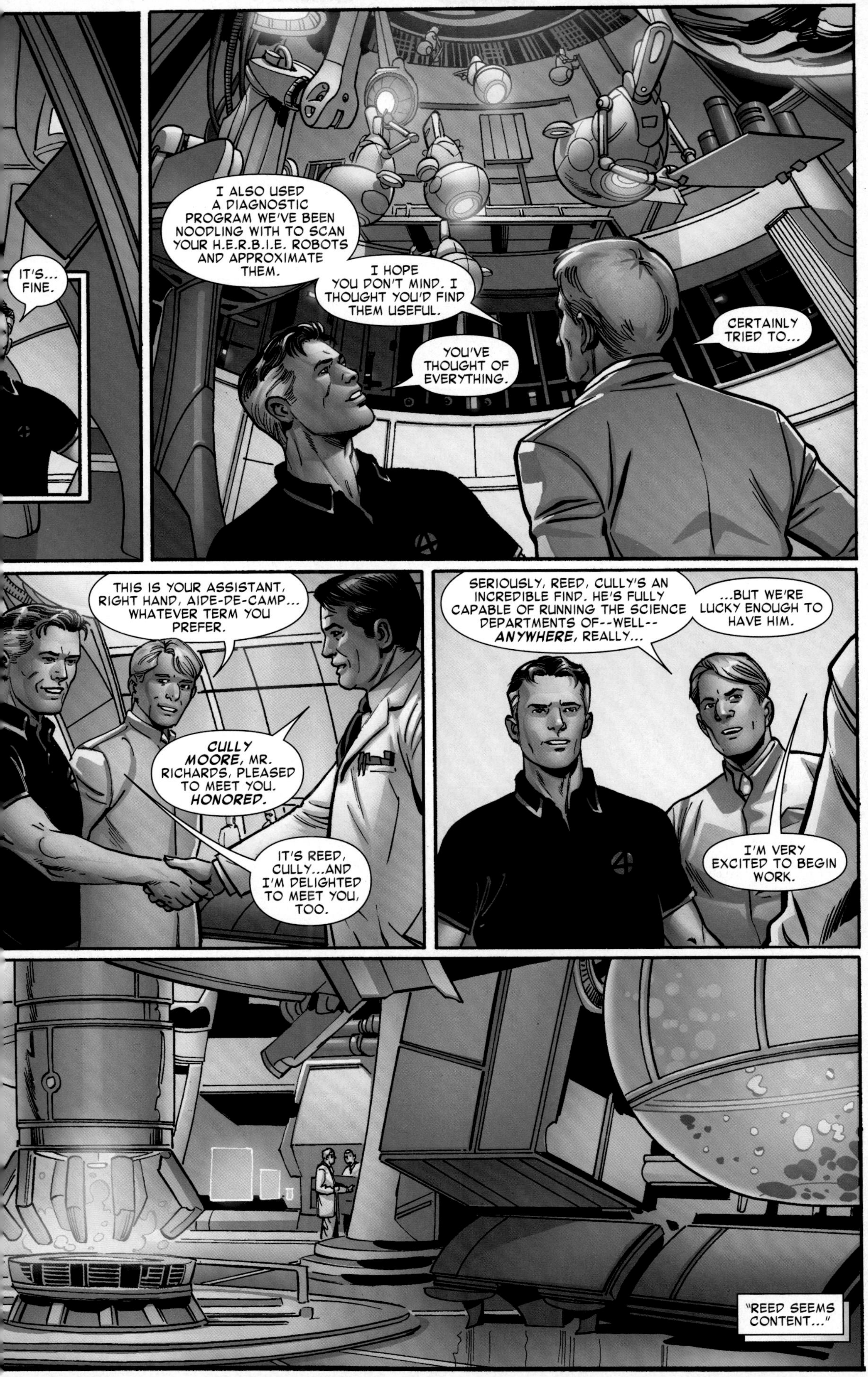
IT'S... FINE.
I ALSO USED A DIAGNOSTIC PROGRAM WE'VE BEEN NOODLING WITH TO SCAN YOUR H.E.R.B.I.E. ROBOTS AND APPROXIMATE THEM.
I HOPE YOU DON'T MIND. I THOUGHT YOU'D FIND THEM USEFUL.
YOU'VE THOUGHT OF EVERYTHING.
CERTAINLY TRIED TO...
THIS IS YOUR ASSISTANT, RIGHT HAND, AIDE-DE-CAMP... WHATEVER TERM YOU PREFER.
CULLY MOORE, MR. RICHARDS, PLEASED TO MEET YOU. HONORED.
IT'S REED, CULLY...AND I'M DELIGHTED TO MEET YOU, TOO.
SERIOUSLY, REED, CULLY'S AN INCREDIBLE FIND. HE'S FULLY CAPABLE OF RUNNING THE SCIENCE DEPARTMENTS OF--WELL--ANYWHERE, REALLY...
...BUT WE'RE LUCKY ENOUGH TO HAVE HIM.
I'M VERY EXCITED TO BEGIN WORK.
"REED SEEMS CONTENT..."

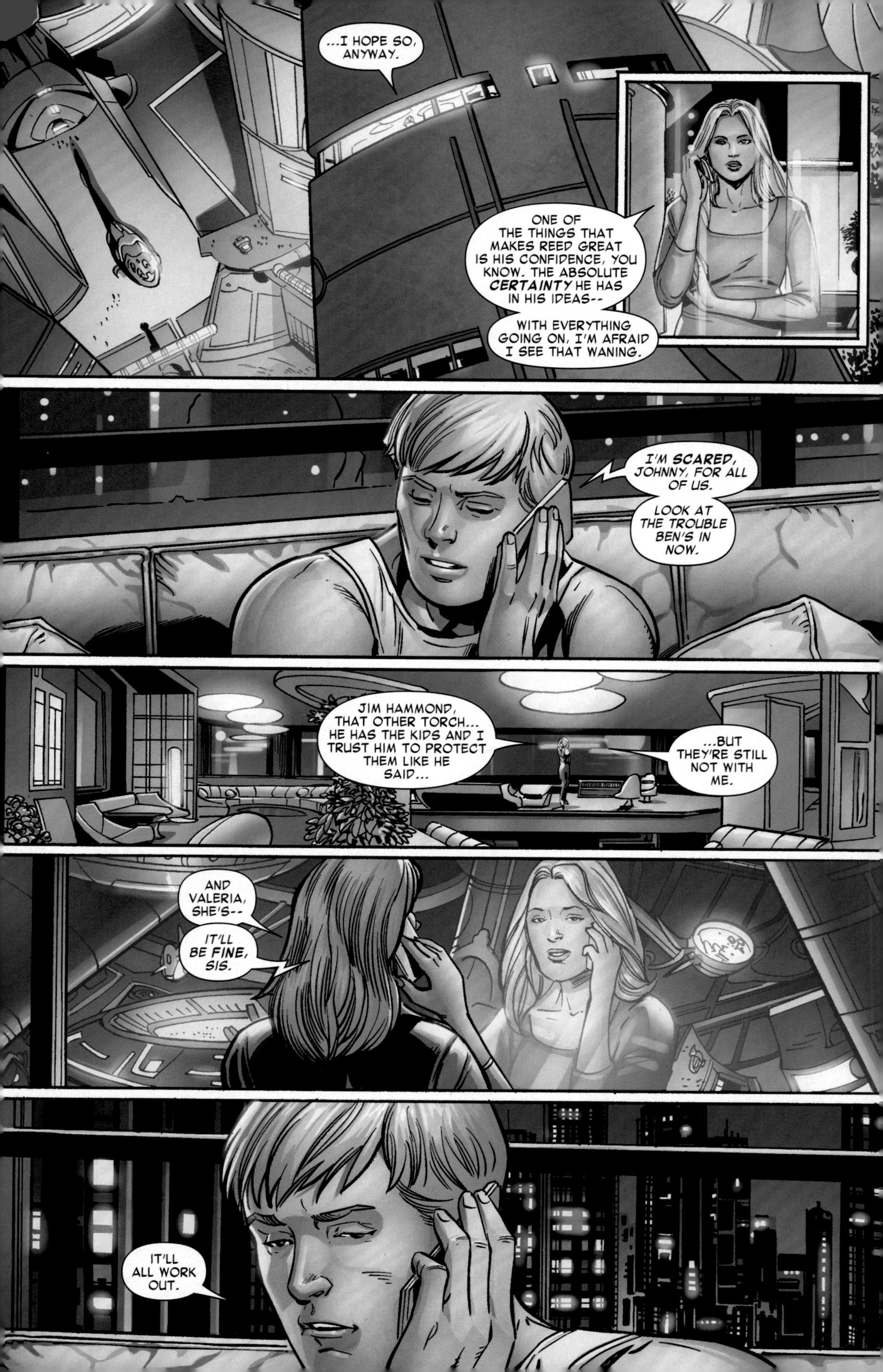
...I HOPE SO, ANYWAY.
ONE OF THE THINGS THAT MAKES REED GREAT IS HIS CONFIDENCE, YOU KNOW. THE ABSOLUTE CERTAINTY HE HAS IN HIS IDEAS--
WITH EVERYTHING GOING ON, I'M AFRAID I SEE THAT WANING.
I'M SCARED, JOHNNY, FOR ALL OF US.
LOOK AT THE TROUBLE BEN'S IN NOW.
JIM HAMMOND, THAT OTHER TORCH... HE HAS THE KIDS AND I TRUST HIM TO PROTECT THEM LIKE HE SAID...
...BUT THEY'RE STILL NOT WITH ME.
AND VALERIA, SHE'S--
IT'LL BE FINE, SIS.
IT'LL ALL WORK OUT.

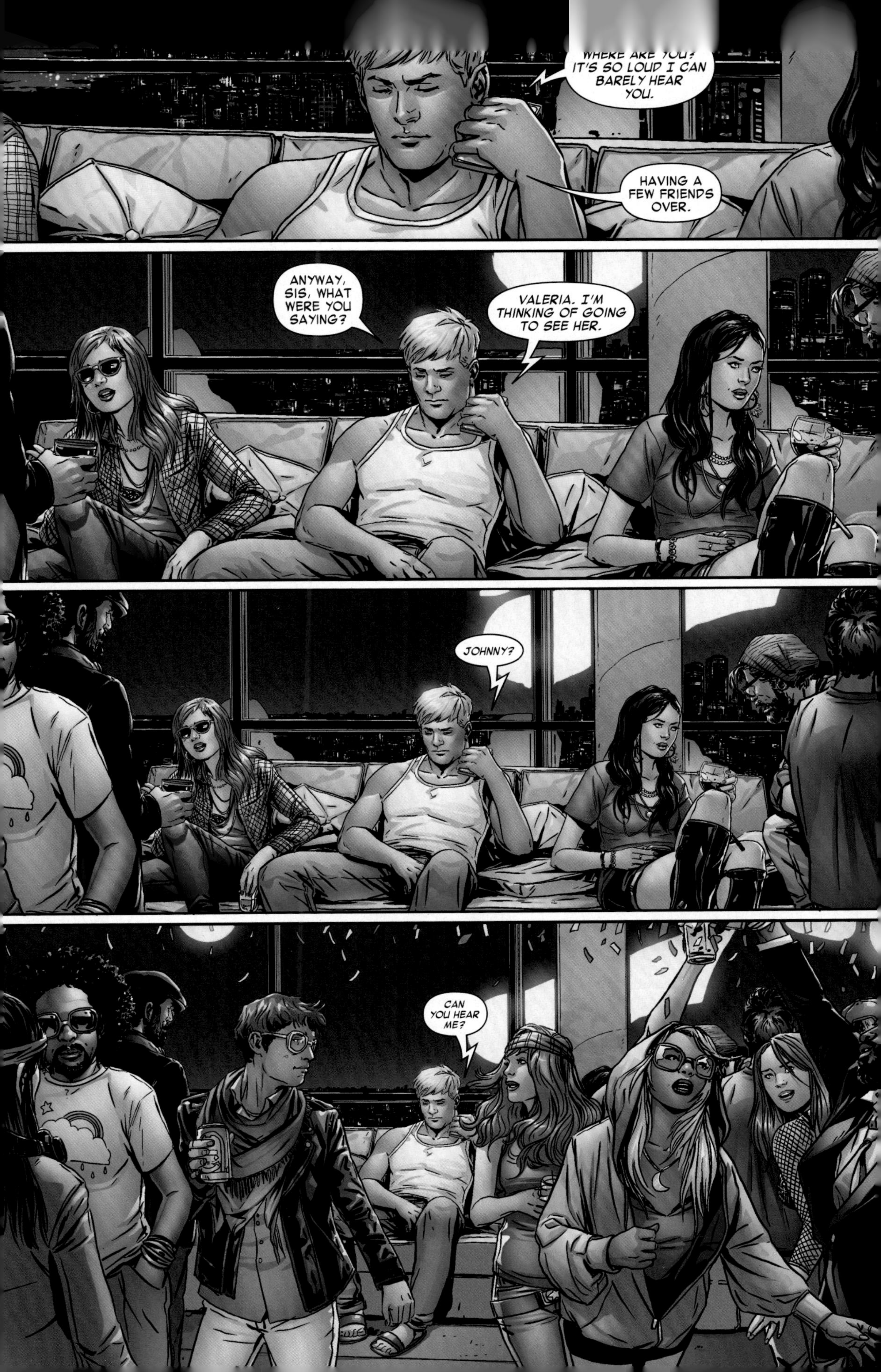
WHERE ARE YOU? IT'S SO LOUD I CAN BARELY HEAR YOU.
HAVING A FEW FRIENDS OVER.
ANYWAY, SIS, WHAT WERE YOU SAYING?
VALERIA. I'M THINKING OF GOING TO SEE HER.
JOHNNY?
CAN YOU HEAR ME?

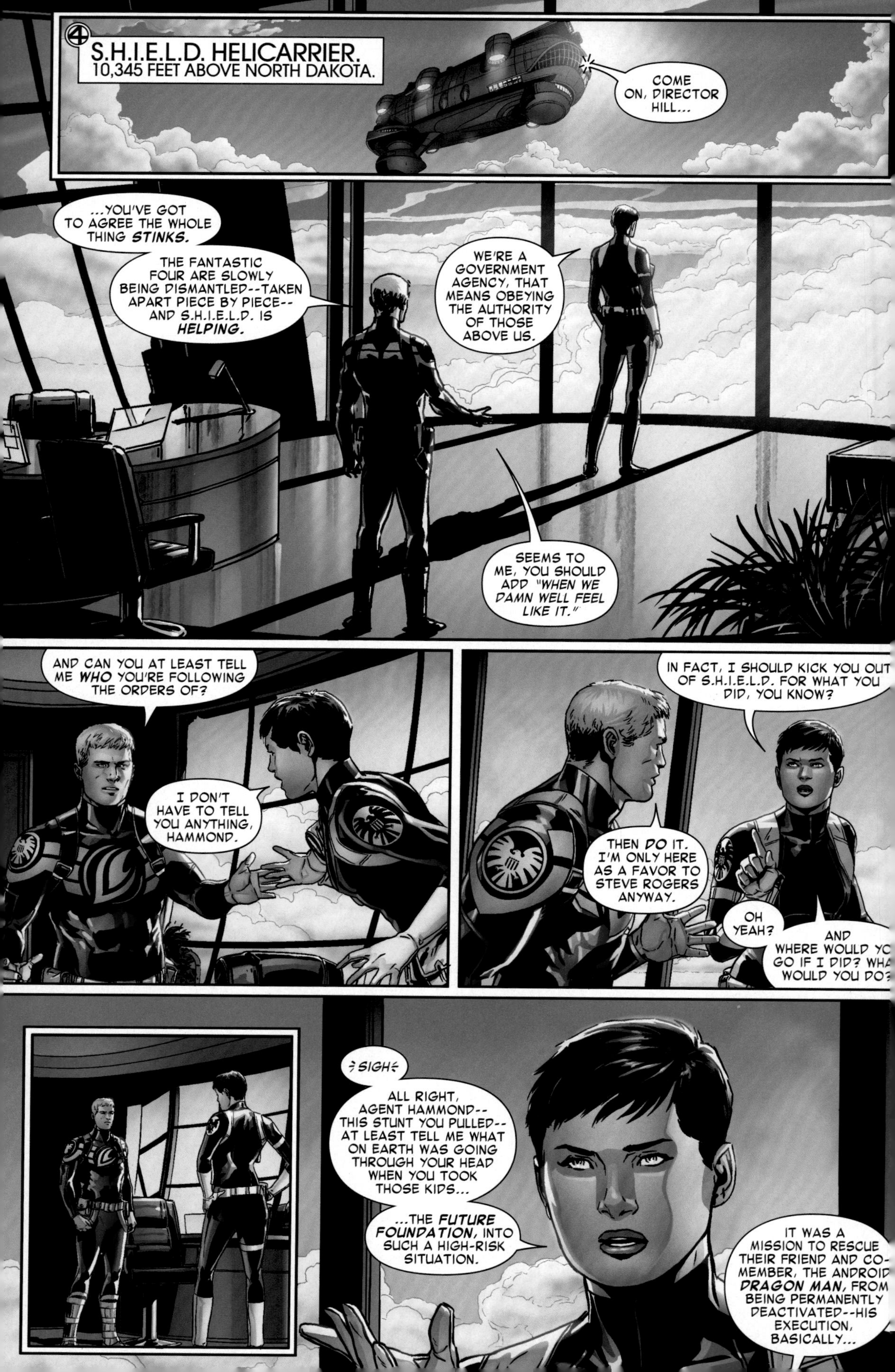
S.H.I.E.L.D. HELICARRIER.
10,345 FEET ABOVE NORTH DAKOTA.
COME ON, DIRECTOR HILL...
...YOU'VE GOT TO AGREE THE WHOLE THING STINKS.
THE FANTASTIC FOUR ARE SLOWLY BEING DISMANTLED--TAKEN APART PIECE BY PIECE--AND S.H.I.E.L.D. IS HELPING.
WE'RE A GOVERNMENT AGENCY, THAT MEANS OBEYING THE AUTHORITY OF THOSE ABOVE US.
SEEMS TO ME, YOU SHOULD ADD "WHEN WE DAMN WELL FEEL LIKE IT."
AND CAN YOU AT LEAST TELL ME WHO YOU'RE FOLLOWING THE ORDERS OF?
I DON'T HAVE TO TELL YOU ANYTHING, HAMMOND.
IN FACT, I SHOULD KICK YOU OUT OF S.H.I.E.L.D. FOR WHAT YOU DID, YOU KNOW?
THEN DO IT. I'M ONLY HERE AS A FAVOR TO STEVE ROGERS ANYWAY.
OH YEAH?
AND WHERE WOULD YO GO IF I DID? WHA WOULD YOU DO?
SIGH
ALL RIGHT, AGENT HAMMOND--THIS STUNT YOU PULLED--AT LEAST TELL ME WHAT ON EARTH WAS GOING THROUGH YOUR HEAD WHEN YOU TOOK THOSE KIDS...
...THE FUTURE FOUNDATION, INTO SUCH A HIGH-RISK SITUATION.
IT WAS A MISSION TO RESCUE THEIR FRIEND AND CO-MEMBER, THE ANDROID DRAGON MAN, FROM BEING PERMANENTLY DEACTIVATED--HIS EXECUTION, BASICALLY...

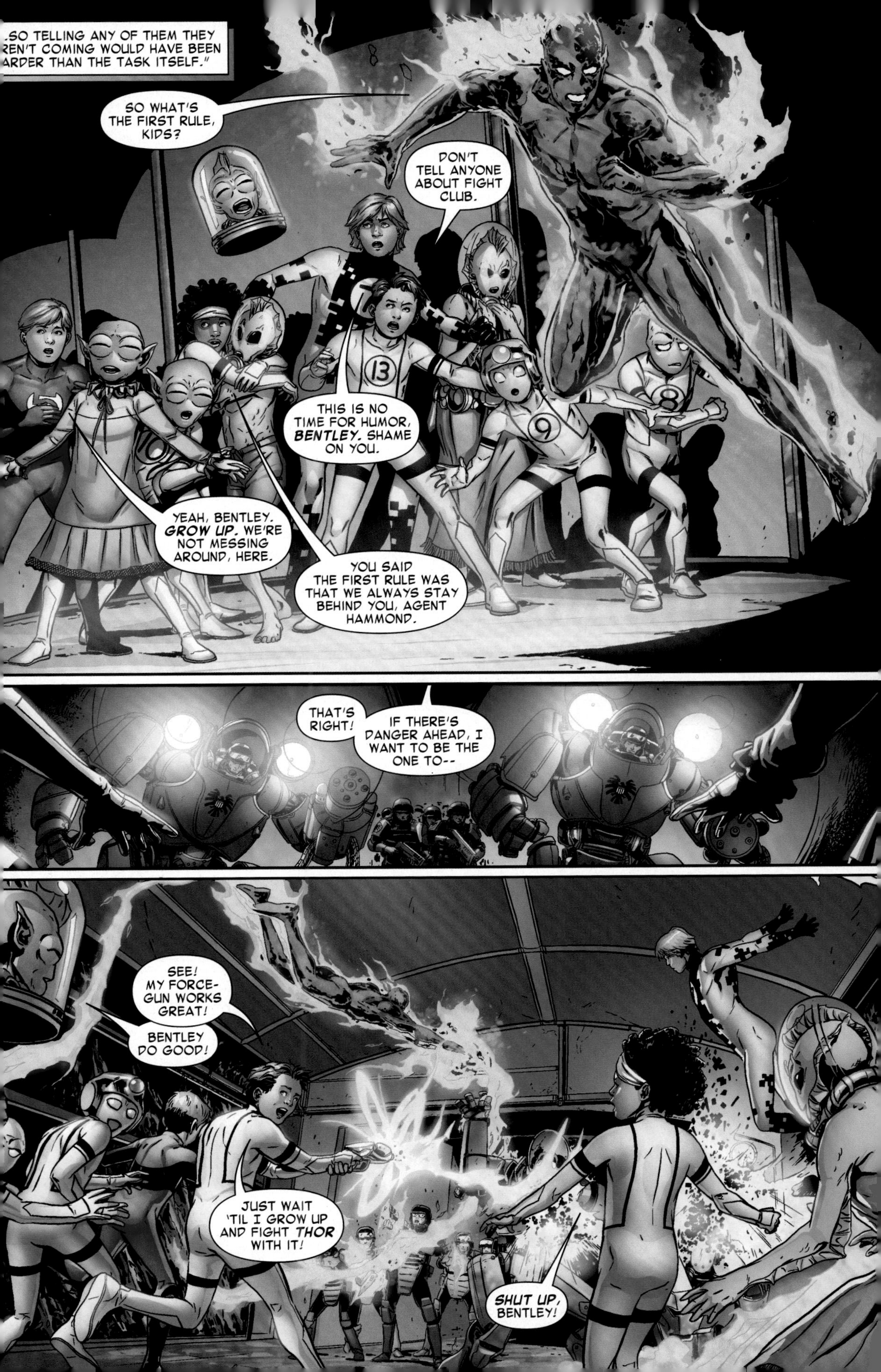
..SO TELLING ANY OF THEM THEY ...REN'T COMING WOULD HAVE BEEN ...ARDER THAN THE TASK ITSELF."
SO WHAT'S THE FIRST RULE, KIDS?
DON'T TELL ANYONE ABOUT FIGHT CLUB.
THIS IS NO TIME FOR HUMOR, BENTLEY. SHAME ON YOU.
YEAH, BENTLEY. GROW UP. WE'RE NOT MESSING AROUND, HERE.
YOU SAID THE FIRST RULE WAS THAT WE ALWAYS STAY BEHIND YOU, AGENT HAMMOND.
THAT'S RIGHT!
IF THERE'S DANGER AHEAD, I WANT TO BE THE ONE TO--
SEE! MY FORCE-GUN WORKS GREAT!
BENTLEY DO GOOD!
JUST WAIT 'TIL I GROW UP AND FIGHT THOR WITH IT!
SHUT UP, BENTLEY!

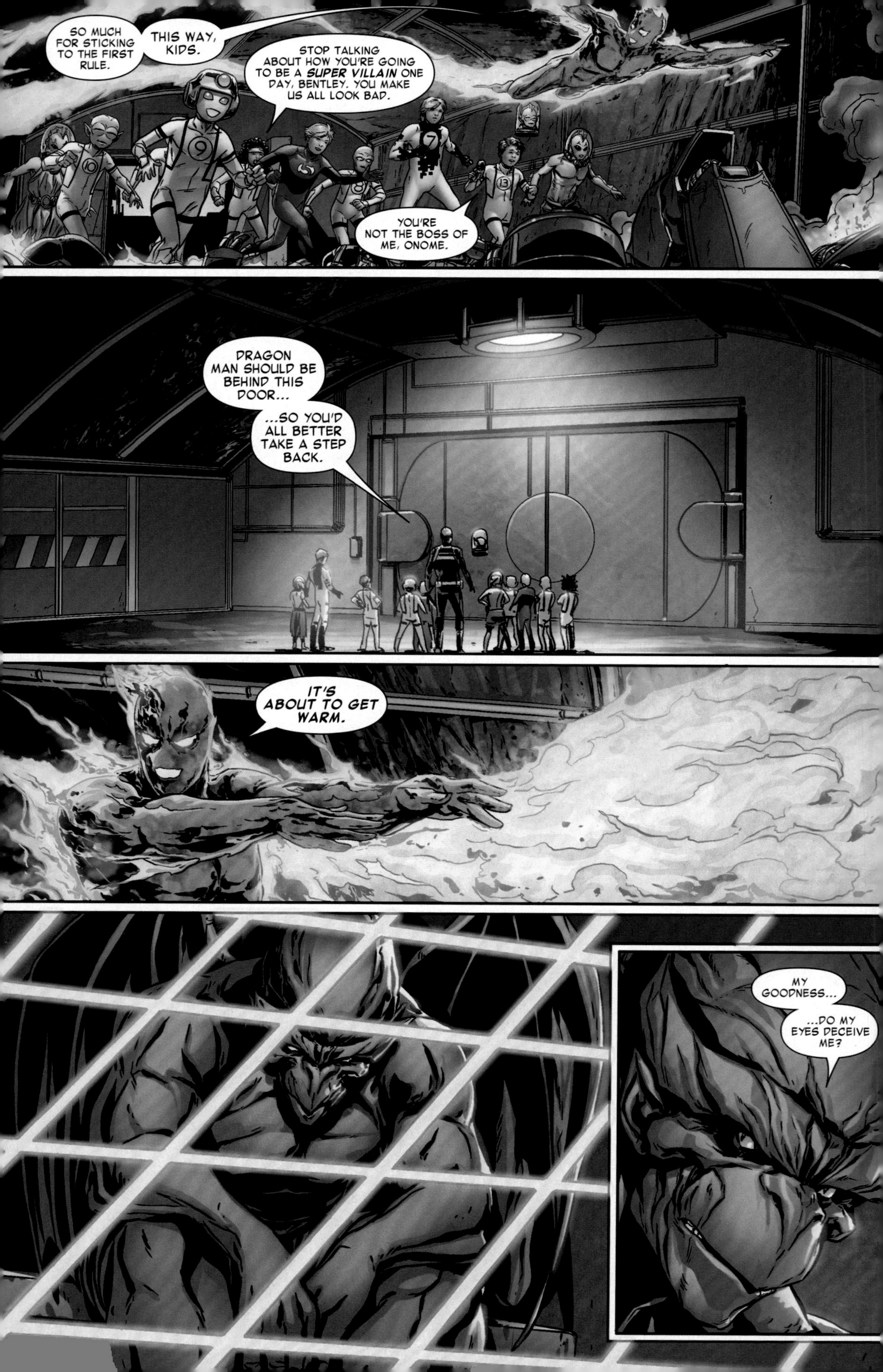
SO MUCH FOR STICKING TO THE FIRST RULE.
THIS WAY, KIDS.
STOP TALKING ABOUT HOW YOU'RE GOING TO BE A SUPER VILLAIN ONE DAY, BENTLEY. YOU MAKE US ALL LOOK BAD.
YOU'RE NOT THE BOSS OF ME, ONOME.
DRAGON MAN SHOULD BE BEHIND THIS DOOR...
...SO YOU'D ALL BETTER TAKE A STEP BACK.
IT'S ABOUT TO GET WARM.
MY GOODNESS...
...DO MY EYES DECEIVE ME?

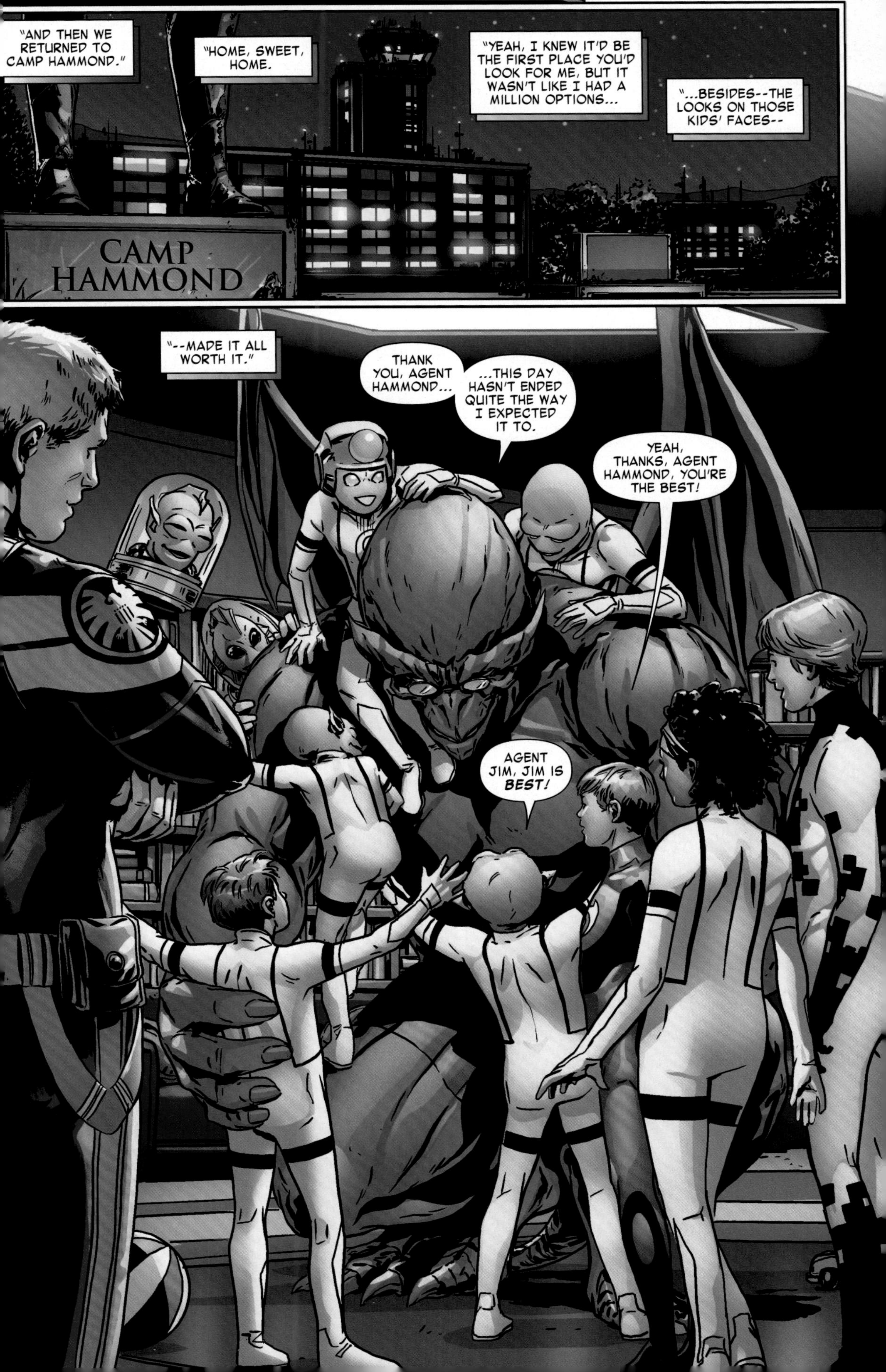
"AND THEN WE RETURNED TO CAMP HAMMOND."
"HOME, SWEET, HOME.
"YEAH, I KNEW IT'D BE THE FIRST PLACE YOU'D LOOK FOR ME, BUT IT WASN'T LIKE I HAD A MILLION OPTIONS...
"...BESIDES--THE LOOKS ON THOSE KIDS' FACES--
CAMP HAMMOND
"--MADE IT ALL WORTH IT."
THANK YOU, AGENT HAMMOND...
...THIS DAY HASN'T ENDED QUITE THE WAY I EXPECTED IT TO.
YEAH, THANKS, AGENT HAMMOND, YOU'RE THE BEST!
AGENT JIM, JIM IS BEST!

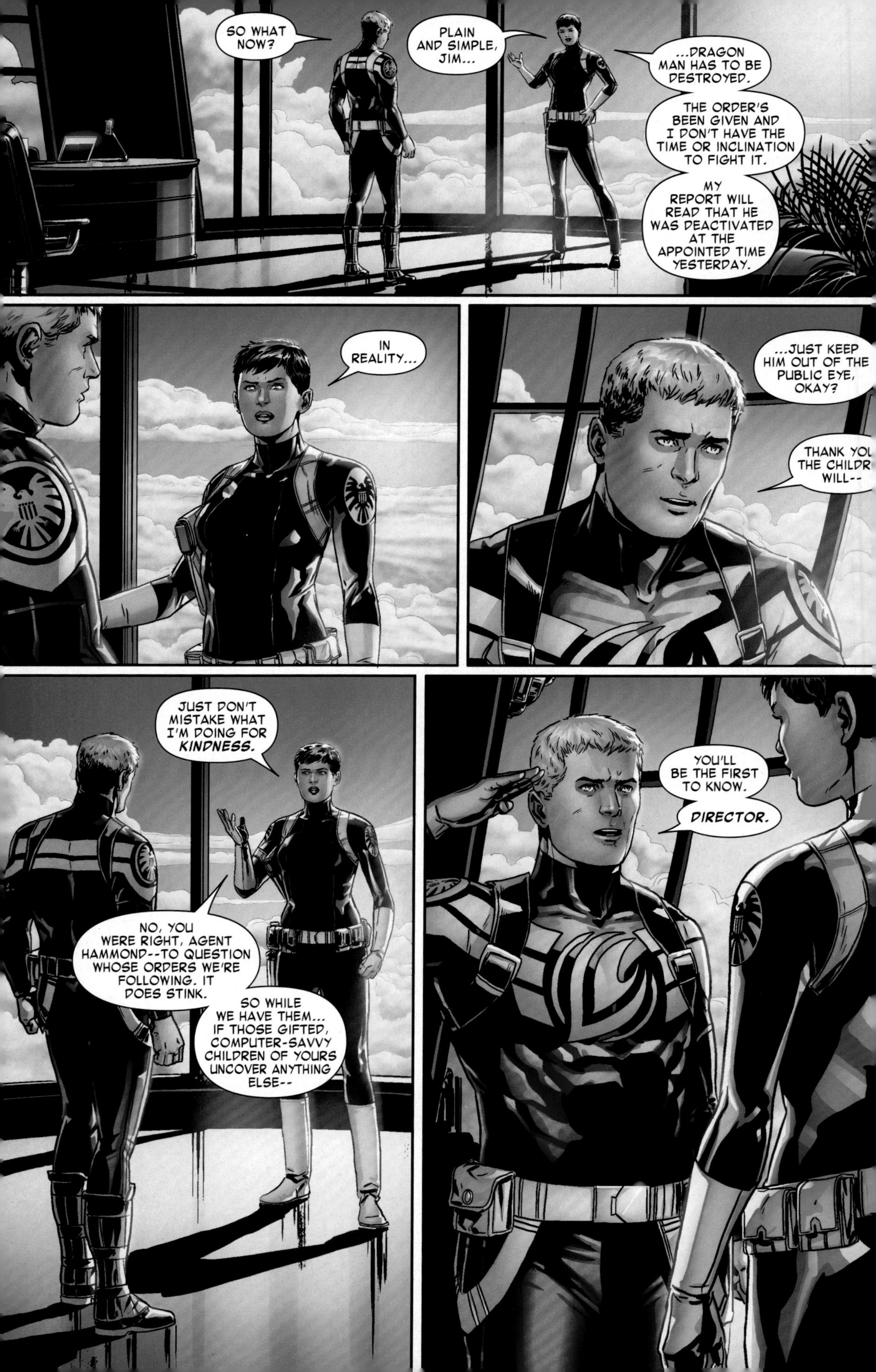

SO WHAT NOW?
PLAIN AND SIMPLE, JIM...
...DRAGON MAN HAS TO BE DESTROYED.
THE ORDER'S BEEN GIVEN AND I DON'T HAVE THE TIME OR INCLINATION TO FIGHT IT.
MY REPORT WILL READ THAT HE WAS DEACTIVATED AT THE APPOINTED TIME YESTERDAY.
IN REALITY...
...JUST KEEP HIM OUT OF THE PUBLIC EYE, OKAY?
THANK YOU THE CHILDR WILL--
JUST DON'T MISTAKE WHAT I'M DOING FOR *KINDNESS.*
NO, YOU WERE RIGHT, AGENT HAMMOND--TO QUESTION WHOSE ORDERS WE'RE FOLLOWING. IT DOES STINK.
SO WHILE WE HAVE THEM... IF THOSE GIFTED, COMPUTER-SAVVY CHILDREN OF YOURS UNCOVER ANYTHING ELSE--
YOU'LL BE THE FIRST TO KNOW.
DIRECTOR.

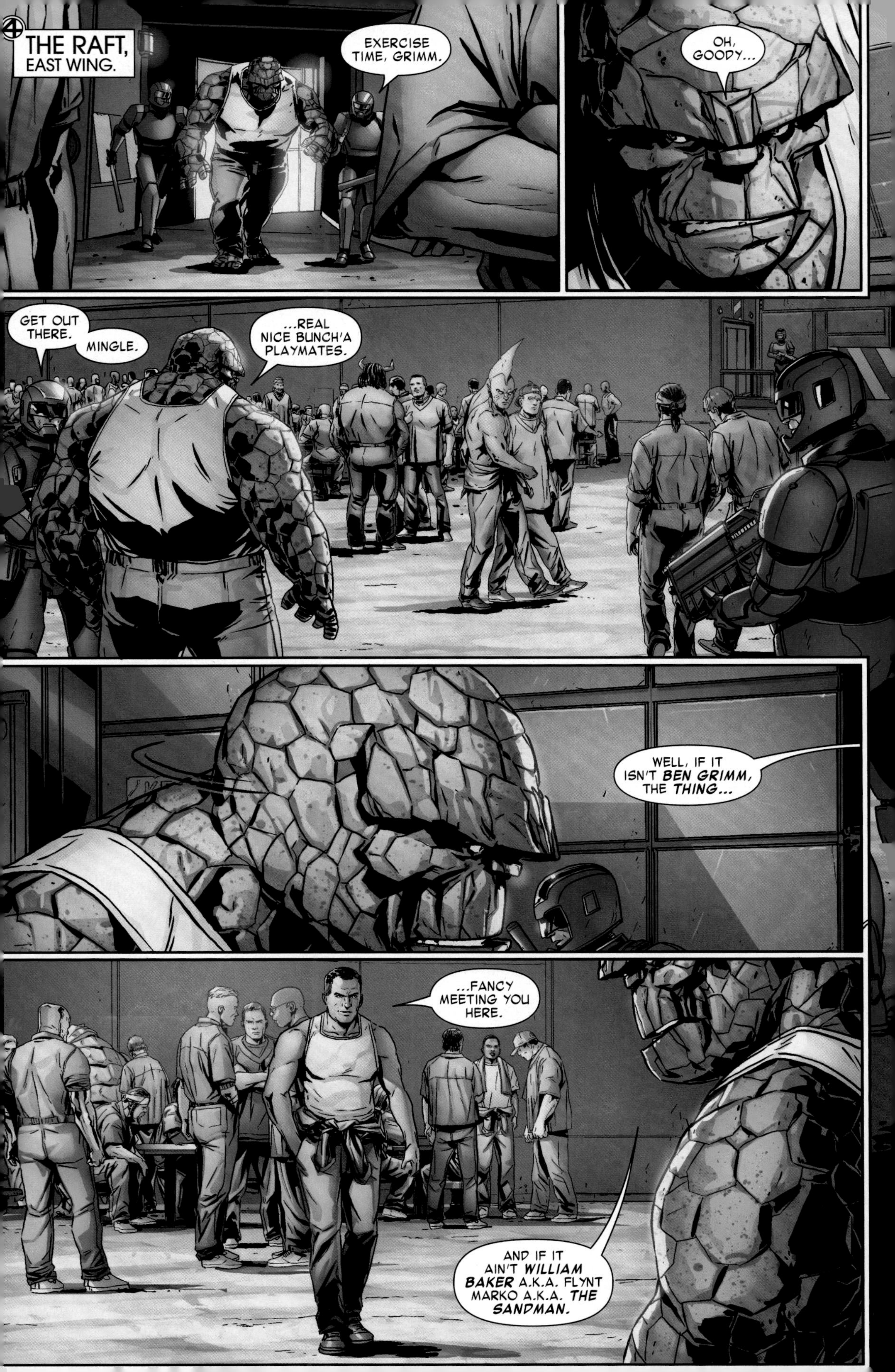
4
THE RAFT, EAST WING.
EXERCISE TIME, GRIMM.
OH, GOODY...
GET OUT THERE.
MINGLE.
...REAL NICE BUNCH'A PLAYMATES.
WELL, IF IT ISN'T BEN GRIMM, THE THING...
...FANCY MEETING YOU HERE.
AND IF IT AIN'T WILLIAM BAKER A.K.A. FLYNT MARKO A.K.A. THE SANDMAN.

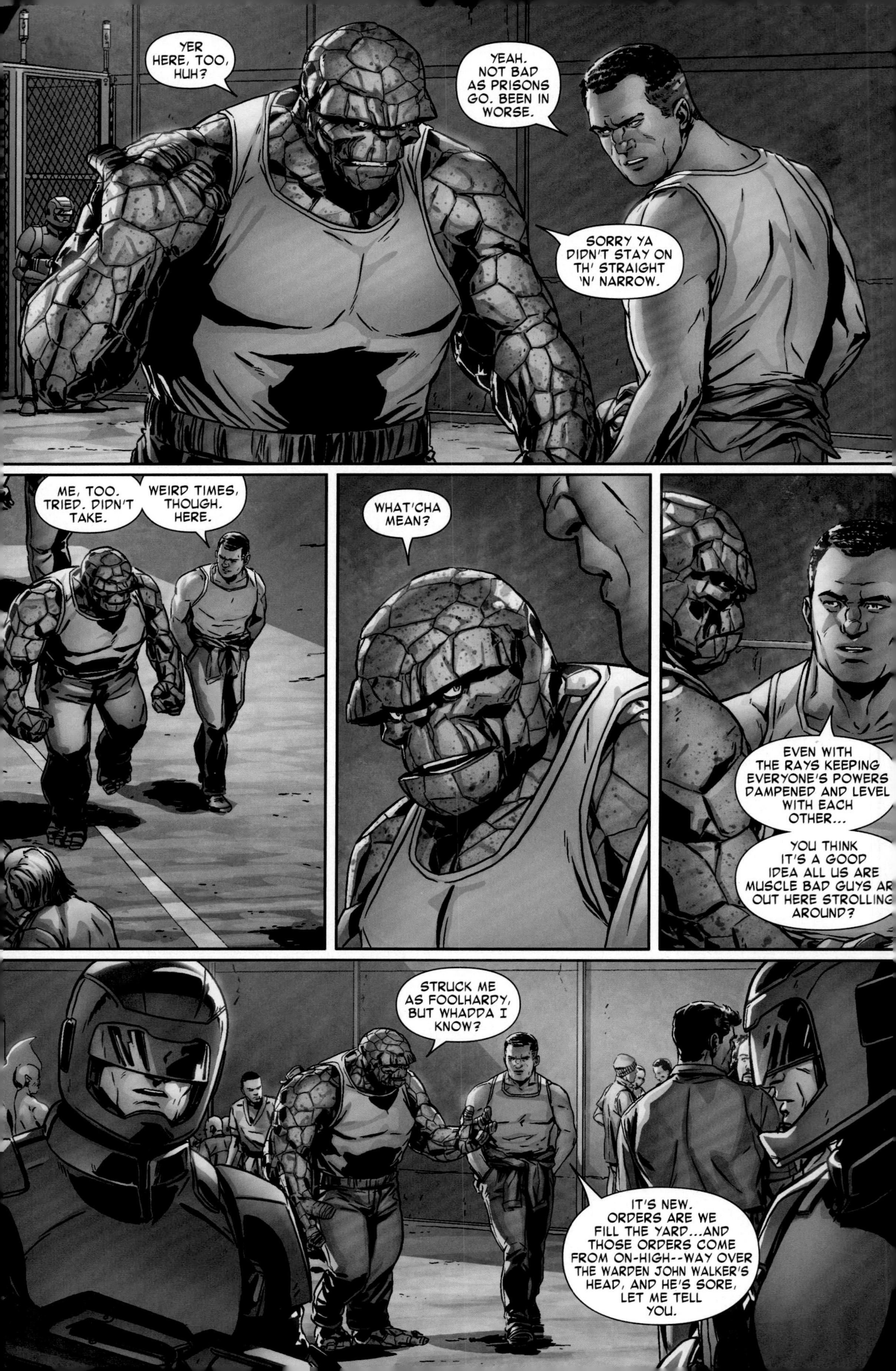

YER HERE, TOO, HUH?
YEAH. NOT BAD AS PRISONS GO. BEEN IN WORSE.
SORRY YA DIDN'T STAY ON TH' STRAIGHT 'N' NARROW.
ME, TOO. TRIED. DIDN'T TAKE.
WEIRD TIMES, THOUGH. HERE.
WHAT'CHA MEAN?
EVEN WITH THE RAYS KEEPING EVERYONE'S POWERS DAMPENED AND LEVEL WITH EACH OTHER...
YOU THINK IT'S A GOOD IDEA ALL US ARE MUSCLE BAD GUYS AR OUT HERE STROLLING AROUND?
STRUCK ME AS FOOLHARDY, BUT WHADDA I KNOW?
IT'S NEW. ORDERS ARE WE FILL THE YARD...AND THOSE ORDERS COME FROM ON-HIGH--WAY OVER THE WARDEN JOHN WALKER'S HEAD, AND HE'S SORE, LET ME TELL YOU.

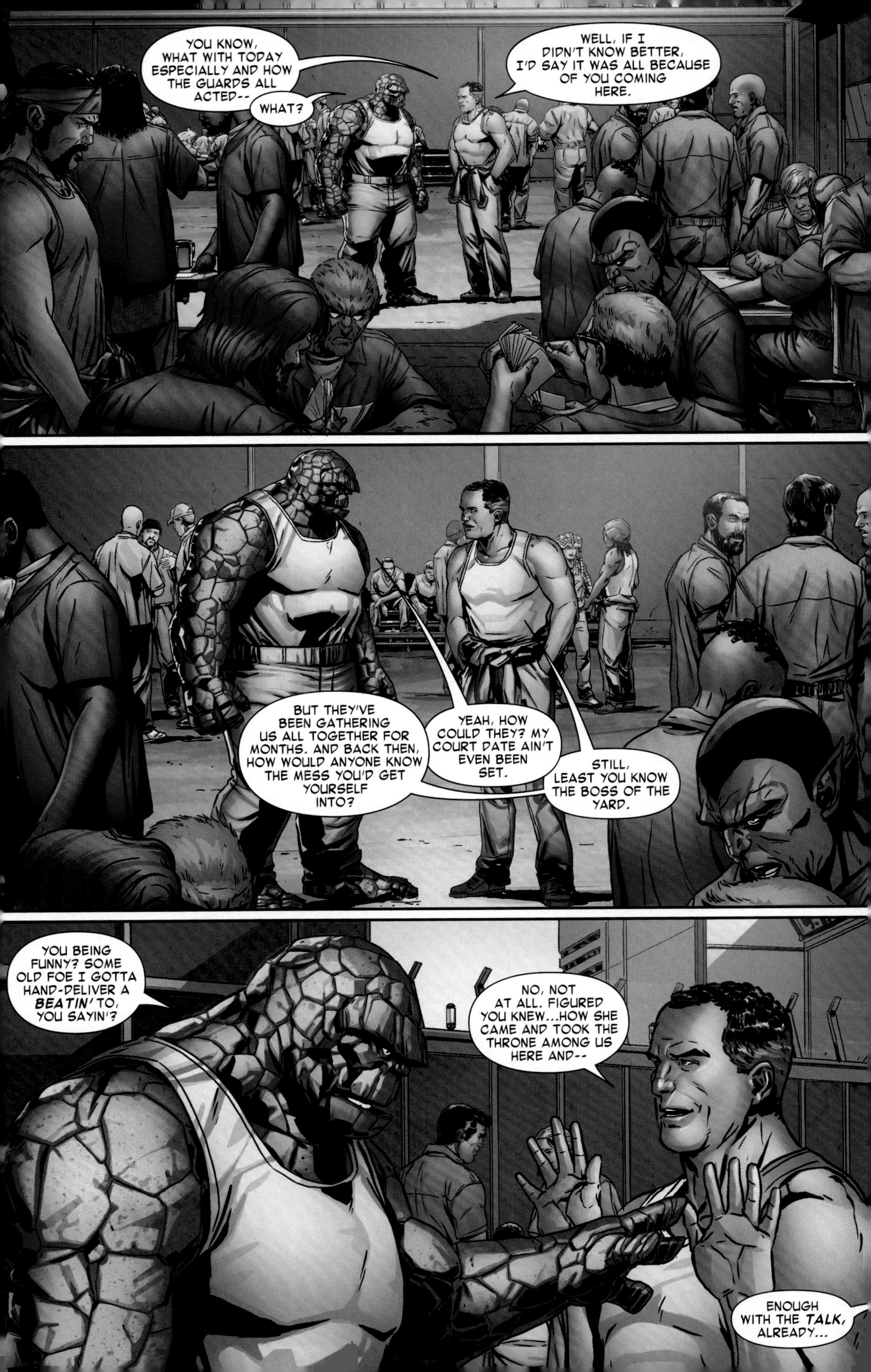

YOU KNOW, WHAT WITH TODAY ESPECIALLY AND HOW THE GUARDS ALL ACTED--
WHAT?
WELL, IF I DIDN'T KNOW BETTER, I'D SAY IT WAS ALL BECAUSE OF YOU COMING HERE.
BUT THEY'VE BEEN GATHERING US ALL TOGETHER FOR MONTHS. AND BACK THEN, HOW WOULD ANYONE KNOW THE MESS YOU'D GET YOURSELF INTO?
YEAH, HOW COULD THEY? MY COURT DATE AIN'T EVEN BEEN SET.
STILL, LEAST YOU KNOW THE BOSS OF THE YARD.
YOU BEING FUNNY? SOME OLD FOE I GOTTA HAND-DELIVER A BEATIN' TO, YOU SAYIN'?
NO, NOT AT ALL. FIGURED YOU KNEW...HOW SHE CAME AND TOOK THE THRONE AMONG US HERE AND--
ENOUGH WITH THE TALK, ALREADY...

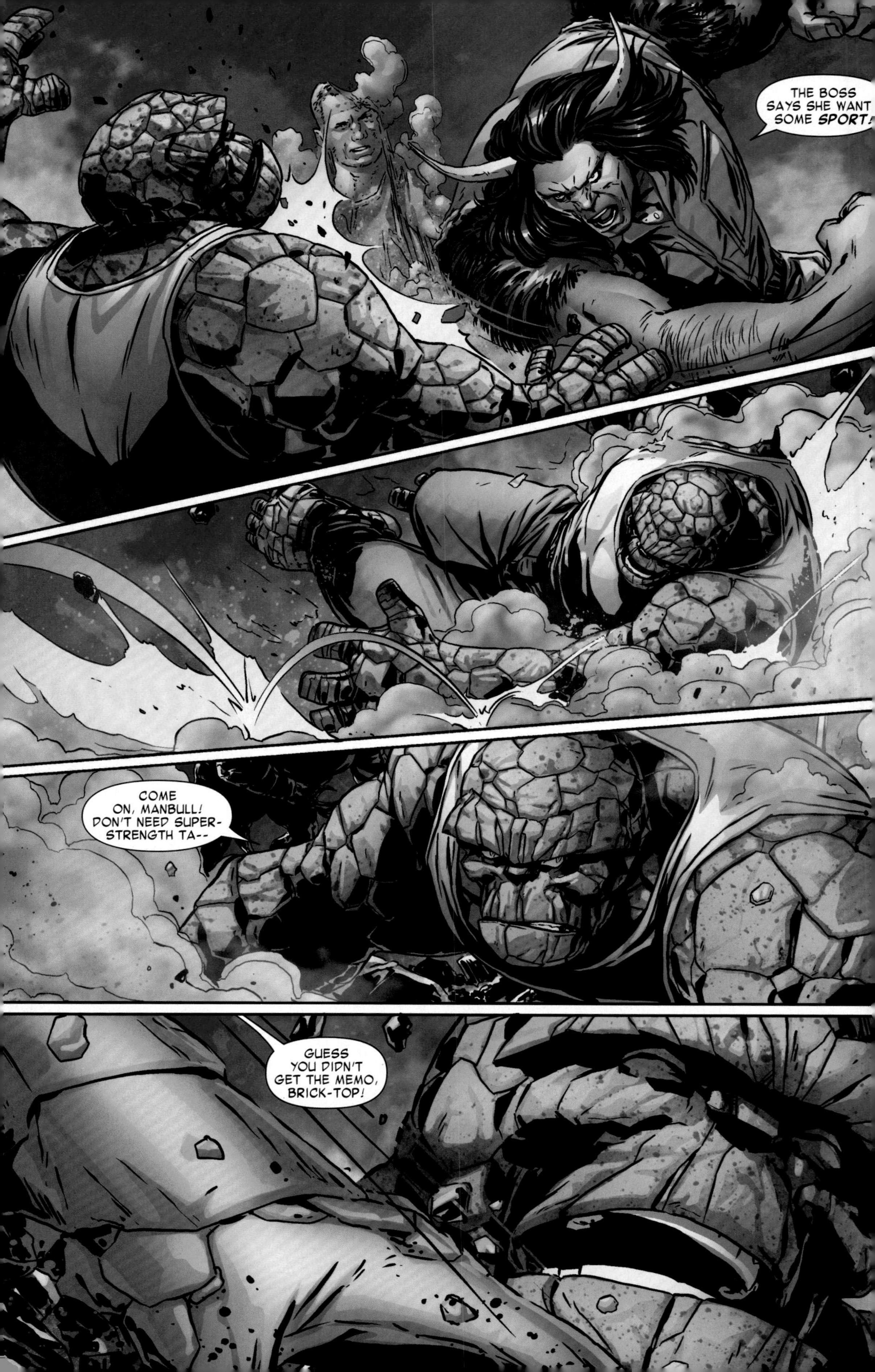
THE BOSS SAYS SHE WANT SOME SPORT!
COME ON, MANBULL! DON'T NEED SUPER-STRENGTH TA--
GUESS YOU DIDN'T GET THE MEMO, BRICK-TOP!

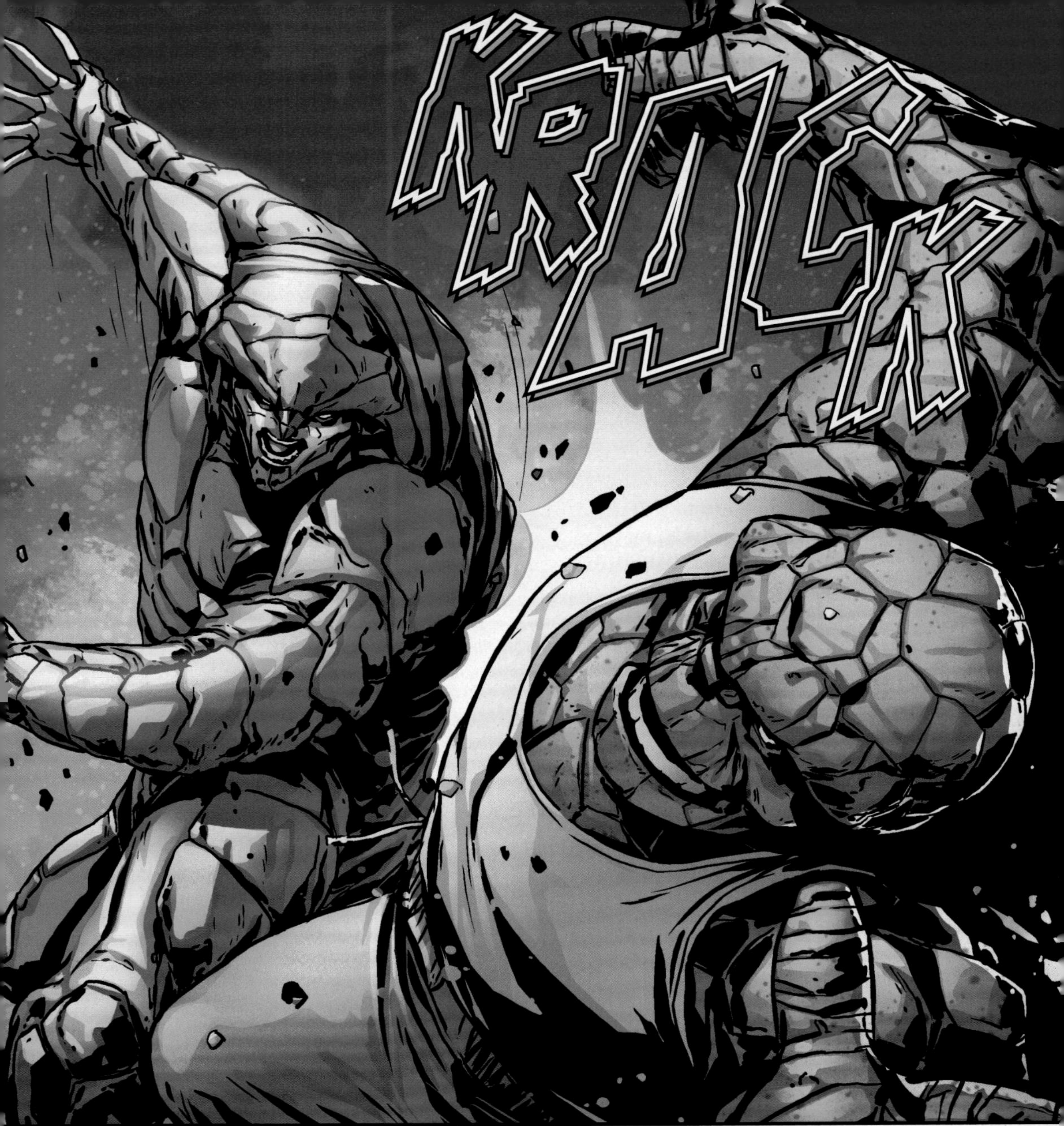

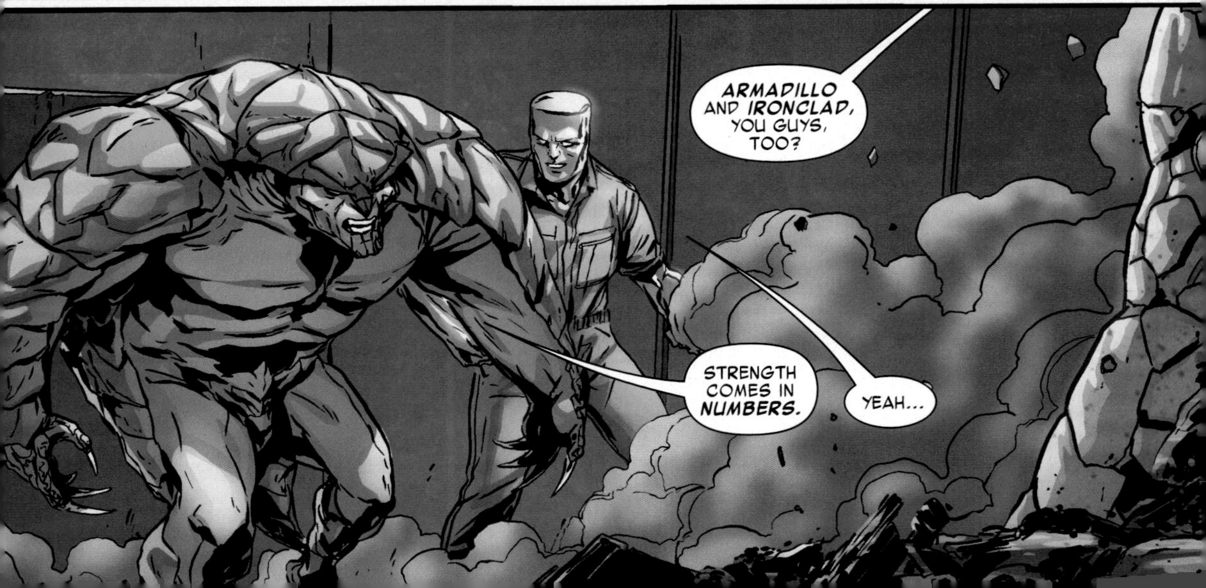
ARMADILLO AND IRONCLAD, YOU GUYS, TOO?
STRENGTH COMES IN NUMBERS.
YEAH...

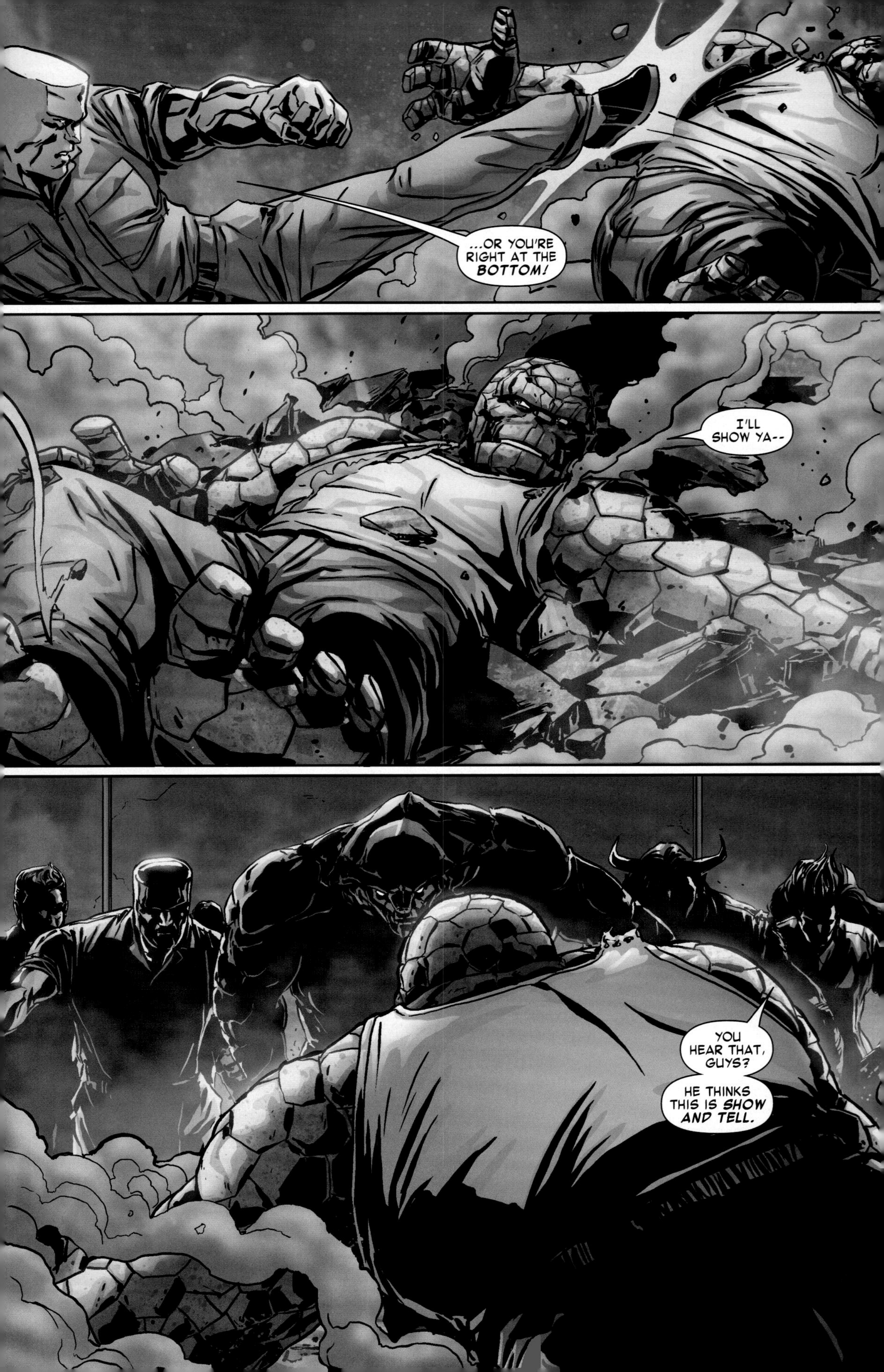
...OR YOU'RE RIGHT AT THE BOTTOM!
I'LL SHOW YA--
YOU HEAR THAT, GUYS?
HE THINKS THIS IS SHOW AND TELL.

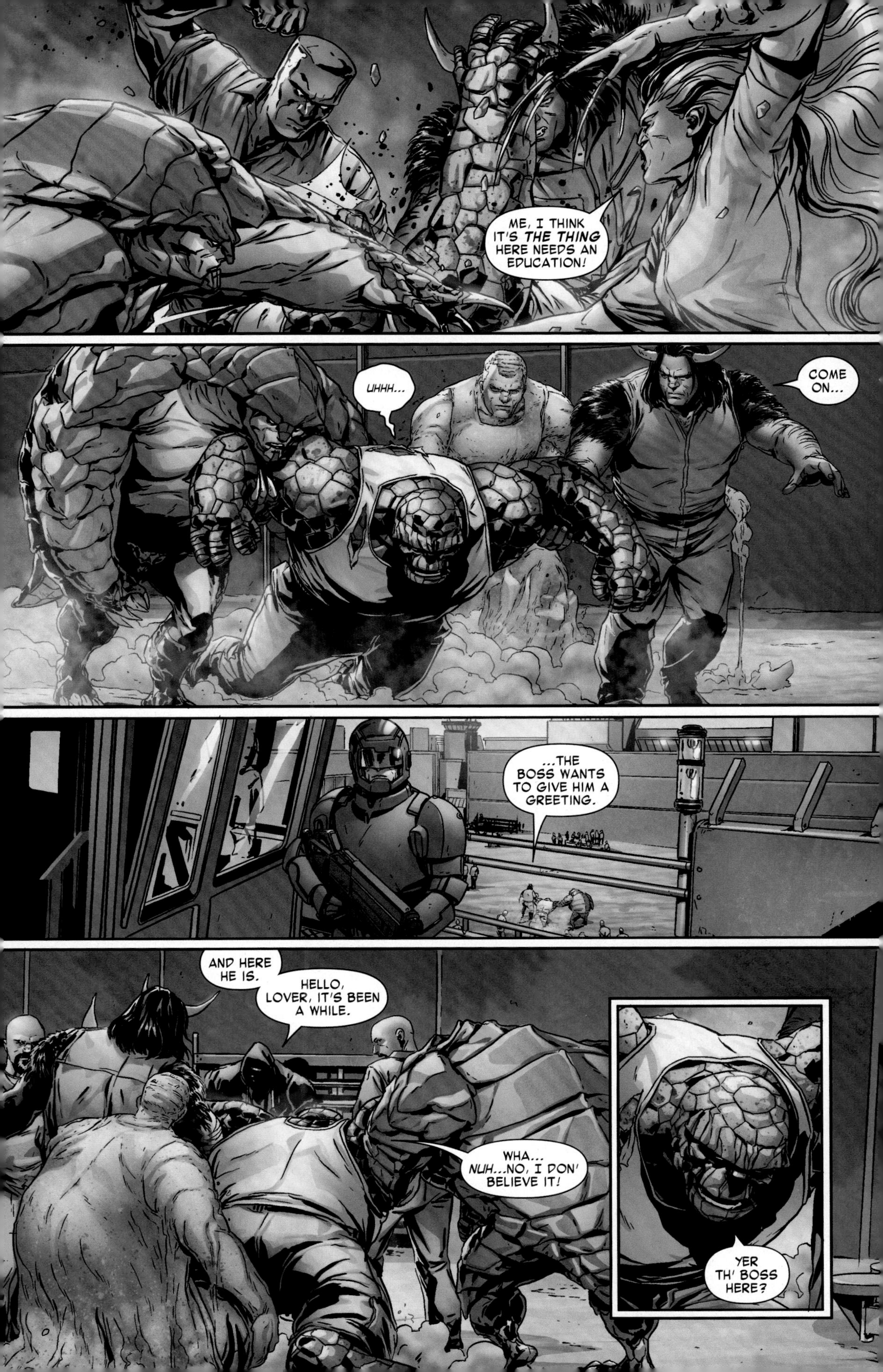
ME, I THINK IT'S *THE THING* HERE NEEDS AN EDUCATION!
UHHH...
COME ON...
...THE BOSS WANTS TO GIVE HIM A GREETING.
AND HERE HE IS.
HELLO, LOVER, IT'S BEEN A WHILE.
WHA... *NUH*...NO, I DON' BELIEVE IT!
YER TH' BOSS HERE?

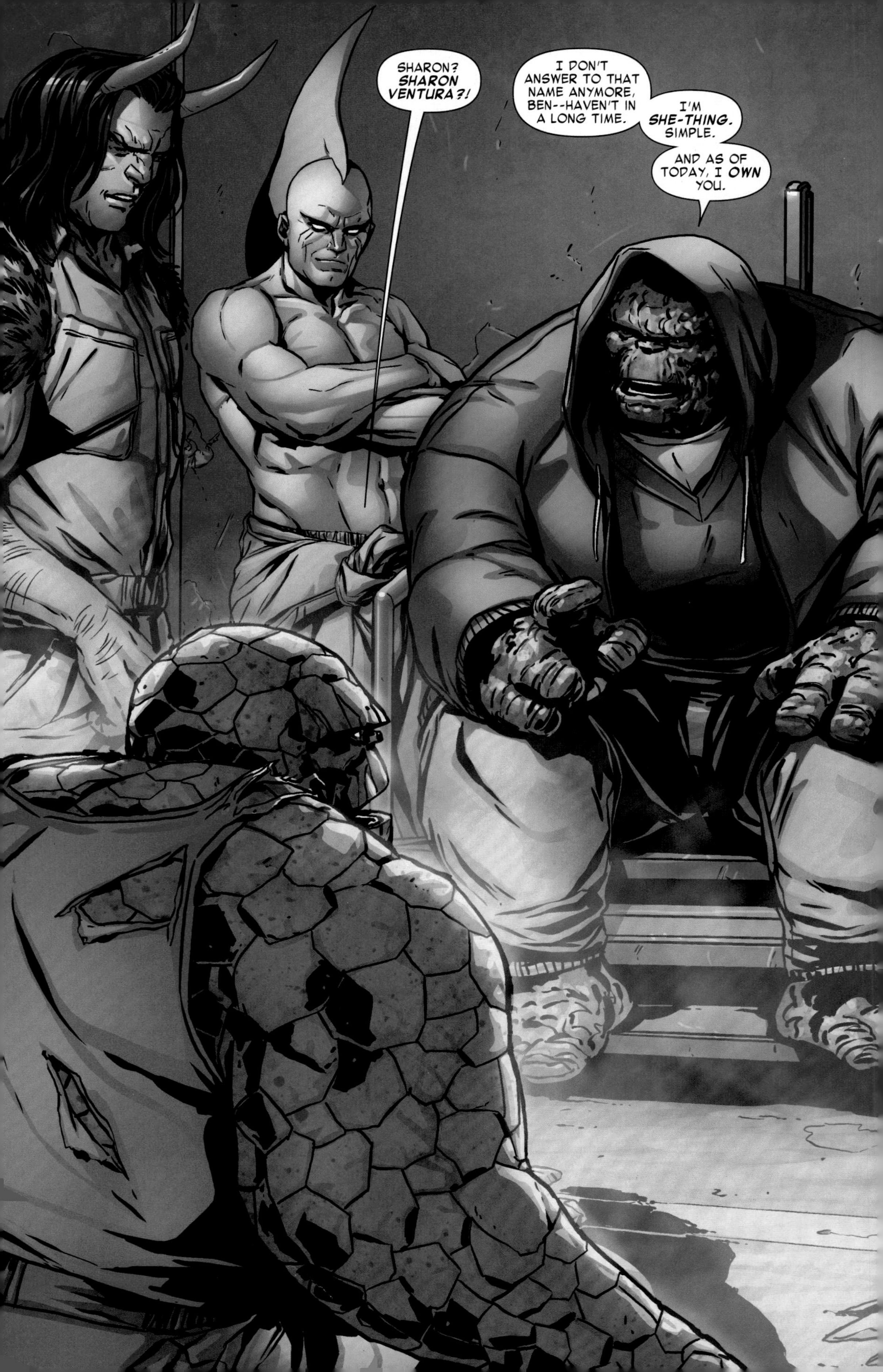
SHARON? SHARON VENTURA?!
I DON'T ANSWER TO THAT NAME ANYMORE, BEN--HAVEN'T IN A LONG TIME.
I'M SHE-THING. SIMPLE.
AND AS OF TODAY, I OWN YOU.

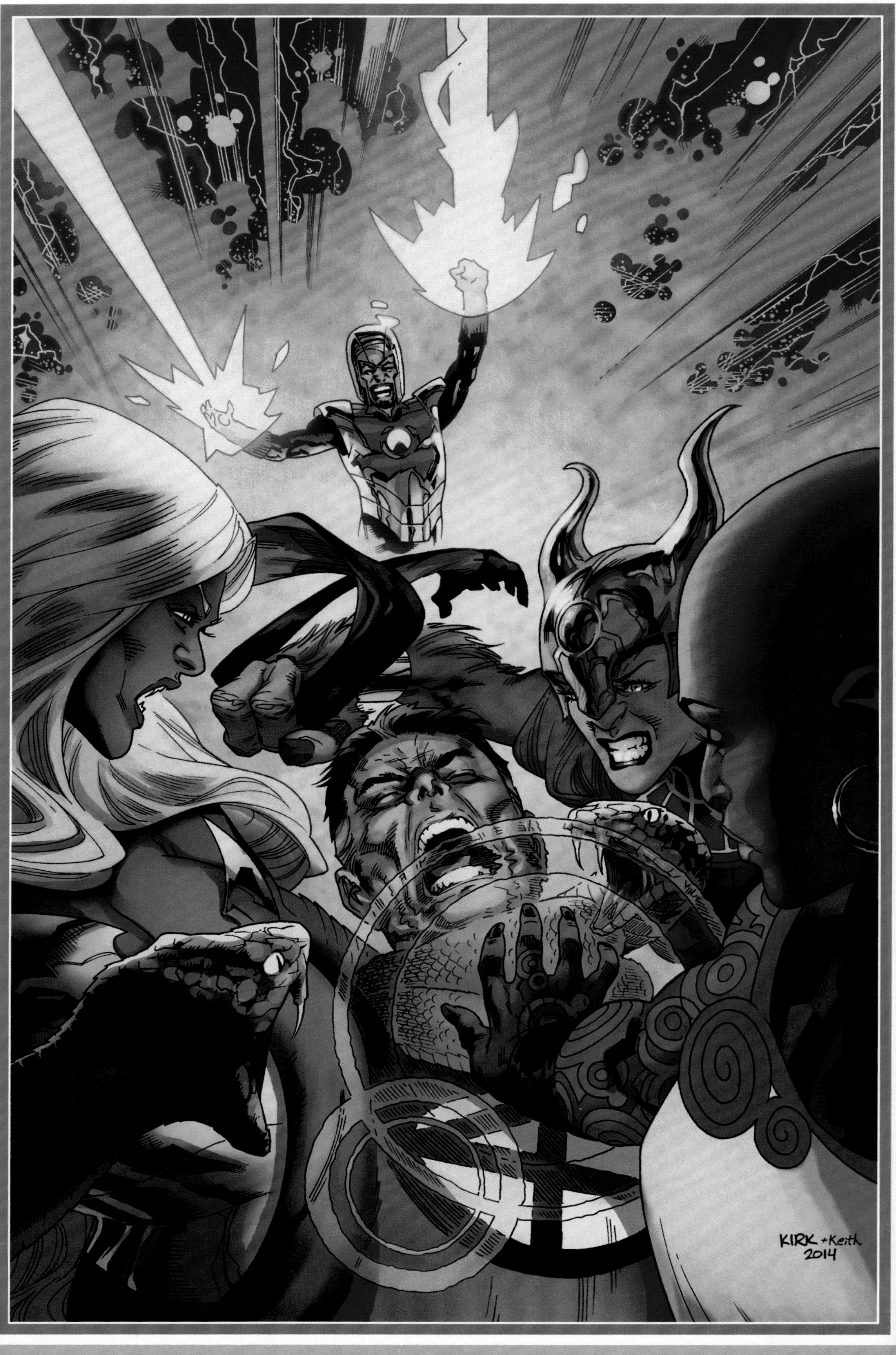
KIRK +Keith
2014

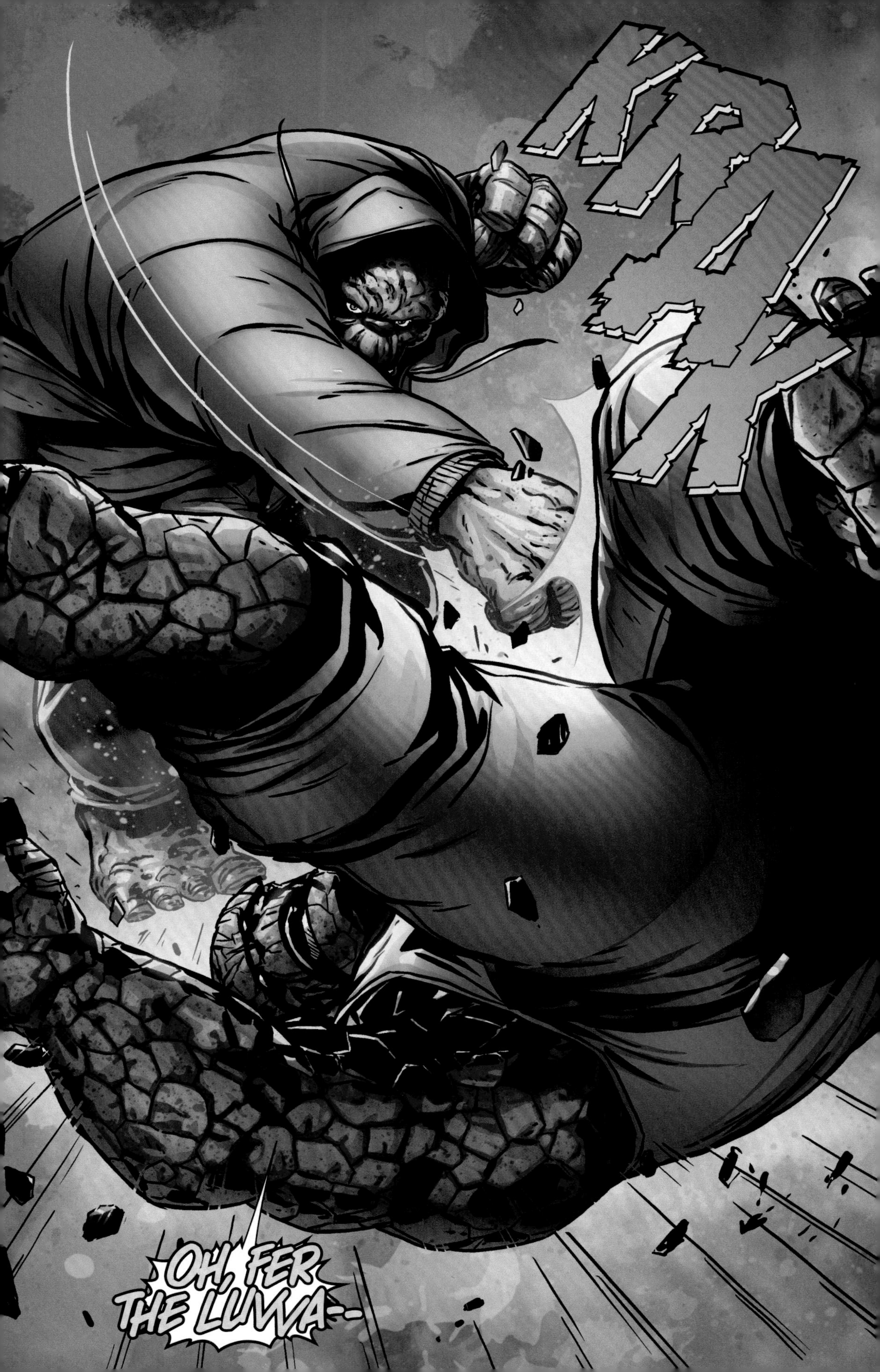
OH, FER THE LUVVA--

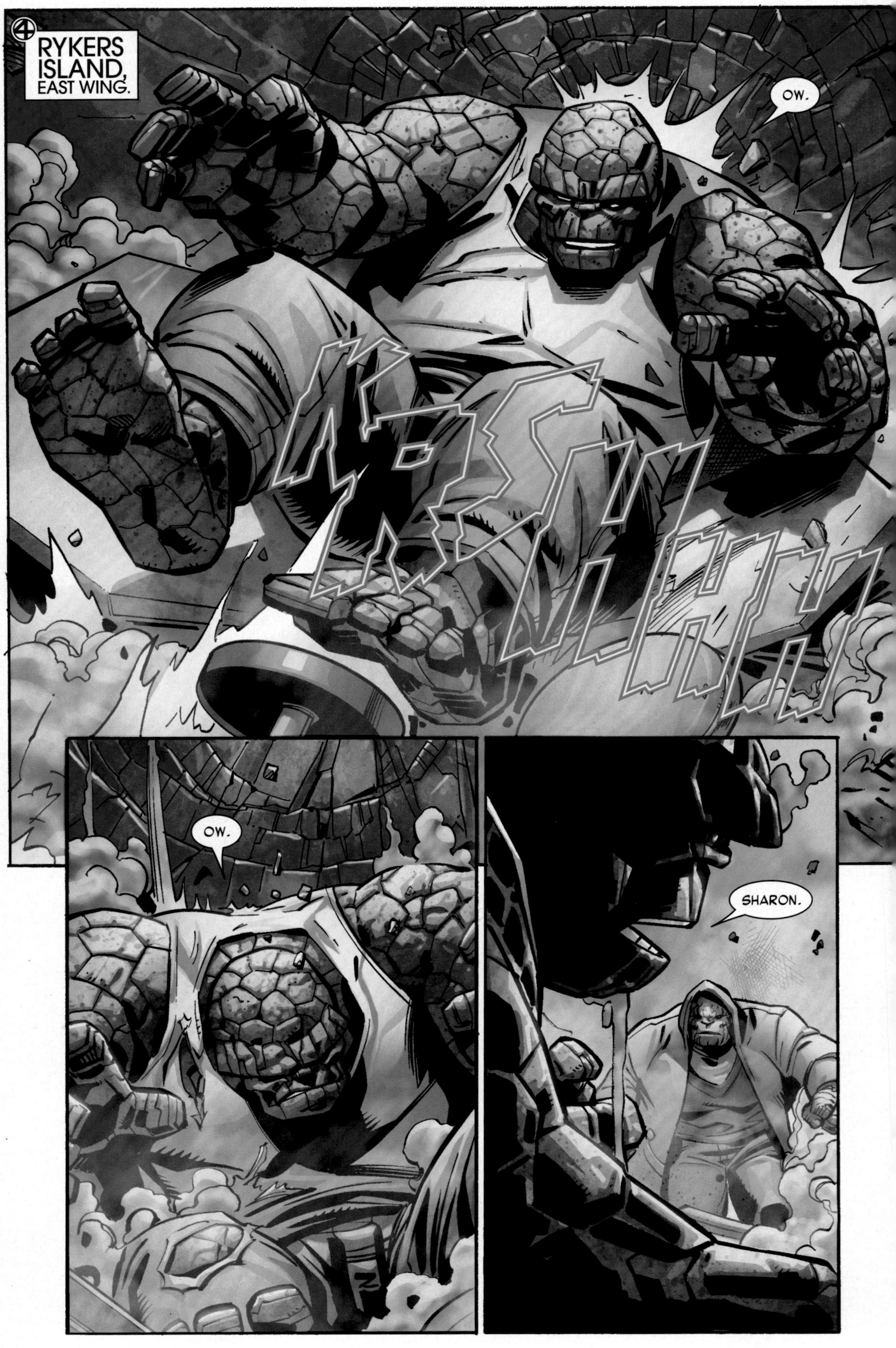
RYKERS ISLAND, EAST WING.
OW.
OW.
SHARON.

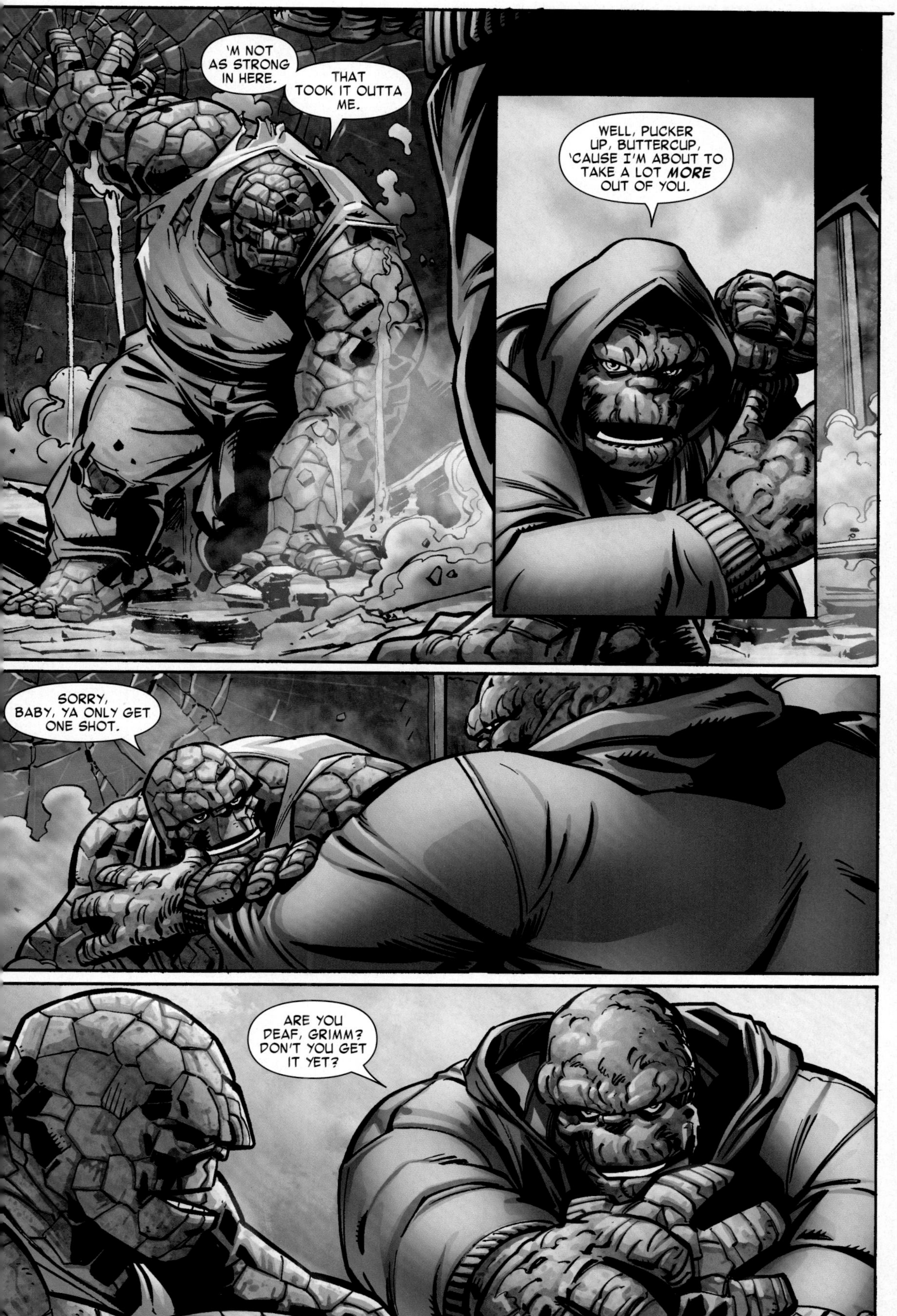
'M NOT AS STRONG IN HERE.
THAT TOOK IT OUTTA ME.
WELL, PUCKER UP, BUTTERCUP, 'CAUSE I'M ABOUT TO TAKE A LOT MORE OUT OF YOU.
SORRY, BABY, YA ONLY GET ONE SHOT.
ARE YOU DEAF, GRIMM? DON'T YOU GET IT YET?

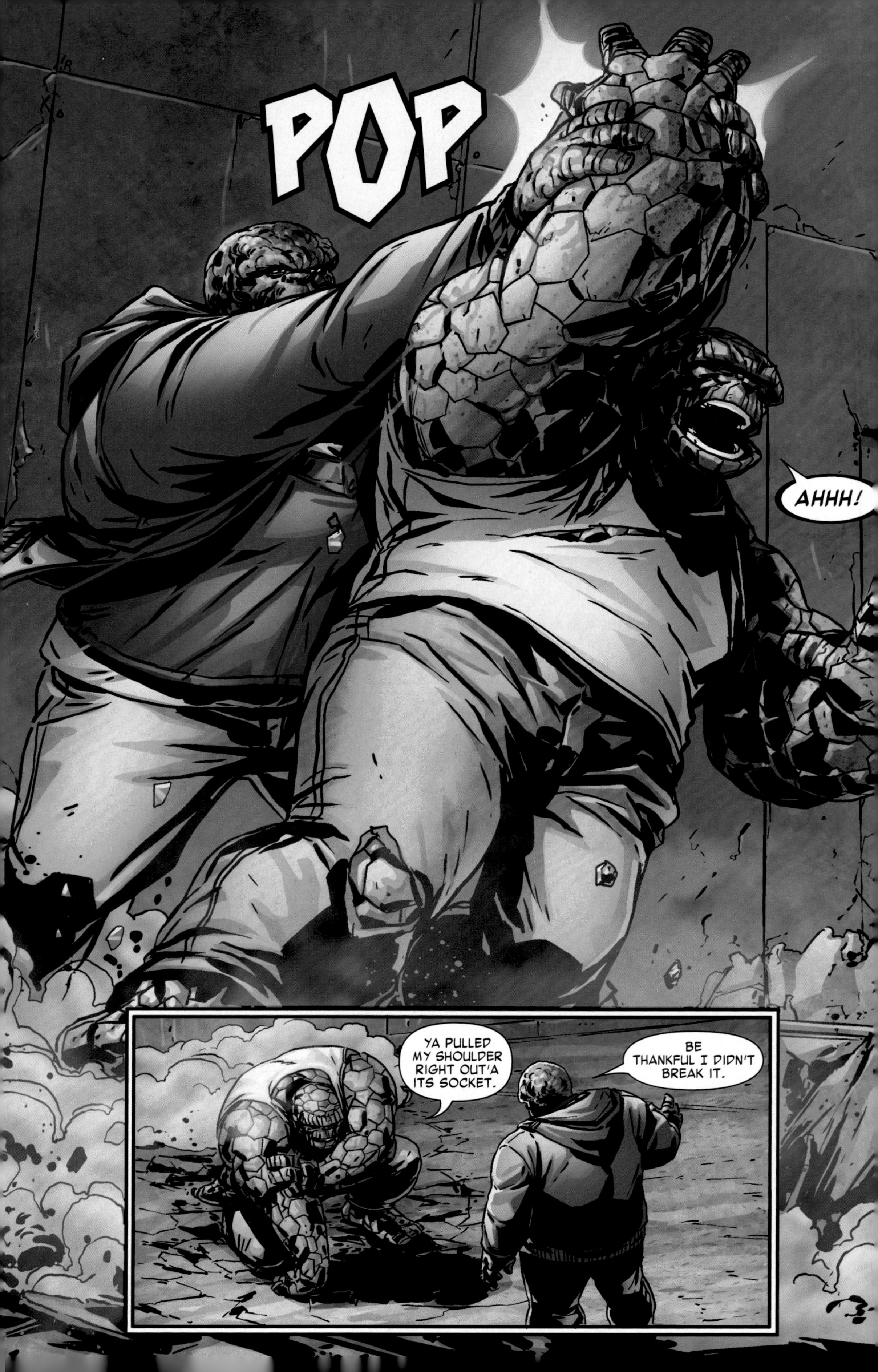
POP
AHHH!
YA PULLED MY SHOULDER RIGHT OUT'A ITS SOCKET.
BE THANKFUL I DIDN'T BREAK IT.

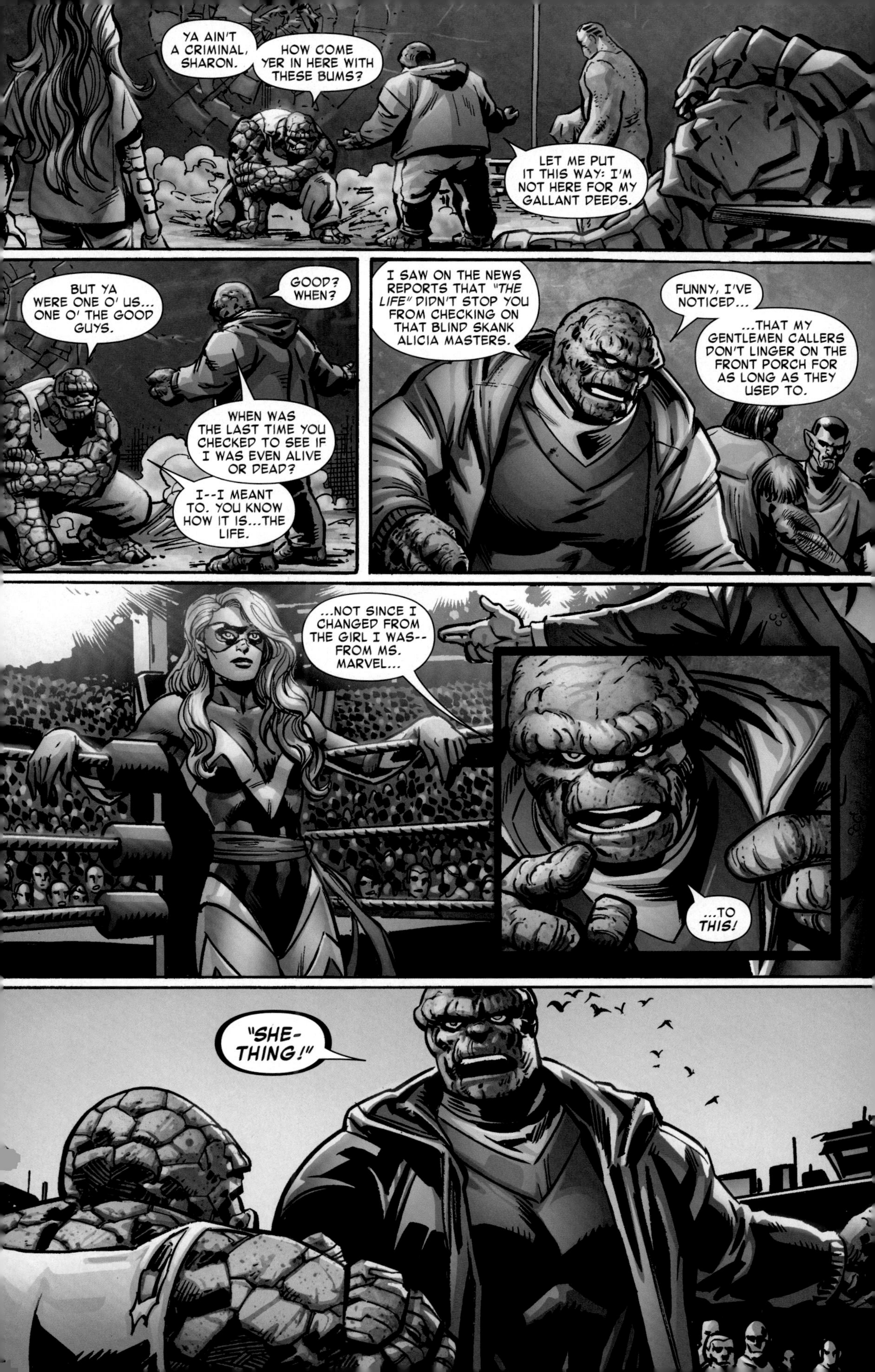
YA AIN'T A CRIMINAL, SHARON.
HOW COME YER IN HERE WITH THESE BUMS?
LET ME PUT IT THIS WAY: I'M NOT HERE FOR MY GALLANT DEEDS.
BUT YA WERE ONE O' US... ONE O' THE GOOD GUYS.
GOOD? WHEN?
WHEN WAS THE LAST TIME YOU CHECKED TO SEE IF I WAS EVEN ALIVE OR DEAD?
I--I MEANT TO. YOU KNOW HOW IT IS...THE LIFE.
I SAW ON THE NEWS REPORTS THAT "THE LIFE" DIDN'T STOP YOU FROM CHECKING ON THAT BLIND SKANK ALICIA MASTERS.
FUNNY, I'VE NOTICED...
...THAT MY GENTLEMEN CALLERS DON'T LINGER ON THE FRONT PORCH FOR AS LONG AS THEY USED TO.
...NOT SINCE I CHANGED FROM THE GIRL I WAS-- FROM MS. MARVEL...
...TO THIS!
"SHE-THING!"

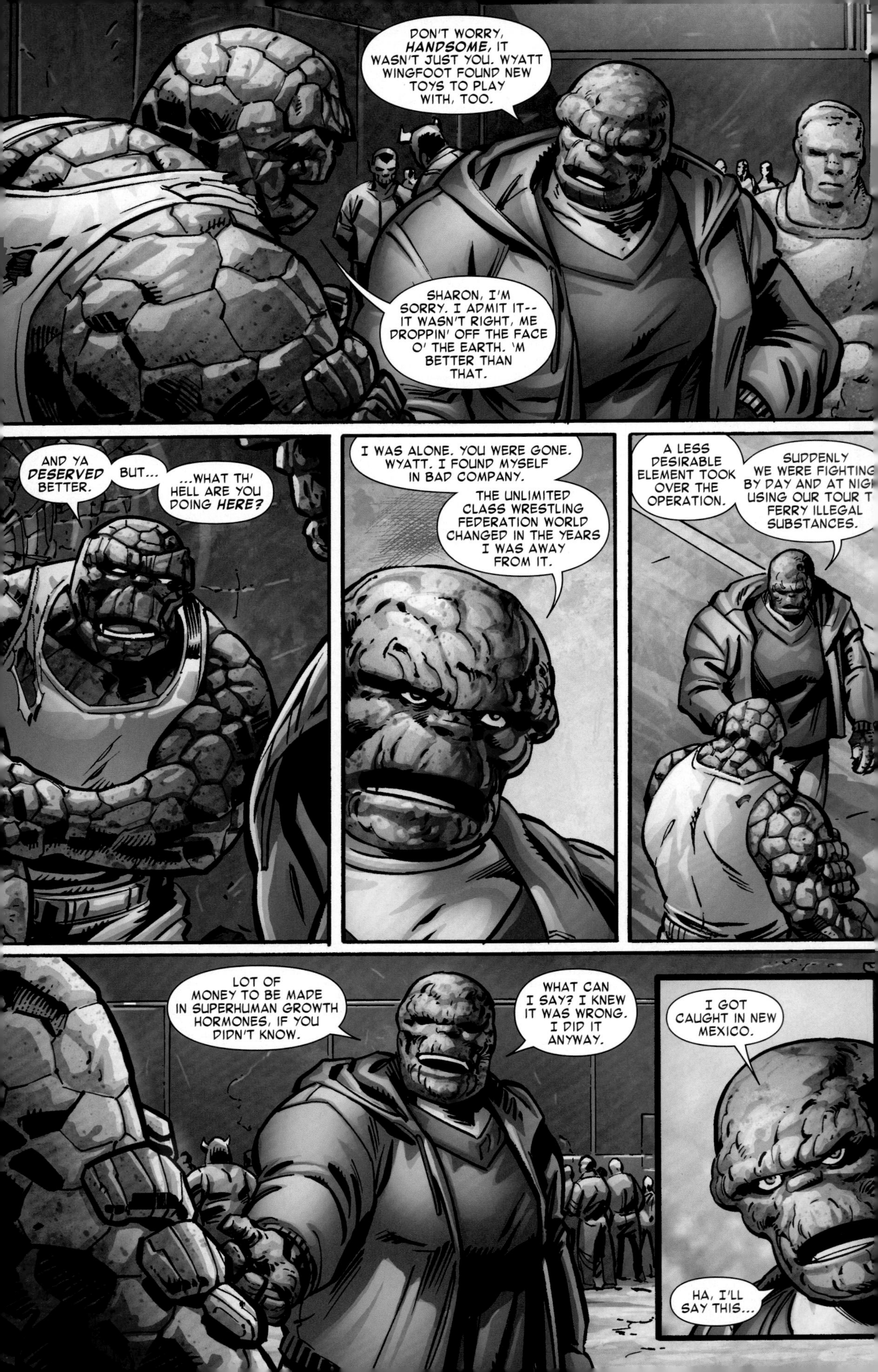
DON'T WORRY, HANDSOME, IT WASN'T JUST YOU. WYATT WINGFOOT FOUND NEW TOYS TO PLAY WITH, TOO.
SHARON, I'M SORRY. I ADMIT IT-- IT WASN'T RIGHT, ME DROPPIN' OFF THE FACE O' THE EARTH. 'M BETTER THAN THAT.
AND YA DESERVED BETTER.
BUT...
...WHAT TH' HELL ARE YOU DOING HERE?
I WAS ALONE. YOU WERE GONE. WYATT. I FOUND MYSELF IN BAD COMPANY.
THE UNLIMITED CLASS WRESTLING FEDERATION WORLD CHANGED IN THE YEARS I WAS AWAY FROM IT.
A LESS DESIRABLE ELEMENT TOOK OVER THE OPERATION.
SUDDENLY WE WERE FIGHTING BY DAY AND AT NIG USING OUR TOUR T FERRY ILLEGAL SUBSTANCES.
LOT OF MONEY TO BE MADE IN SUPERHUMAN GROWTH HORMONES, IF YOU DIDN'T KNOW.
WHAT CAN I SAY? I KNEW IT WAS WRONG. I DID IT ANYWAY.
I GOT CAUGHT IN NEW MEXICO.
HA, I'LL SAY THIS...

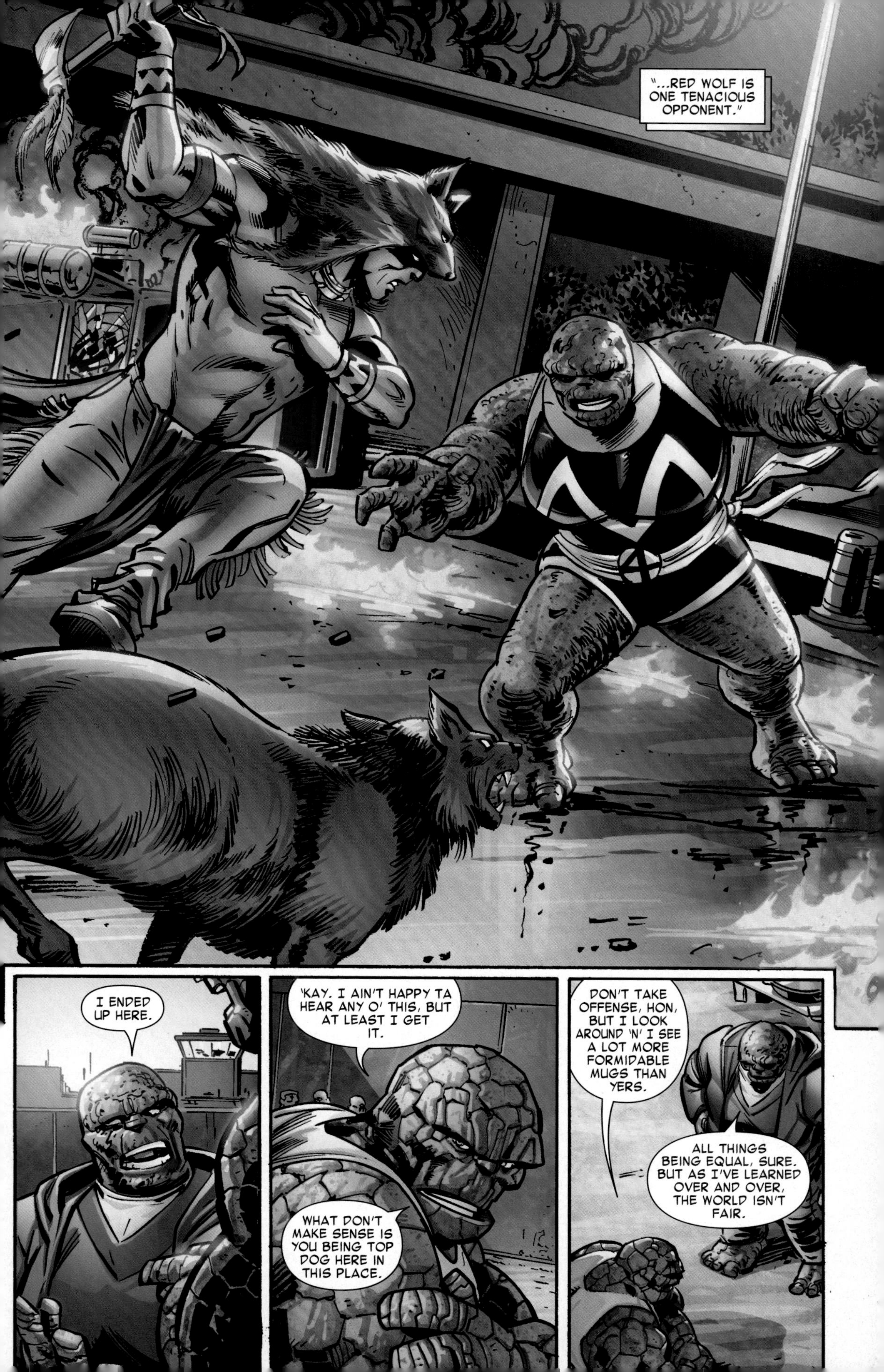
"...RED WOLF IS ONE TENACIOUS OPPONENT."
I ENDED UP HERE.
'KAY. I AIN'T HAPPY TA HEAR ANY O' THIS, BUT AT LEAST I GET IT.
WHAT DON'T MAKE SENSE IS YOU BEING TOP DOG HERE IN THIS PLACE.
DON'T TAKE OFFENSE, HON, BUT I LOOK AROUND 'N' I SEE A LOT MORE FORMIDABLE MUGS THAN YERS.
ALL THINGS BEING EQUAL, SURE. BUT AS I'VE LEARNED OVER AND OVER, THE WORLD ISN'T FAIR.

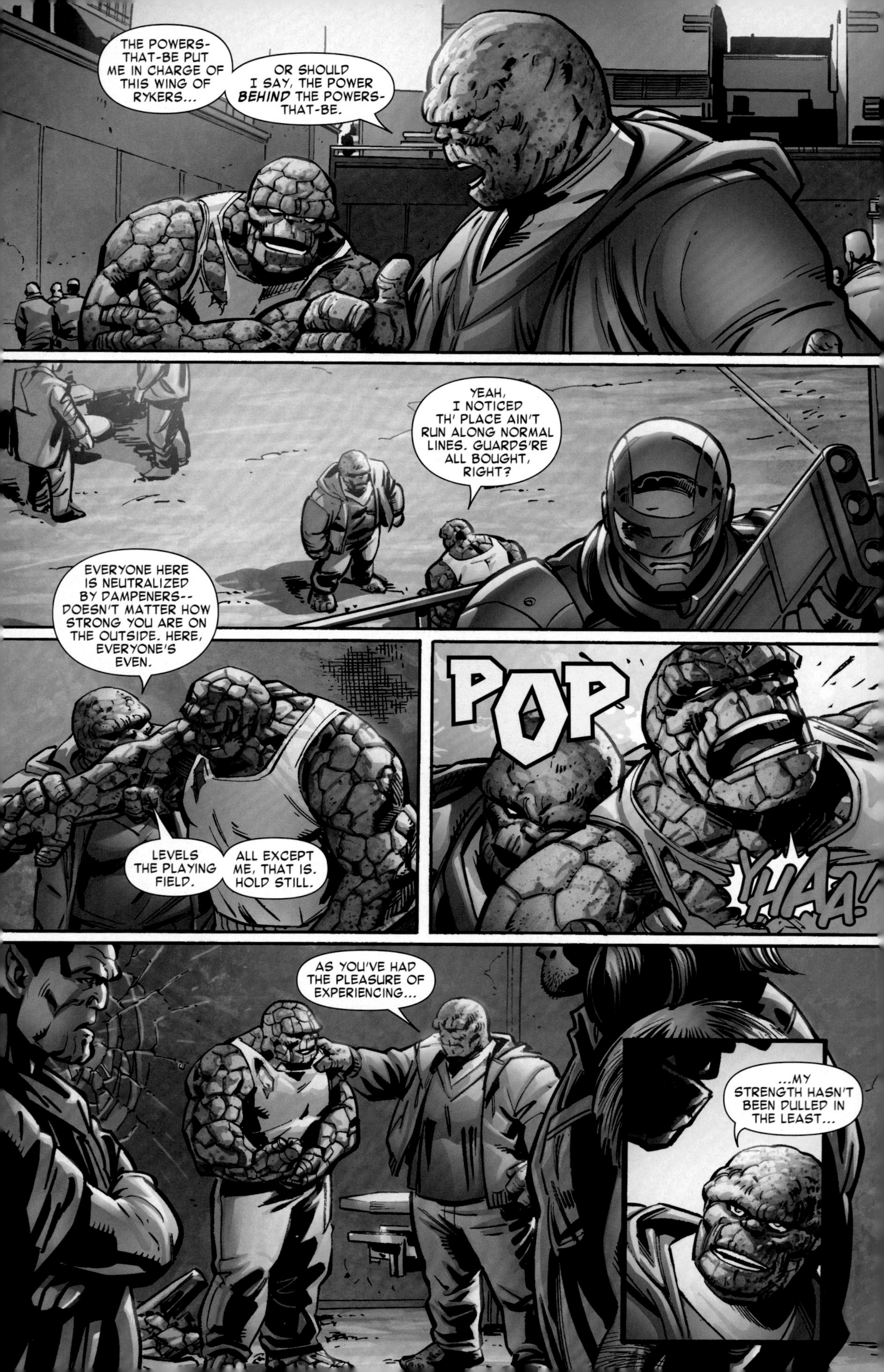
THE POWERS-THAT-BE PUT ME IN CHARGE OF THIS WING OF RYKERS...
OR SHOULD I SAY, THE POWER *BEHIND* THE POWERS-THAT-BE.
YEAH, I NOTICED TH' PLACE AIN'T RUN ALONG NORMAL LINES. GUARDS'RE ALL BOUGHT, RIGHT?
EVERYONE HERE IS NEUTRALIZED BY DAMPENERS--DOESN'T MATTER HOW STRONG YOU ARE ON THE OUTSIDE. HERE, EVERYONE'S EVEN.
LEVELS THE PLAYING FIELD.
ALL EXCEPT ME, THAT IS. HOLD STILL.
POP
YHAA!
AS YOU'VE HAD THE PLEASURE OF EXPERIENCING...
...MY STRENGTH HASN'T BEEN DULLED IN THE LEAST...

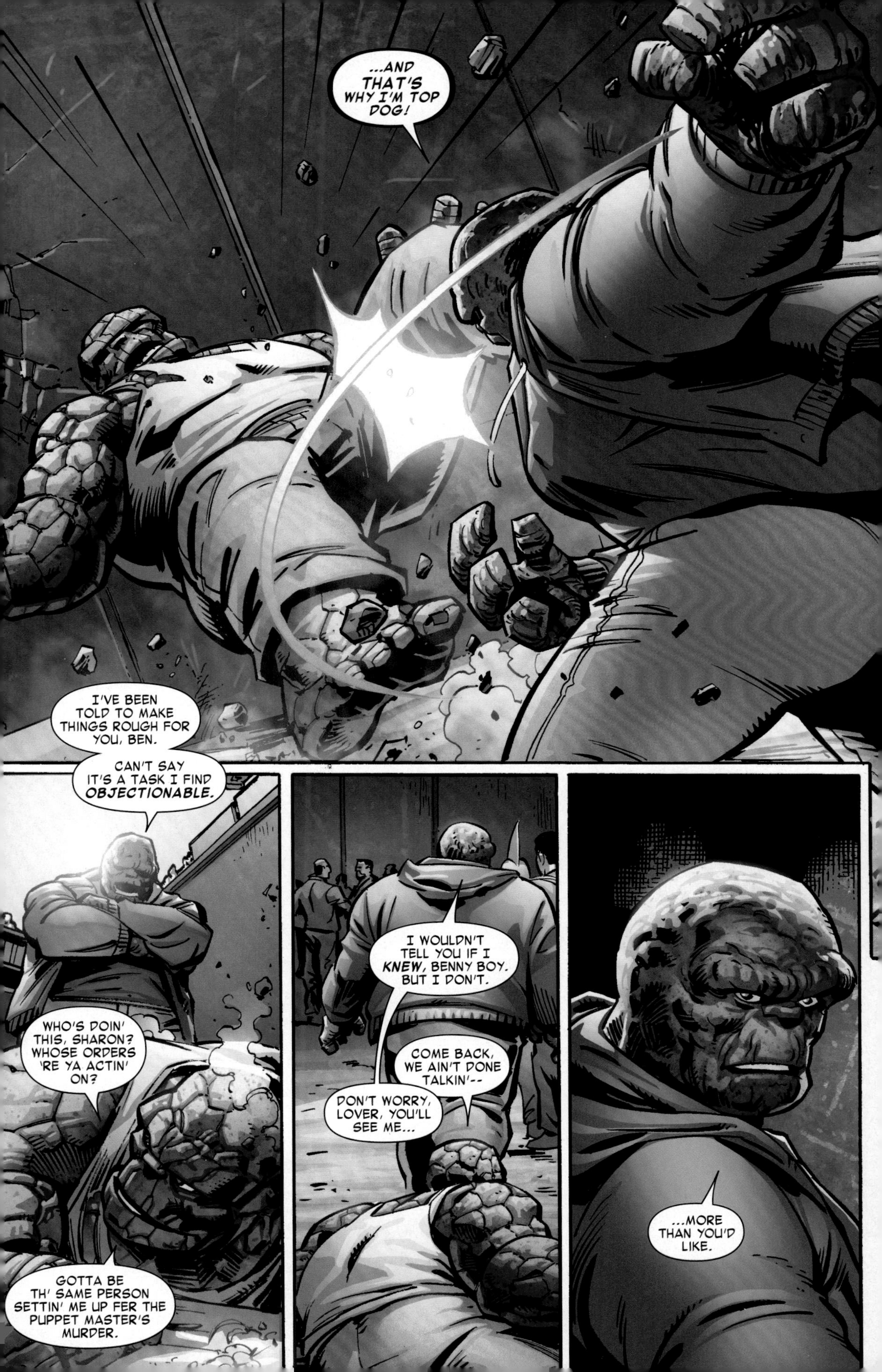
...AND THAT'S WHY I'M TOP DOG!
I'VE BEEN TOLD TO MAKE THINGS ROUGH FOR YOU, BEN.
CAN'T SAY IT'S A TASK I FIND OBJECTIONABLE.
WHO'S DOIN' THIS, SHARON? WHOSE ORDERS 'RE YA ACTIN' ON?
GOTTA BE TH' SAME PERSON SETTIN' ME UP FER THE PUPPET MASTER'S MURDER.
I WOULDN'T TELL YOU IF I KNEW, BENNY BOY. BUT I DON'T.
COME BACK, WE AIN'T DONE TALKIN'--
DON'T WORRY, LOVER, YOU'LL SEE ME...
...MORE THAN YOU'D LIKE.

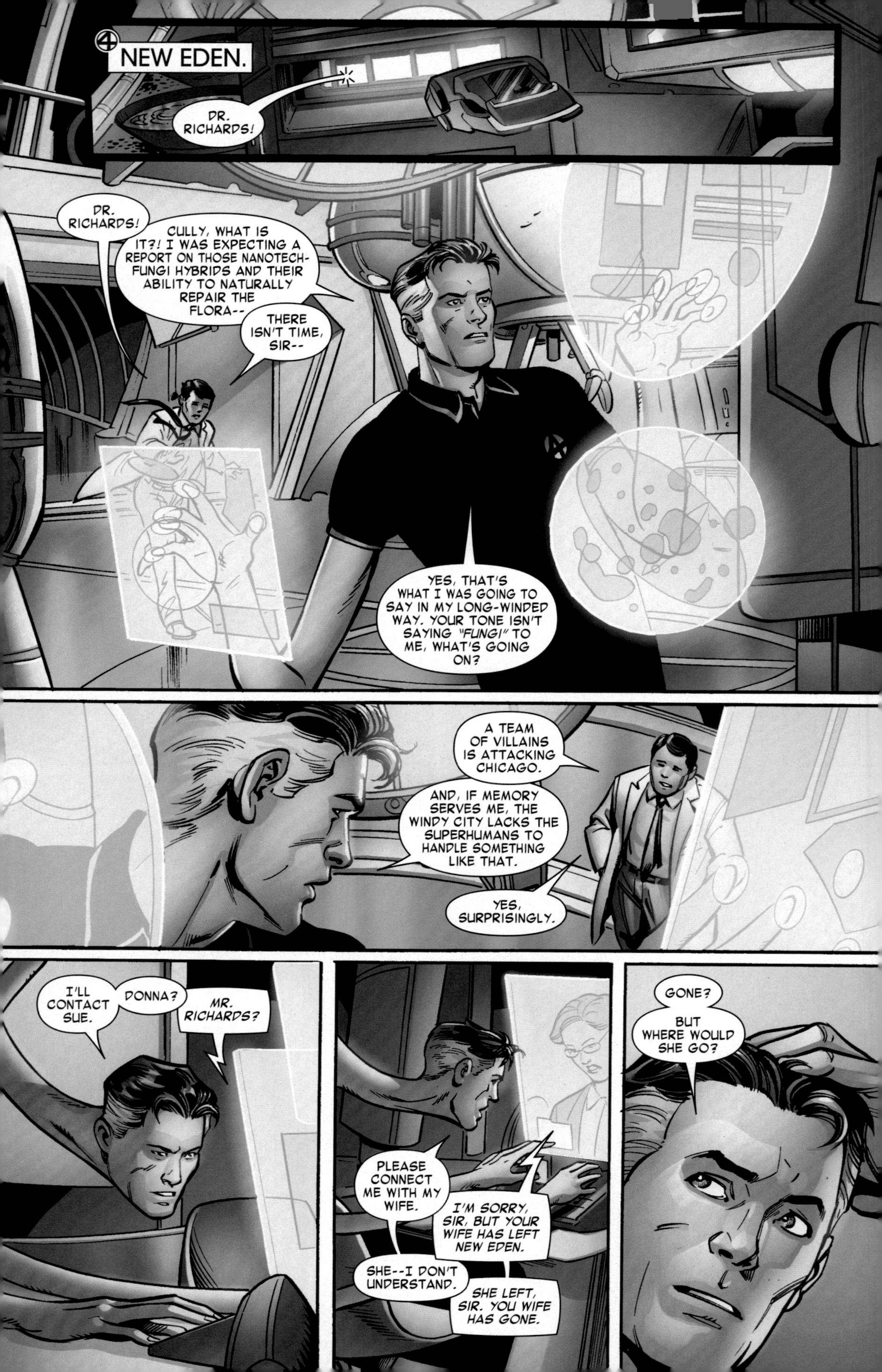
NEW EDEN.
DR. RICHARDS!
DR. RICHARDS!
CULLY, WHAT IS IT?! I WAS EXPECTING A REPORT ON THOSE NANOTECH-FUNGI HYBRIDS AND THEIR ABILITY TO NATURALLY REPAIR THE FLORA--
THERE ISN'T TIME, SIR--
YES, THAT'S WHAT I WAS GOING TO SAY IN MY LONG-WINDED WAY. YOUR TONE ISN'T SAYING "FUNGI" TO ME, WHAT'S GOING ON?
A TEAM OF VILLAINS IS ATTACKING CHICAGO.
AND, IF MEMORY SERVES ME, THE WINDY CITY LACKS THE SUPERHUMANS TO HANDLE SOMETHING LIKE THAT.
YES, SURPRISINGLY.
I'LL CONTACT SUE.
DONNA?
MR. RICHARDS?
PLEASE CONNECT ME WITH MY WIFE.
I'M SORRY, SIR, BUT YOUR WIFE HAS LEFT NEW EDEN.
SHE--I DON'T UNDERSTAND.
SHE LEFT, SIR. YOU WIFE HAS GONE.
GONE?
BUT WHERE WOULD SHE GO?

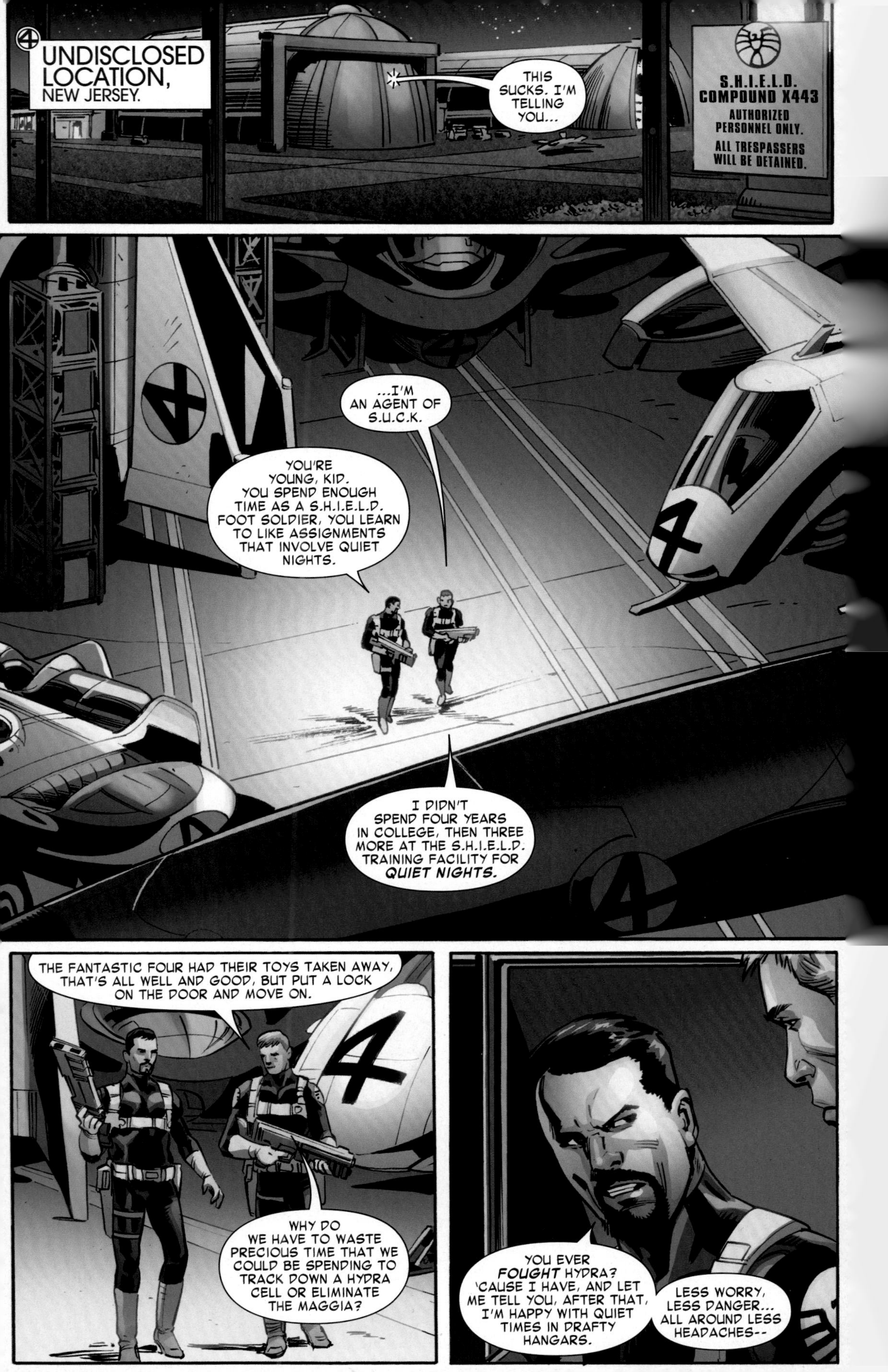

UNDISCLOSED LOCATION, NEW JERSEY.
THIS SUCKS. I'M TELLING YOU...
S.H.I.E.L.D. COMPOUND X443
AUTHORIZED PERSONNEL ONLY.
ALL TRESPASSERS WILL BE DETAINED.
...I'M AN AGENT OF S.U.C.K.
YOU'RE YOUNG, KID. YOU SPEND ENOUGH TIME AS A S.H.I.E.L.D. FOOT SOLDIER, YOU LEARN TO LIKE ASSIGNMENTS THAT INVOLVE QUIET NIGHTS.
I DIDN'T SPEND FOUR YEARS IN COLLEGE, THEN THREE MORE AT THE S.H.I.E.L.D. TRAINING FACILITY FOR QUIET NIGHTS.
THE FANTASTIC FOUR HAD THEIR TOYS TAKEN AWAY, THAT'S ALL WELL AND GOOD, BUT PUT A LOCK ON THE DOOR AND MOVE ON.
WHY DO WE HAVE TO WASTE PRECIOUS TIME THAT WE COULD BE SPENDING TO TRACK DOWN A HYDRA CELL OR ELIMINATE THE MAGGIA?
YOU EVER FOUGHT HYDRA? 'CAUSE I HAVE, AND LET ME TELL YOU, AFTER THAT, I'M HAPPY WITH QUIET TIMES IN DRAFTY HANGARS.
LESS WORRY, LESS DANGER... ALL AROUND LESS HEADACHES--

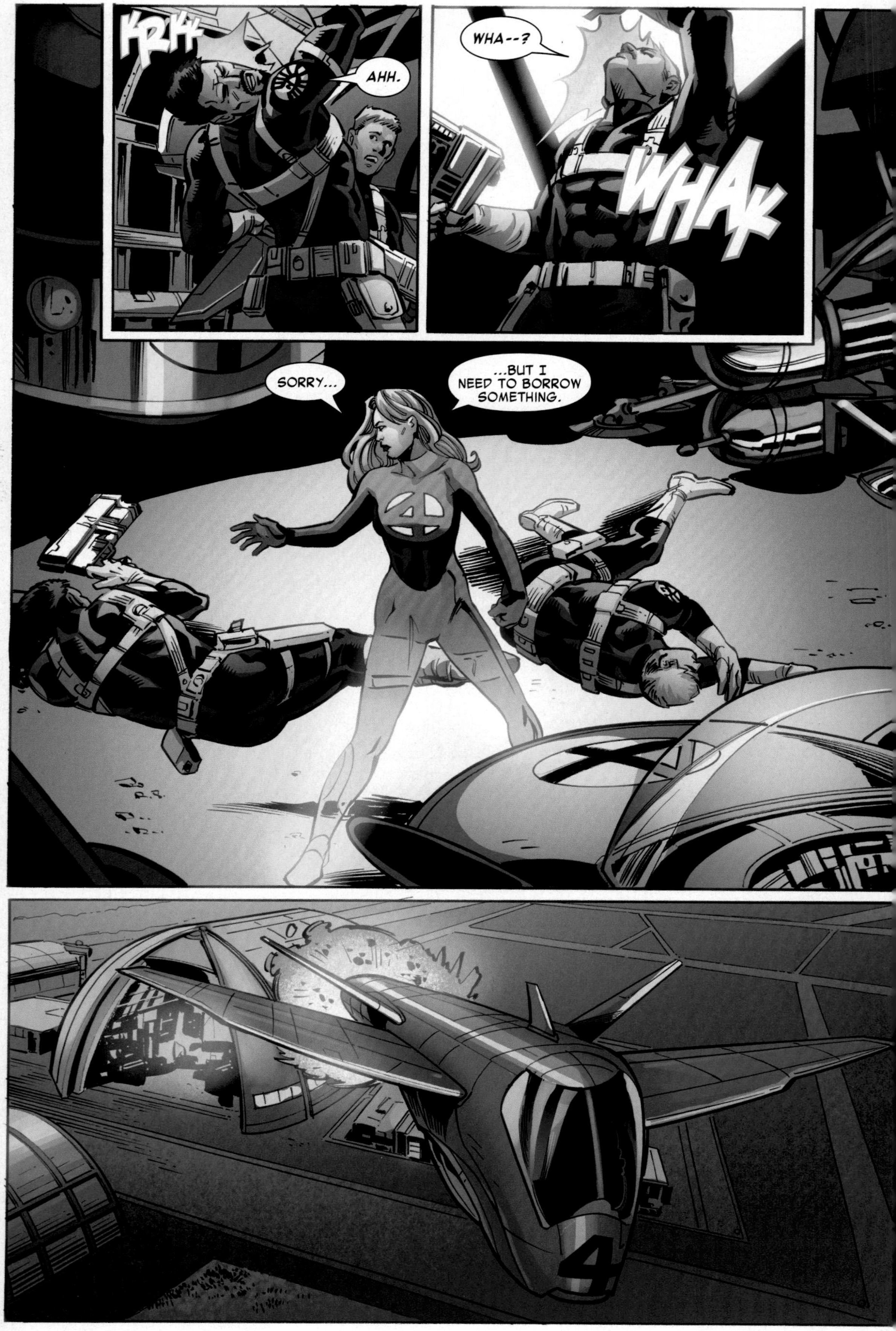
KRKK
AHH.
WHA--?
WHAK
SORRY...
...BUT I NEED TO BORROW SOMETHING.

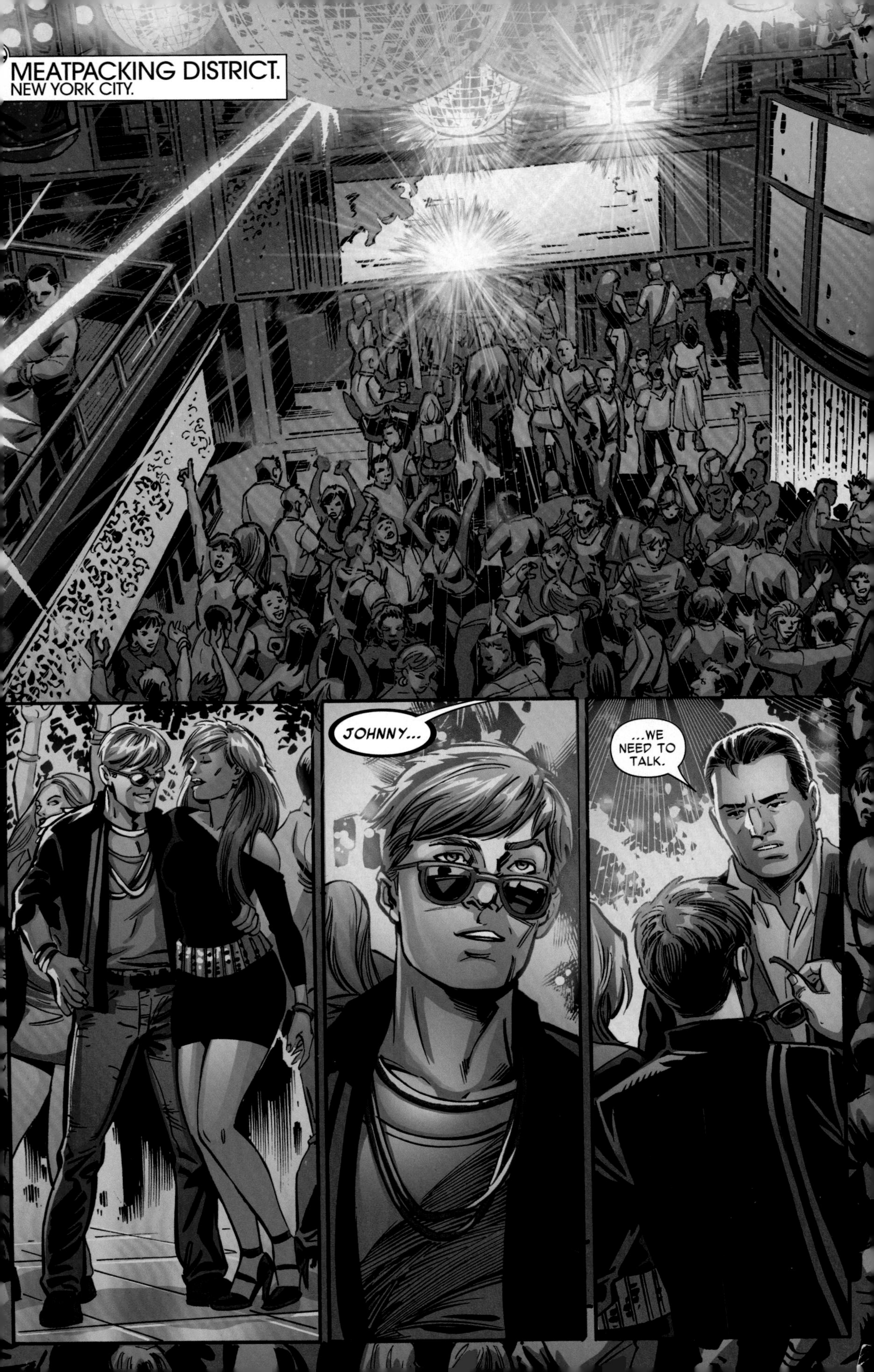
MEATPACKING DISTRICT.
NEW YORK CITY.
JOHNNY...
...WE NEED TO TALK.

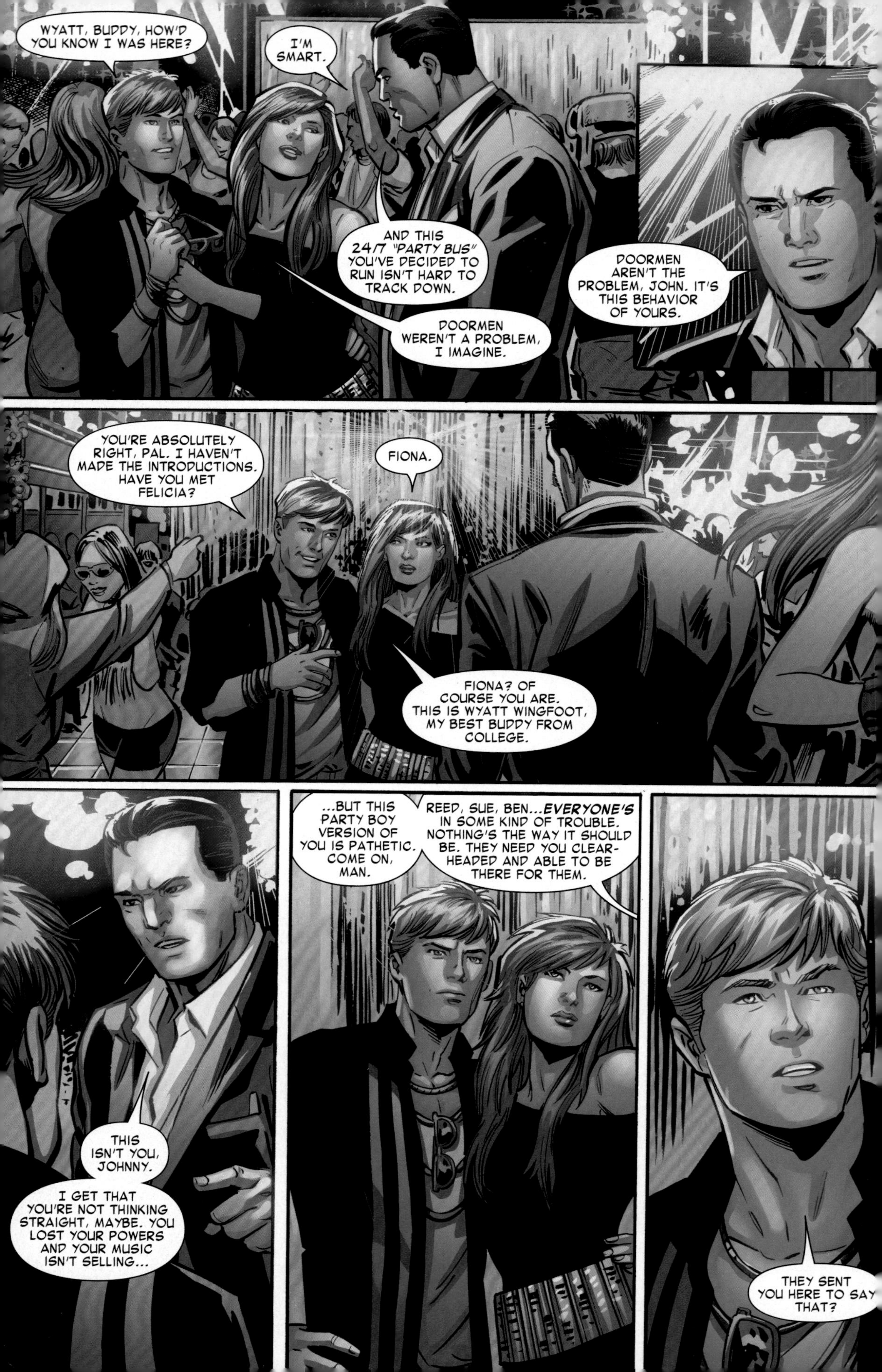
WYATT, BUDDY, HOW'D YOU KNOW I WAS HERE?
I'M SMART.
AND THIS 24/7 "PARTY BUS" YOU'VE DECIDED TO RUN ISN'T HARD TO TRACK DOWN.
DOORMEN WEREN'T A PROBLEM, I IMAGINE.
DOORMEN AREN'T THE PROBLEM, JOHN. IT'S THIS BEHAVIOR OF YOURS.
YOU'RE ABSOLUTELY RIGHT, PAL. I HAVEN'T MADE THE INTRODUCTIONS. HAVE YOU MET FELICIA?
FIONA.
FIONA? OF COURSE YOU ARE. THIS IS WYATT WINGFOOT, MY BEST BUDDY FROM COLLEGE.
THIS ISN'T YOU, JOHNNY.
I GET THAT YOU'RE NOT THINKING STRAIGHT, MAYBE. YOU LOST YOUR POWERS AND YOUR MUSIC ISN'T SELLING...
...BUT THIS PARTY BOY VERSION OF YOU IS PATHETIC. COME ON, MAN.
REED, SUE, BEN...EVERYONE'S IN SOME KIND OF TROUBLE. NOTHING'S THE WAY IT SHOULD BE. THEY NEED YOU CLEAR-HEADED AND ABLE TO BE THERE FOR THEM.
THEY SENT YOU HERE TO SAY THAT?

WELL, YES, I TALKED TO SUE. BUT MAINLY I'VE JUST BEEN AROUND LONG ENOUGH TO KNOW THAT--

YOU LIVE ON THE *SIDELINES*, WYATT. YOU KNOW ONLY AS MUCH OF OUR LIVES AS WE *LET* YOU.

YOU DON'T KNOW *ANYTHING* ABOUT ME OR MY FAMILY.

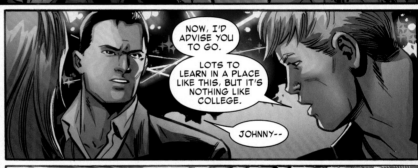

NOW, I'D ADVISE YOU TO GO.

LOTS TO LEARN IN A PLACE LIKE THIS, BUT IT'S NOTHING LIKE COLLEGE.

JOHNNY--

JOHNNY'S GONE, WYATT. JOHNNY'S DEAD. DIDN'T YOU HEAR? I "DIED" A WHILE BACK.

JUST GO ON THINKING THAT.

THAT'S WHAT I DO.

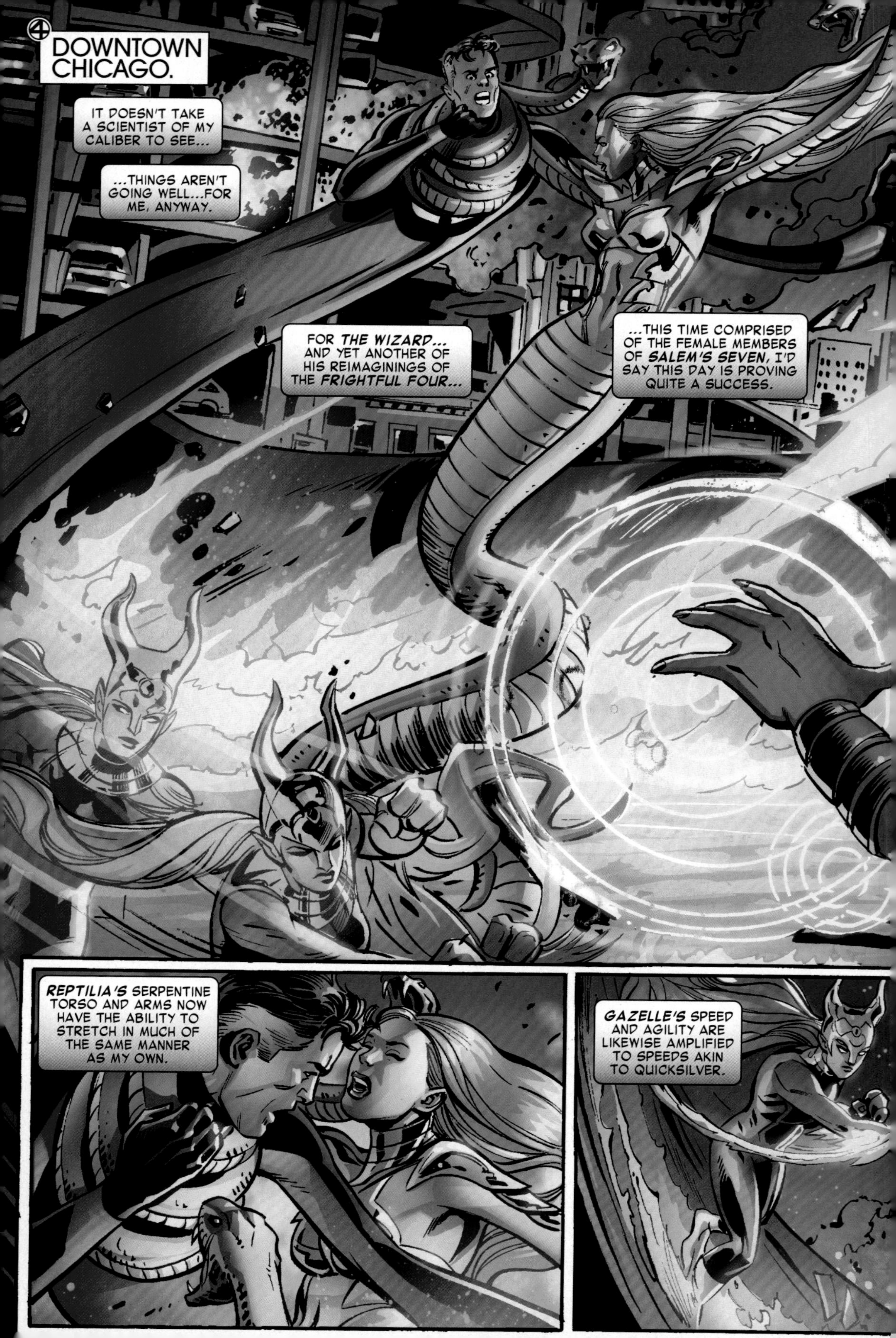
DOWNTOWN CHICAGO.
IT DOESN'T TAKE A SCIENTIST OF MY CALIBER TO SEE...
...THINGS AREN'T GOING WELL...FOR ME, ANYWAY.
FOR THE WIZARD... AND YET ANOTHER OF HIS REIMAGININGS OF THE FRIGHTFUL FOUR...
...THIS TIME COMPRISED OF THE FEMALE MEMBERS OF SALEM'S SEVEN, I'D SAY THIS DAY IS PROVING QUITE A SUCCESS.
REPTILIA'S SERPENTINE TORSO AND ARMS NOW HAVE THE ABILITY TO STRETCH IN MUCH OF THE SAME MANNER AS MY OWN.
GAZELLE'S SPEED AND AGILITY ARE LIKEWISE AMPLIFIED TO SPEEDS AKIN TO QUICKSILVER.

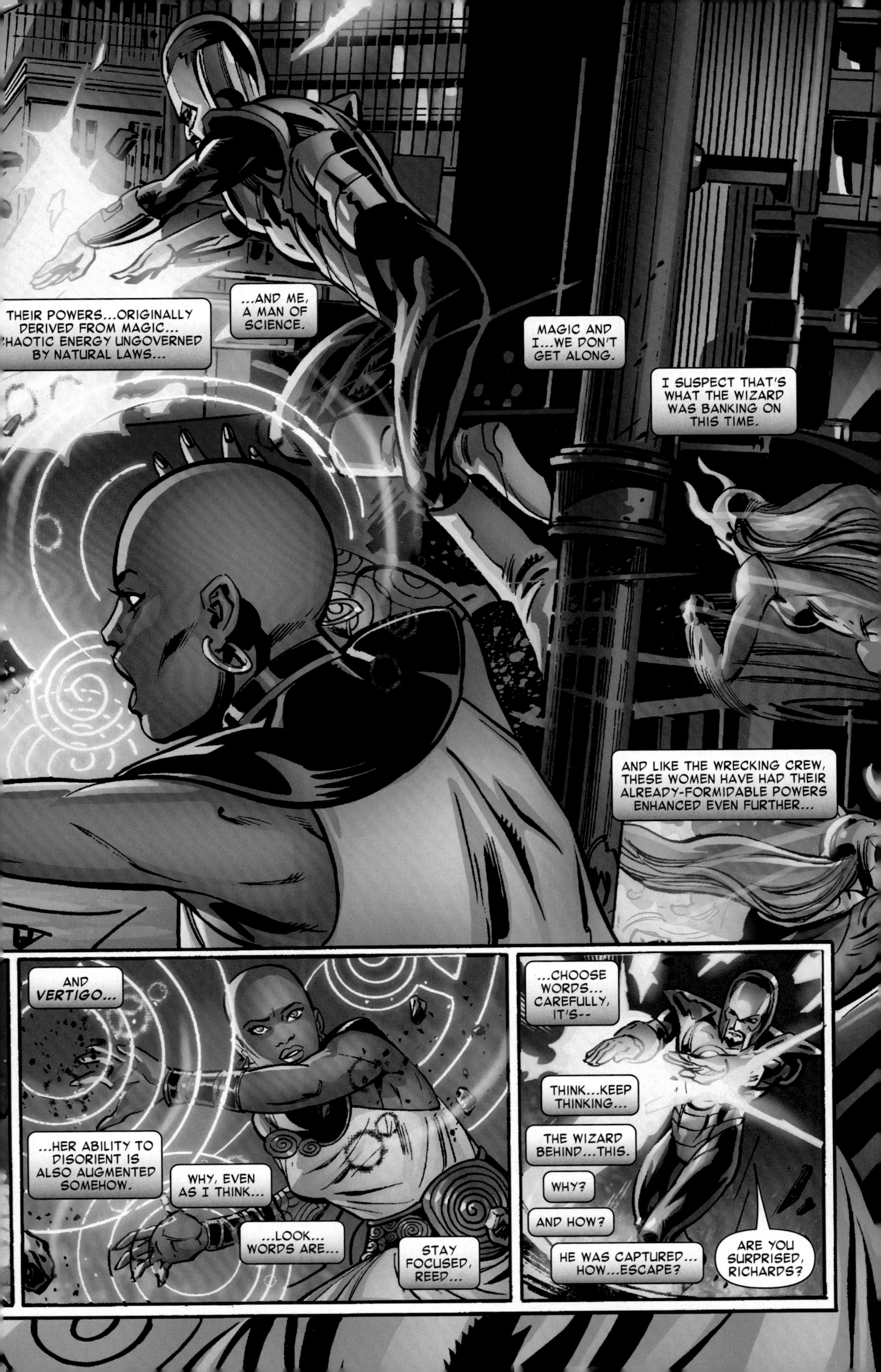
THEIR POWERS...ORIGINALLY DERIVED FROM MAGIC... CHAOTIC ENERGY UNGOVERNED BY NATURAL LAWS...
...AND ME, A MAN OF SCIENCE.
MAGIC AND I...WE DON'T GET ALONG.
I SUSPECT THAT'S WHAT THE WIZARD WAS BANKING ON THIS TIME.
AND LIKE THE WRECKING CREW, THESE WOMEN HAVE HAD THEIR ALREADY-FORMIDABLE POWERS ENHANCED EVEN FURTHER...
AND VERTIGO...
...HER ABILITY TO DISORIENT IS ALSO AUGMENTED SOMEHOW.
WHY, EVEN AS I THINK...
...LOOK... WORDS ARE...
STAY FOCUSED, REED...
...CHOOSE WORDS... CAREFULLY, IT'S--
THINK...KEEP THINKING...
THE WIZARD BEHIND...THIS.
WHY?
AND HOW?
HE WAS CAPTURED... HOW...ESCAPE?
ARE YOU SURPRISED, RICHARDS?

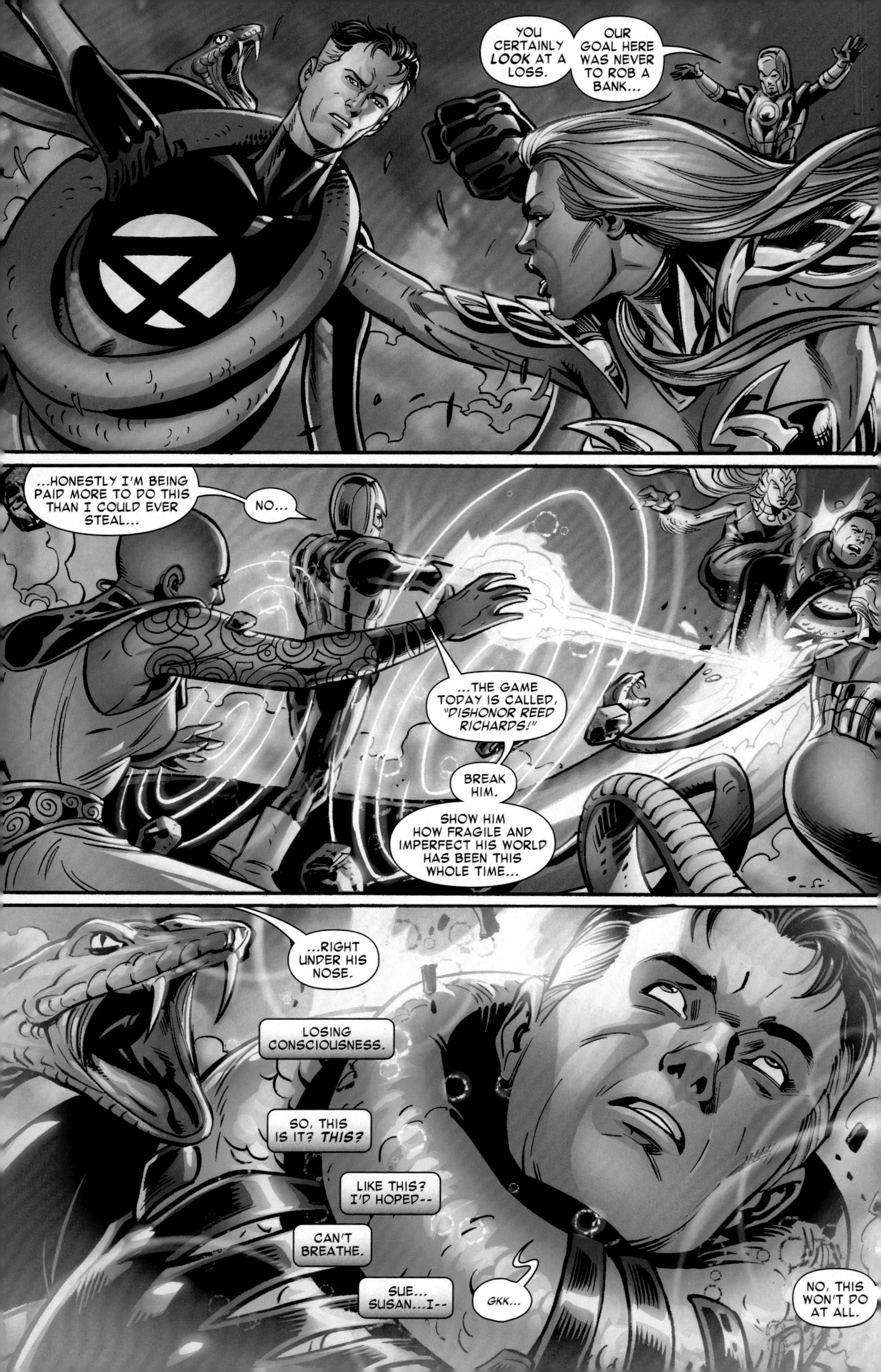
YOU CERTAINLY LOOK AT A LOSS.
OUR GOAL HERE WAS NEVER TO ROB A BANK...
...HONESTLY I'M BEING PAID MORE TO DO THIS THAN I COULD EVER STEAL...
NO...
...THE GAME TODAY IS CALLED, "DISHONOR REED RICHARDS!"
BREAK HIM.
SHOW HIM HOW FRAGILE AND IMPERFECT HIS WORLD HAS BEEN THIS WHOLE TIME...
...RIGHT UNDER HIS NOSE.
LOSING CONSCIOUSNESS.
SO, THIS IS IT? THIS?
LIKE THIS? I'D HOPED--
CAN'T BREATHE.
SUE... SUSAN...I--
GKK...
NO, THIS WON'T DO AT ALL.

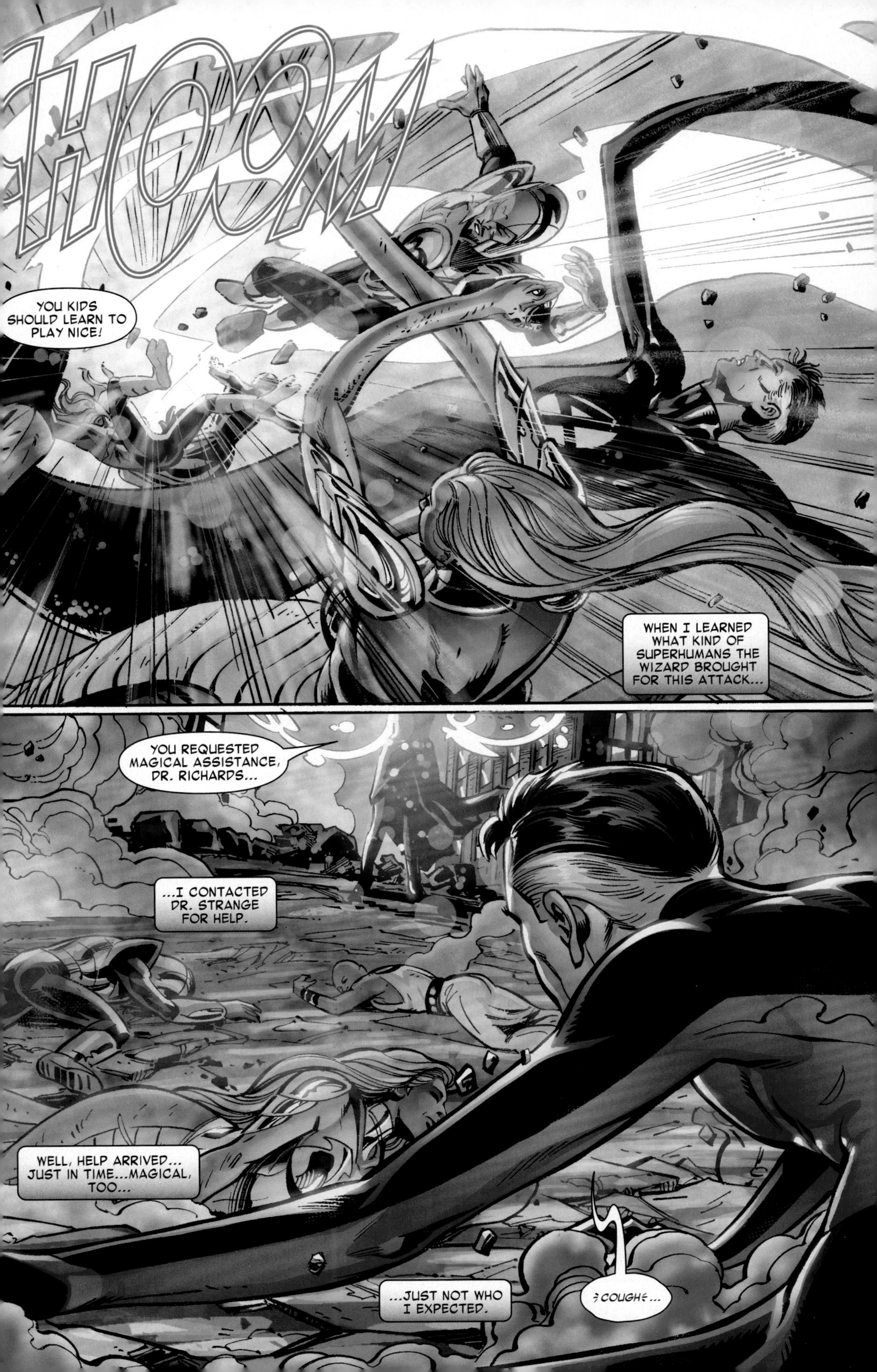
CHOOM
YOU KIDS SHOULD LEARN TO PLAY NICE!
WHEN I LEARNED WHAT KIND OF SUPERHUMANS THE WIZARD BROUGHT FOR THIS ATTACK...
YOU REQUESTED MAGICAL ASSISTANCE, DR. RICHARDS...
...I CONTACTED DR. STRANGE FOR HELP.
WELL, HELP ARRIVED... JUST IN TIME...MAGICAL, TOO...
...JUST NOT WHO I EXPECTED.
COUGH...

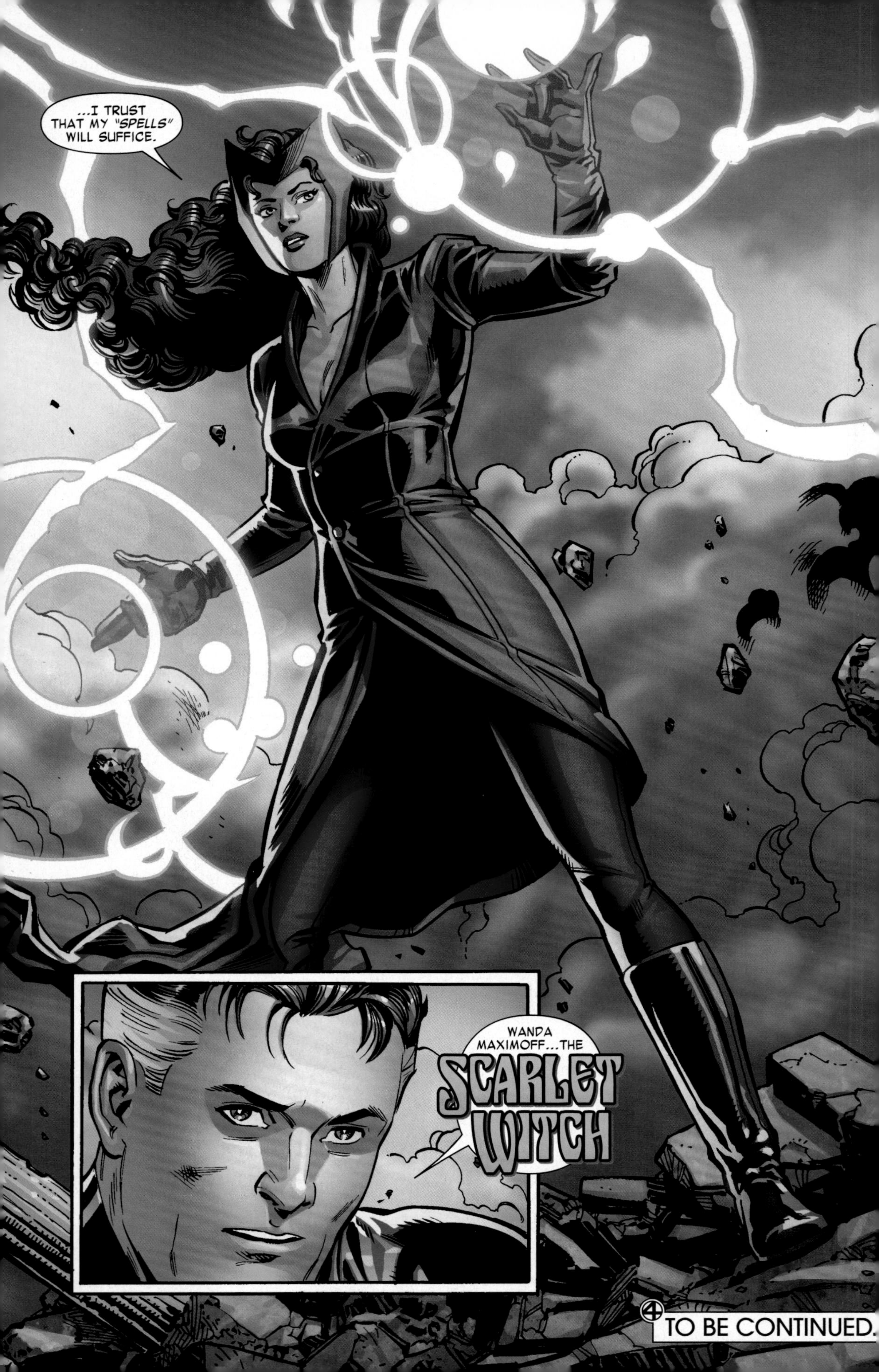
...I TRUST THAT MY "SPELLS" WILL SUFFICE.
WANDA MAXIMOFF... THE
SCARLET WITCH
TO BE CONTINUED.

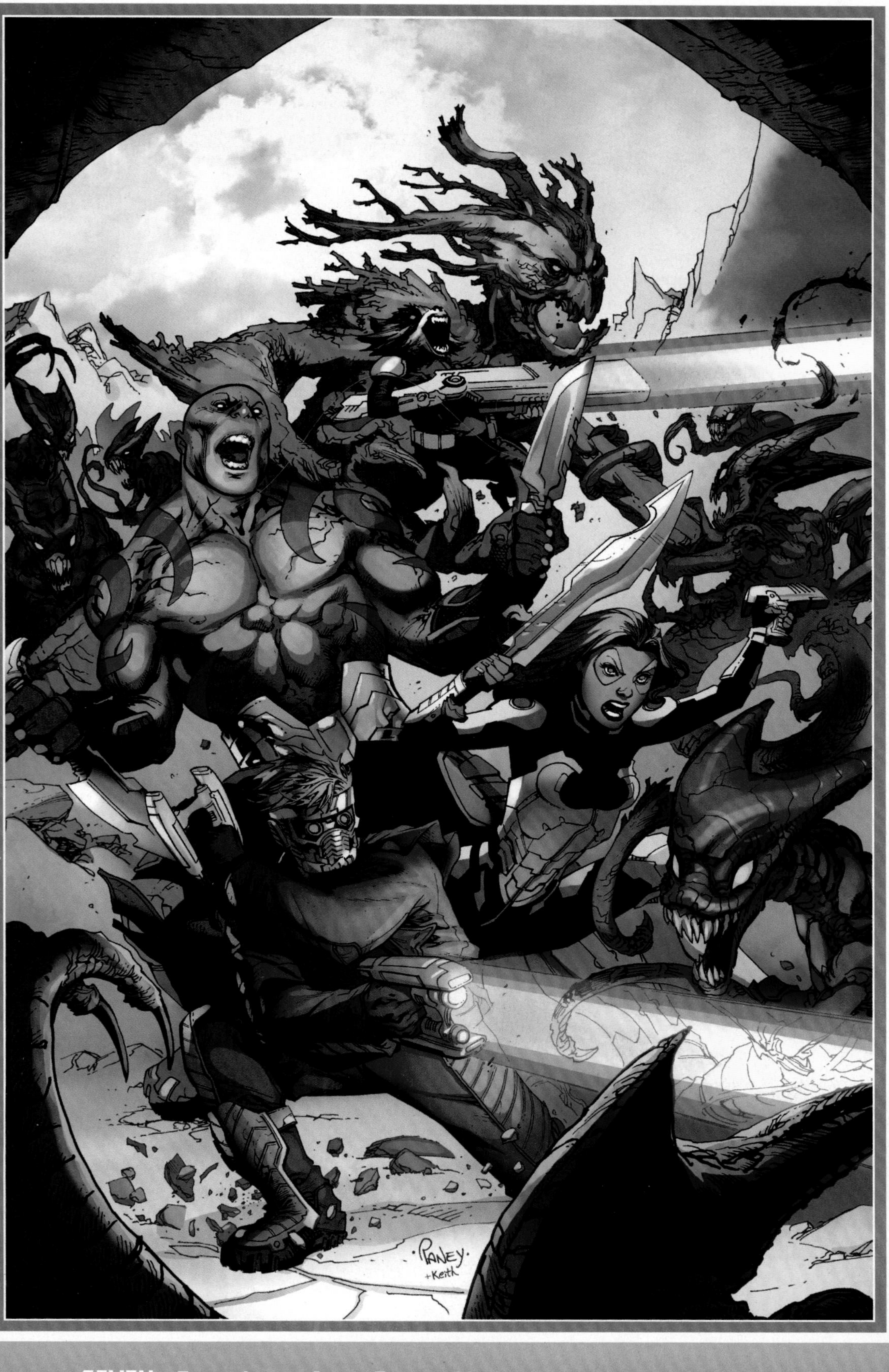
RANEY
+Keith

SEVEN · Guardians of the Galaxy Variant by Tom Raney & Jason Keith

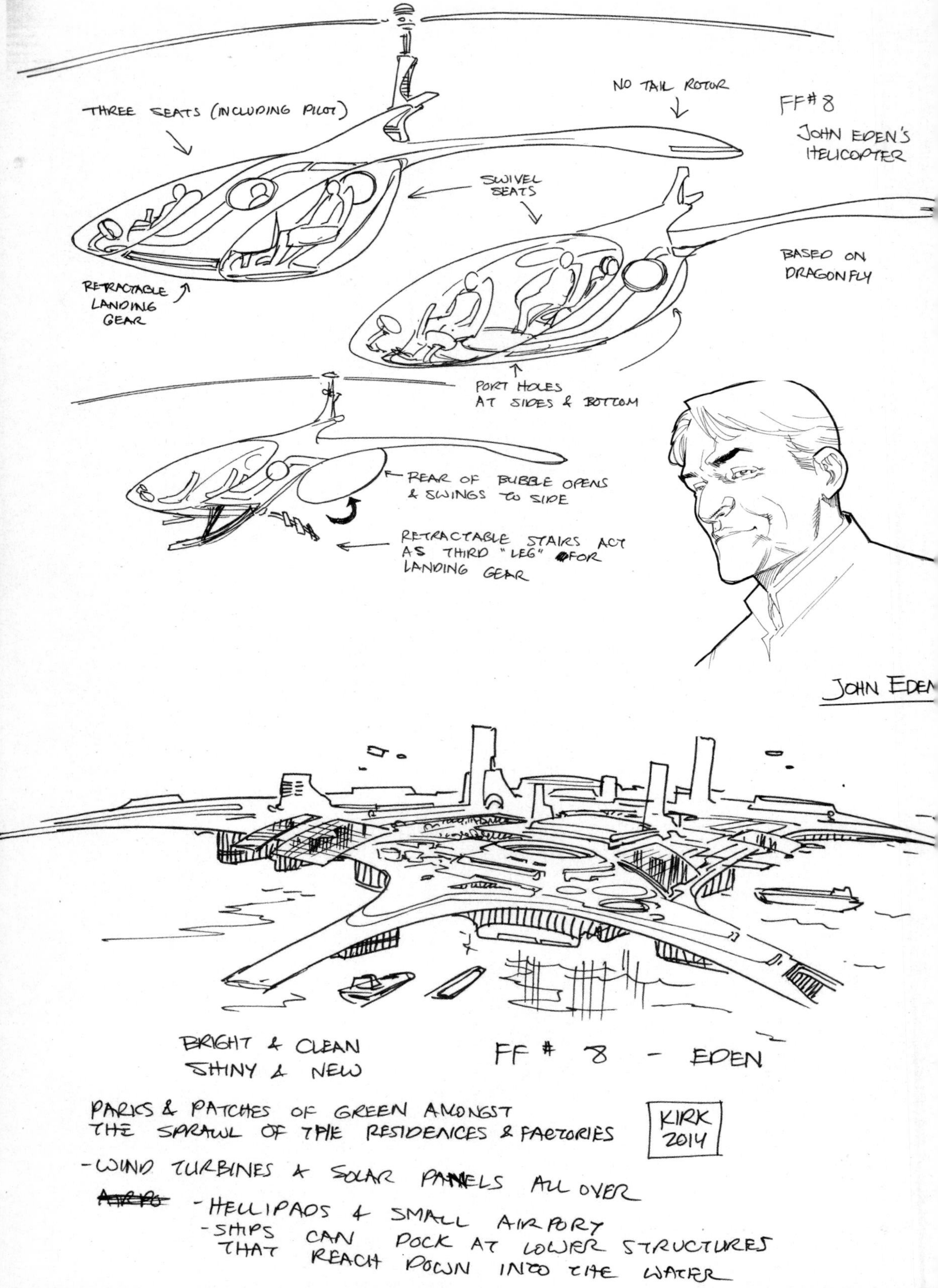
NO TAIL ROTOR
FF#8
JOHN EDEN'S HELICOPTER
THREE SEATS (INCLUDING PILOT)
SWIVEL SEATS
BASED ON DRAGONFLY
RETRACTABLE LANDING GEAR
PORT HOLES AT SIDES & BOTTOM
REAR OF BUBBLE OPENS & SWINGS TO SIDE
RETRACTABLE STAIRS ACT AS THIRD "LEG" FOR LANDING GEAR
JOHN EDEN
BRIGHT & CLEAN
SHINY & NEW
FF # 8 - EDEN
PARKS & PATCHES OF GREEN AMONGST THE SPRAWL OF THE RESIDENCES & FACTORIES
KIRK 2014
-WIND TURBINES & SOLAR PANELS ALL OVER
-HELLIPADS & SMALL AIRPORT
-SHIPS CAN DOCK AT LOWER STRUCTURES THAT REACH DOWN INTO THE WATER

John Eden, helicopter and location designs by Leonard Kirk